A HANDBOOK FOR NEWS AGENCY REPORTER

A HANDBOOK FOR NEWS AGENCY REPORTER

Shashikant Swami

CYBER TECH PUBLICATIONS
4264/3, Ansari Road, Daryaganj, New Delhi-110002 (India)
Ph.: 011-23244078, 011-43559448 Fax: 011-23280028
E-Mail: cyberpublicationsdelhi@yahoo.com
Website: www.cybertechpublications.com

A HANDBOOK FOR NEWS AGENCY REPORTER

Shashikant Swami

First Edition 2010

Published by : Asian Offset Printers

G.S. Rawat for **Cyber Tech Publications**

4264/3, Ansari Road, Daryaganj, New Delhi-110002 (India)

Ph.: 011-23244078, 011-43559448 Fax: 011-23280028

E-Mail: cyberpublicationsdelhi@yahoo.com

Website: www.cybertechpublications.com

Preface

A news agency is an organization of journalists established to supply news reports to organizations in the news trade: newspapers, magazines, and radio and television broadcasters. These are known as wire services or news services. The purpose of this book is to provide a guideline for the communication of health risk information to diverse audiences in response to the risks posed by bioterrorism and emerging infectious diseases. It is intended for public information staff and state public health officials who must respond to media and public concerns about public health emergencies – natural or manmade. It is critical to have a plan in place to deal with a crisis before it happens. This workbook and the accompanying webcasts are intended to help state health officials and public information officers work together to create crisis communication plans and messages.

The workbook includes specific suggestions for mapping responses to anticipated questions, for presenting information, and for interacting effectively with the media and the public. A section is devoted specifically to communications guidelines for dealing with a smallpox incident. Much of the material in this workbook deals with establishing trust and credibility – two of the cornerstones of effective risk communications. When an issue is of high concern, such as the 2001 anthrax incidents or the threat of a smallpox outbreak, trust and credibility on the part of communicators is essential. Without them your message will not be heard, people will not make informed decisions, and problems can escalate. Communicating information about possible life threatening issues can be difficult, but if it is not done well, the communicator can put the public at greater risk by creating misunderstanding or possibly inciting panic. Professional communicators owe it to the people and agencies they represent, as well as to the public, to be prepared to deal with a crisis – natural or man made.

— Author

CONTENTS

1

Introduction

Journalism inherently requires that stories be told in-depth. Many newspapers have cut out long articles, even before the Internet. They've followed the example set by television news. They've been hit by the rising price of newsprint, and the renewed emphasis on cost-cutting. They're convinced that readers are pressed for time, impatient with detail, and conditioned to ingest the news in pellet-like form. Of course, the same readers are not so pressed for time that they can't watch the O.J. Simpson trial, or the Olympics, or reruns of very bad movies. People who choose not to read are not cut off from the news. The movies, radio, and later television have deepened the public's acquaintance with the wider world - at least with its memorable horrors and tragedies.

The bulk of broadcast news is reporting, in the sense that I used it earlier, rather than journalism. It is epitomized by the two-minute wire service radio bulletin on the hour, already a fast disappearing format. "German armies marched into Poland today from five directions." "President Kennedy was shot and killed today in Dallas." Just the facts, ma'am.

Electronic news carries the danger of egenerating into the equivalent of the old stock market ticker tape, spewing out an endless series of figures and symbols geared to the transitory and the insignificant. Occasionally the stream of numbers was interrupted by a terse headline announcing an unexpected calamity that might affect the market. Information isn't knowledge, and facts don't add up to wisdom. The preoccupation with data is at odds with the journalistic quest for meaning, a quest that can only be met through the insights that come from accumulated experience.

I know an economic journalist who has spent a long and distinguished career specializing in one of the world's leading industries. He has interviewed and hobnobbed with all of the principal players and has acquired an intimate familiarity with the technology, economics and politics of an extraordinarily complex global business.

To keep active after his retirement from a senior editorial position, he has become a consultant to one of the many electronic news services that have sprung up in the last few years. He is stunned by the emphasis on up-to-the-minute reports on pricing, trading, transactions, investments, personnel shifts and all the other evanescent minutiae of the market.

He faces a profound distrust of intelligent interpretation of the big forces and long term trends that shape the industry's future direction. The management suspects his motives in wanting to attend a major industry conference he has covered for years. "We have a stringer in London. He can handle it!" Sure, he can summarize the handouts. Are we entering an age of universal access to massive amounts of raw, unbundled information, which anyone can take or leave in any quantities desired? In electronic databases, the public has at its disposal an incredible reference facility, with innumerable business and scholarly uses. But it's not going to make journalism an obsolete skill.

You can put "War and Peace" on a Web site, but who's going to read it all the way through? When people read for fun, they want to sit back in a relaxed posture, not all keyed up at the keyboard. That tense position goes well for an active information-search, but it's not the way people consume news. Computers lend themselves well to the display of terse factual data, like financial tables or sports results, but they are a far less comfortable medium for communicating narrative. Readers savor both the content and style of a good story, and print lets them move back and forth instantaneously from what they are reading to what they have read and are about to read.

Few private individuals have reason or inclination to conduct their own investigative search of secondary sources; people want information professionally picked, processed and interpreted. They want this done with an understanding of the human dramas that mere facts disguise and distort; they want it done with literary style, through the use of language that evokes imagery and emotions.

The Challenges in Prosecuting Print Media for Incitement to Genocide

It is up to the Inyenzis now to demonstrate that they are courageous and to know what will happen in the future. They should understand that if they commit the slightest mistake, then all of them will perish, and that if they make a mistake of once again attacking, launching an attack, no accomplice will survive in Rwanda. They should know that today all Hutus have become united; we're united as one man.

The standard arguments for free speech are well known. We cannot know the truth or the value of an hypothesis if its opponents are forbidden to challenge it or if its proponents are not allowed to defend it. Most of an individual's beliefs, including his or her scientific beliefs, are justified by his or her perception that they have emerged unscathed from the free confrontation of ideas and the unrestrained search for facts. We would be hard pressed to find a single idea now generally accepted that was not offensive to the majority at some time in history.

Throughout history, institutions and individuals have engaged in large-scale efforts to persuade and convince others of the rightness of their ideological views, cultural values and beliefs. The truth is that there have always been excuses and rationales for slavery, for the genocide of Jews, Gypsies and American Indians, with racial and cultural terms of 'us and them' and with the theft of land and resources.

The crime of 'incitement to genocide' knocks against the right to freedom of expression. The challenge is how to counter future war propaganda and speeches that jeopardize the lives of minority groups. Some parameters are laid down in the international law, especially in the landmark judgment in The

Prosecutor v. Ferdinand Nahimana, Jean-Bosco Barayagwiza and Hassan Ngeze, case no. ICTR-99-52-T (the 'Media Trial') on the responsibility of the media and journalists and their role in the crimes committed in conflict situations without jeopardizing press freedom. The definition of genocide set forth in the genocide convention (UN 1951) is authoritative and has been incorporated verbatim into the statutes of the Yugoslavian and Rwandan tribunals as well as those of the permanent International Criminal Court. In addition to the crime of genocide itself, the genocide convention provides that the following acts shall be punishable: conspiracy to commit genocide, direct and public incitement to commit genocide, attempt to commit genocide, and complicity in genocide.

Article III(c) of the convention prohibits 'direct and public incitement to commit genocide'. In specifying this distinct act, the crime is crafted in such a way as to preclude any defence of freedom of expression. The crime of direct and public incitement to commit genocide, like conspiracy, is an inchoate crime, in that the prosecution need not make proof of any result. It is sufficient to establish that:

- The act of direct and public incitement took place.
- The direct and public incitement was intentional.
- It was carried out with the intent to destroy a protected group in whole or in part.

The genocide convention is not the only international document that speaks to the concept of freedom of expression. During the relevant period in 1994, Rwanda was a party to the following international conventions and treaties that directly address the limits of freedom of expression:

- Convention on the Prevention and Punishment of the Crime of Genocide (UN 1951) - ratified by Rwanda 16 April 1975.
- International Covenant on Civil and Political Rights (UN 1966a) - ratified by Rwanda 16 April 1975; Articles 19 and 20 specifically identify the right of freedom of expression, its limits and the responsibilities that are associated with this right.

- Optional Protocol to the International Covenant on Civil and Political Rights (UN 1966b) - ratified by Rwanda 16 April 1975.
- International Covenant on Economic, Social and Cultural Rights (UN 1966c) - ratified by Rwanda 16 April 1975.
- International Convention on the Elimination of All Forms of Racial Discrimination (UN 1965) - ratified by Rwanda 16 April 1975; in Article 5, 'state parties undertake to prohibit and eliminate racial discrimination in all its forms and to guarantee the right of everyone, without distinction as to race, colour, or national or ethnic origin, to equality before the law'.
- African Charter on Human and Peoples' Rights (OAU 1981) - ratified by Rwanda 15 July 1983; Article 9 provides that 'every individual shall have the right to receive information' and 'every individual shall have the right to express and disseminate his opinions within the law'.

These conventions show that freedom of expression is not absolute and can be limited in instances where it conflicts with the rights of others. Attaining the right balance between freedom of expression and its limits had indeed proved difficult in international law. 'International law ... requires a contextual analysis ... The use of the right to freedom of expression, if aimed to destroy the rights of others, constitutes an abuse of that right and as such may be restricted by law' (Farrior 1996). Although under international conventions and treaties all speech is protected, every one of these instruments also recognizes that certain restrictions on speech are permissible and are, in fact, often required to uphold certain other fundamental rights.

A Brief Comparison of Kangura and Der Sturmer

On 20 April 1923, the first copy of Der Stürmer ('The Attacker') was published; 71 years later in Rwanda the newspaper Kangura1 ('Awake') first appeared. Fifty-nine issues of Kangura were published, more or less monthly, as well as a number of international issues. Publication ceased during the genocide and resumed in September 1994.

Circulation

Der Stürmer circulation amounted to a few thousand, fluctuating throughout the years of its publication. However, the sales figures do not reflect the number of people who actually read Der Stürmer or Kangura. Der Stürmer was displayed in specially constructed cases all over Germany. Constructed by local supporters in places where people naturally congregated - bus stops, parks, street corners, etc. - these display cases were often large and adorned with phrases from the paper such as 'Die Juden Sind Unser Unglück' ('The Jews are our misfortune') (Bytwerk 2001).

Before the genocide, approximately 66 per cent of Rwandans were literate. Kangura was printed in relatively small numbers, but each issue was circulated to numerous readers. It was common practice for a person to buy a newspaper, photocopy it and distribute it, read it to his neighbour who could not read and read it in public places for people to listen (ICTR transcript, Marcel Kabanda, 13 May 2001: 58-9).

In January 1992, an article written by François Akimana, president of the Executive Committee of the National Parti pour la libération du peuple Hutu (PALIPEHUTU), describes the circulation of Kangura's international edition:

I do not have words to describe the prevailing situation. When this issue of the Kangura newspaper appeared, in some areas of Bujumbura, all the Hutus, particularly PALIPEHUTU members, heaved a deep sigh of relief. They distributed the newspaper everywhere, including prisons, to the extent that a copy could cost up to a 1,000 Burundi francs, that is, if you are lucky enough to get one because some people preferred to frame them so they could enlighten all family members. (Akimana 1992)

During the Media Trial, several witnesses gave evidence of this system of oral reporting. Witness FS (ICTR transcript, 7 February 2000: 40-1) stated that in Rwanda, people commonly read to each other. For example, he said an illiterate person might ask his child who goes to school to help him read articles from newspapers. Thus, people who could not read bought

Kangura and asked others to read it for them. Witness ABE (ICTR transcript, 27 February 2000: 49-50) stated that the literacy levels in Rwanda were very low; however, those who could read Kangura were able to explain it to those who could not read and thus the messages were widely disseminated. Witness AGX (ICTR transcript, 21 June 2001: 74) testified that although he did not buy Kangura, he borrowed copies from his neighbours and friends to read. Witness AFB (ICTR transcript, 6 March 2001: 23) stated that he did not buy Kangura but people who bought it would tell him the main points in each issue. Defence witness RM 10 (ICTR transcript, 20 January 2003: 34), who was illiterate, said that she would buy Kangura and ask someone to read it to her; she stated that this was a common practice in Rwanda.

Style

Like Der Stürmer, Kangura was filled with stories of scandal and crime. The articles were written by the editor Hassan Ngeze, a couple of staff writers and readers who submitted articles. Like Der Stürmer, the quality of the publication from a purely journalistic standpoint was lamentable. Nevertheless, both Kangura and Der Stürmer enjoyed enormous influence and support from leading authorities. Both were written in a style that the average person could easily understand. The writing was simple and straightforward, using short sentences and basic vocabulary. Ideas were repeated. Headlines, such as 'Inhabitants of Kigali remain vigilant: the enemy is still among us' (Kangura no. 20, August 1991) grabbed the reader's attention. And the cartoons were easily understood. Both journals adopted their local community's style of speaking, and had a similar effect.

In Der Stürmer, caricatures were used to present various themes of anti-Semitism. Jews were depicted as unshaven, short and fat with large, hooked noses and bulging eyes. They were also shown as vermin, snakes and spiders. The female form was often displayed nude or partly nude. In Der Stürmer, 'Aryan' women were often illustrated as the victims of Jews. These nude women made the paper especially attractive to young males (Bytwerk 2001).

Kangura also printed caricatures that were easy to comprehend by a largely illiterate community. The images were graphic and reinforce its message of morbid psychological antagonism of the Hutu masses against the Tutsi ethnic group. In Kangura, Tutsi women were depicted as seductress spies, and the Tutsi feudal regime was a consistent theme.

While Der Stürmer focused on a worldwide conspiracy of the Jews to take over the world based on the protocols of the elders of Zion,2 Kangura propagated the ancient plan of the Tutsi to conquer the Central Africa region.3 This was a theory based on the 19 Tutsi commandments.4 It linked Tutsis living inside Rwanda with those who had exploited Hutus in the past, with the Rwandan Patriotic Front (RPF) and with all the Tutsi in the diaspora.

For example, in a Kangura editorial in July 1991, Hassan Ngeze (1991) asserts: 'Tutsis always seek to reconquer power which Gahutu seized.'5 He states that it can be proven that 85 per cent of Tutsis within the country have close or loose ties with the refugees and have become Inyenzi-inkotanyi. He warns that Tutsis within the country always help their brothers, work day and night and never surrender. His message was clear that the Inyenzi were supported by Tutsis the world over.

Impact

Albert Forster, Gauleiter of Danzig, wrote:

> *With pleasure I say that the Stürmer, more than any other daily or weekly newspaper, has made clear to the people in simple ways the danger of Jewry. Without Julius Streicher and his Stürmer, the importance of a solution to the Jewish question would not be seen to be as critical as it actually is by many citizens. It is therefore to be hoped that those who want to learn the unvarnished truth about the Jewish question will read the Stürmer. (Bytwerk 2001)*

Similar letters came from Heinrich Himmler (1937) and other prominent Nazis. In a leading article in Der Stürmer, Streicher wrote about the paper's impact and goal:

The continued work of the Stürmer will help to ensure that every German down to the last man will, with heart and hand, join the ranks of those whose aim is to crush the head of the serpent Pan-Juda beneath their heels. He who helps to bring this about helps to eliminate the devil. And this devil is the Jew. (Streicher 1937)

Similarly the impact of Kangura in shaping public opinion about the Tutsis in Rwanda and neighbouring countries was phenomenal. In Kangura no. 54 published in January of 1994, Hassan Ngeze informs the readers of Kangura that he has fulfilled his self-appointed task of uniting the Hutu and revealing to the people who the Tutsi is. He states this in a section titled 'The role of Kangura in the salvation of Rwanda':

Before Rwanda was attacked, Kangura revealed the plan. We started urging the Hutus to unite, not to listen to what the enemy was asking them to do, especially as the enemy was the cause of the war amongst them. From that time, the truth preached by KANGURA has played a remarkable role in the reconciliation of Hutus and the return of those who had been misled. Today, Hutus from different parties meet, discuss and share a drink. The irrefutable proof of this is the speech Justin MUGENZI delivered during the MRND meeting the day before yesterday in Nyamirambo. Who could have thought that MUGENZI will one day become an Interahamwe? Kangura's role will be studied in the history of Rwanda and that of the region we live in where a lot of Tutsis reside; Besides, Kangura has revealed to the coming generation who the Tutsi is. (ICTR transcript, Marcel Kabanda, 16 May 2002: 176, emphasis added; Ngeze 1994) It was clear that the message in Kangura was read and taken seriously by the Rwandan community. In the Akayesu case, the Trial Chamber held that, 'In light of the culture of Rwanda, acts of incitement can be viewed as direct or not, by focusing mainly on the issue of whether the persons for whom the message was intended immediately grasped the implication thereof' (ICTR 1998a: para. 558).

The message in an article signed by François Akimana, the president of PALIPEHUTU, reflects the effect of Kangura. In reference to international issue 3, he states that for the

Hutus, 'Kangura has become a culture, an extraordinary culture which reassured them in the same manner as Baby Jesus, and when Christmas Day came' (Akimana 1992: 5; ICTR transcript, Kabanda, 14 May 2002: 131-4). He goes on to describe the reaction of the Tutsis in Burundi when they saw the issue: 'They fell sick, they had liver crisis. They died because of the truth that they had come to see in Kangura newspapers.'

Call for Extermination

In December 1941, Julius Streicher wrote that 'if the danger of ... reproduction of that curse of God in the Jewish blood is finally to come to an end, then there is only one way - the extermination of that people whose father is the devil' (Taylor 1992: 378).

Issue 26 (November 1991) of Kangura was titled 'Tutsi: race Of God!? What arms shall we use to conquer the Inyenzi once and for all?' (ICTR exhibit P7 translated in P115/26/A: K015110).

In this issue, the Tutsi ethnic group was ironically referred to as 'the race of God'.6 The question about conquering the Inyenzi once and for all carried an ominous message calling for a final solution to the evil that, according to Kangura, the Tutsi ethnic group posed in Rwanda.

Historians and sociologists tell us that Rwanda is inhabited by three ethnic groups, which are the Twas, the Hutu, and the Tutsi. They say that these ethnic groups can co-exist in harmony and work together if Tutsis do not behave themselves in a bragging manner, people who like to boast, talk a lot, tell lies and are hypocrites, people who are never satisfied and people who want to have everything, they're thieves, they are involved in intrigues, they are wicked, they are killers. And they are people who have grudges just like serpents. (ICTR transcript, Hassan Ngeze, 2 April 2003: 87-8; Moustapha 1991)

CHALLENGES FACED DURING THE MEDIA TRIAL

One of the greatest challenges was that not all 73 Kangura issues were translated into English and French. This was and still is a subject in contention with the defence. When litigated before the Trial Chamber, it was held that such an exercise would stretch the resources of the Tribunal beyond its capacity. The Trial Chamber noted that the resources of the tribunal were not unlimited and that only the relevant portions need be translated. The defence attourneys were asked to explore less expensive measures, such as securing the cooperation of their clients who were fluent in Kinyarwanda and French or using Kinyarwanda investigators.

Addressing this matter in the judgement, the Chamber noted that: defence counsel availed themselves of the opportunity to select issues for translation and that copies of all issues within the custody of the prosecution were furnished years ago to the defence in hard copy and electronically on a CD-ROM. The Chamber also noted that the extracts of Kangura relied on by both the prosecution and the defence were read into the trial record during presentation of both their cases. This included simultaneous translations into English and French. Thus, the relevant translations were provided to the Chamber for its consideration (ICTR 2003a: para. 44).

Temporal Jurisdiction of the Tribunal

Article 7 of the statute of the ICTR states:

The territorial jurisdiction of the International Tribunal for Rwanda shall extend to the territory of Rwanda including its land surface and airspace as well as to the territory of neighboring States in respect of serious violations of international humanitarian law committed by Rwandan citizens. The temporal jurisdiction of the International Tribunal for Rwanda shall extend to a period beginning on 1 January 1994 and ending on 31 December 1994. (ICTR 1994: article 7)

Only five issues of Kangura were published in 1994 before the genocide. The famous ten commandments of the Hutu were only republished in December 1990. The 19 Tutsi commandments were also republished in Kangura in November 1990. The defence contention, which is still a matter of appeal, was that the Chamber had no jurisdiction over Kangura issues published before 1994. In pre-trial rulings, the Court held that although many of the events referred to in the indictment preceded 1 January 1994, such events 'provide a relevant background and a basis for understanding the Accused's alleged conduct in relation to the Rwanda Genocide of 1994' (ICTR 1999: para. 3). The Appeals Chamber confirmed the Trial Chamber's decision that an accused could not be held accountable for crimes committed before 1994 and that such events would not be referred to 'except for historical purposes or information' (ICTR 2000a: 6). Evidence was adduced that, in March 1994 (issues 58 and 59: 7-11), Kangura called on and directed its readers to read almost all editions of the newspaper by publishing ten questions, whose answers could be found in previous issues, and offered several prizes. In its judgement, the Trial Chamber held that 'the competition was designed to direct participants to any and to all of these issues of the publication and that in this manner in March 1994 Kangura effectively and purposely brought these issues back into circulation' (ICTR 2003a: para. 257).

Prosecution of Journalism at Nuremburg

The Media Trial marked the first time since Nuremberg that hate speech had been prosecuted internationally as a war crime. The trial of Julius Streicher was characterized in the Akayesu judgement of the tribunal as the 'most famous conviction for incitement' (ICTR 1998a: para. 550). The different treatment of two Nazi defendants at Nuremberg - the publicist Julius Streicher and head of the radio division of the propaganda ministry, Hans Fritzsche - was an early indication of ambiguity in international law regarding the incitement that would well outlast the Nuremberg trials.

Streicher, a committed Nazi and the publisher of Der Stürmer, was convicted of crimes against humanity and hanged for having provoked hatred against the Jews and having called for the annihilation of the Jewish race. He received this punishment even though he had held no official government or party position and his journal was not an official party or state organ.

The International Military Tribunal at Nuremberg linked Streicher's propaganda with the war crimes that had been carried out to establish a parallel to the specific intent requirement in criminal law. The tribunal held that Streicher's incitement to murder and extermination at the time when Jews in the East were being killed under the most horrible conditions clearly constitutes persecution on political and racial grounds in connection with War Crimes, as defined by the Charter, and constitutes a Crime against Humanity. (Avalon Project 2005). The tribunal's reference to 'crimes committed in the East', and not those committed within Germany, implicitly linked the alleged crimes against humanity with war crimes. The link to the actual killing in the East also established an element of causation in the definition of actionable incitement, which seemed to require both inciting words and the physical realization of their message.

Although not charged with 'direct incitement', Hans Fritzsche was accused of inciting and encouraging the commission of war crimes 'by deliberately falsifying news to arouse in the German people those passions which led them to the commission of atrocities'. The Nuremberg Tribunal held that there was definite evidence of anti-Semitism in his broadcasts, and that he had blamed the war on the Jews. But, said the tribunal, 'these speeches did not urge persecution or extermination of Jews.' Consequently, it was 'not prepared to hold that they were intended to incite the German people to commit atrocities on conquered peoples'. In effect, Fritzsche's anti-Semitic propaganda was not 'direct' enough to consist of incitement to commit genocide.

The Fritzsche holding set a tough standard of causality between targeted words and specific events. Although the tribunal characterized Fritzsche's virulently anti-Semitic statements in his broadcasts as 'strong statements of a propagandist nature', it found no evidence of explicit calls for the extermination of the Jews (Avalon Project 2005).

Accordingly, it concluded that it was 'not prepared to hold that [these statements] were intended to incite the German people to commit atrocities on conquered people', and that

Fritzsche 'cannot be held to have been a participant in the crimes charged'. His aim was rather to arouse popular sentiment in support of Hitler and the German war effort. The term 'on conquered people' again suggests a focus on crimes against the peace.

The tribunal held that Fritzsche was not aware that the information was false. It also noted that he was not aware of the extermination of the Jews in the East. His position and official duties were also held not to be sufficiently important to infer that he took part in the originating or formulating propaganda campaigns. Fritzsche was considered a 'conduit' of propaganda, not a liable participant.

Direct and Public Incitement and the International Criminal Tribunals for Yugoslavia and Rwanda

The crime of direct and public incitement to commit genocide is punishable under Article 2(3)(C) of the Statute of the ICTR and Article 4 (3)(e) of the Statute of the International Criminal Tribunal for the (former) Yugoslavia (ICTY). The ICTY has issued no indictments against journalists.

In the first conviction of the ICTR, for direct and public incitement to commit genocide, the Trial Chamber described the essential elements of the crime of direct and public incitement to commit genocide: directly provoking the perpetrator(s) to commit genocide, whether through speeches, shouting or threats uttered in public places or at public gatherings, or through the sale or dissemination, offer for sale or display of written material or printed matter in public places or at public gatherings, or through the public display of placards or posters, or through any other means of audiovisual communication. (ICTR 1998a: para. 559)

The Akayesu case determined that the mens rea required for the crime of direct and public incitement to commit genocide lies in the intent to prompt directly or to provoke another to commit genocide. It implies a desire on the part of the perpetrator to create by his or her actions a particular state of mind necessary to commit such a crime in the minds of the person(s) he or she is engaging. That is to say that the person who is inciting to commit genocide must have the specific intent to commit genocide, that is, to destroy, in whole or in part, a national, ethnical, racial or religious group, as such (ICTR 1998a: para. 560).

The Trial Chamber held that genocide fell within the category of crimes so serious that direct and public incitement to commit such a crime must be punished as such, even when such incitement fails to produce the result expected by the perpetrator (ICTR 1998a: para. 552). Whether a communication constituted incitement depended on the context in Rwanda at the time of these events. The Chamber noted that the facts should be considered on a case-by-case basis whether, in light of the culture of Rwanda and the specific circumstances of the instant case, acts of incitement can be viewed as direct or not, by focusing mainly on the issue of whether the persons for whom the message was intended immediately grasped the implication thereof. (ICTR 1998a: para. 558)

The Akayesu Trial Chamber opined that the direct element of incitement should be viewed in light of its cultural and linguistic content. It noted that a particular speech may be perceived as 'direct' in one country, but not in another depending on the audience (ICTR 1998a: para. 557).

The next conviction for the crime of direct and public incitement was in the case of the Prosecutor v. Georges Ruggiu (ICTR 2000b). Others include: The Prosecutor v. Jean Kambanda (ICTR 1998b); The Prosecutor v. Eliézer Niyitegeka (ICTR 2003b); The Prosecutor v. Juvénal Kajelijeli (ICTR 2003c).

PARAMETERS OF PRESS FREEDOM

During the Media Trial, the Chamber examined a number of articles and excerpts from Kangura, focusing primarily on those that addressed issues of ethnicity and on those that called on readers to take action. During its deliberations, the Chamber accepted that the media has a role to play in the protection of democracy and, where necessary, the mobilization of civil defence for the protection of a nation and its people. The Chamber noted that what distinguished both Kangura and RTLM from an initiative to this end was their consistent identification of the enemy as the Tutsi population. Readers and listeners were not directed against individuals who were clearly defined as armed and dangerous. Instead, Tutsi civilians and in fact the Tutsi population as a whole were targeted (ICTR 2003a: para. 1025).

The Chamber considered that it was critical to distinguish between the discussion of ethnic consciousness and the promotion of ethnic hatred (ICTR 2003a: para. 1020). It also held that speech constituting ethnic hatred results from the stereotyping of ethnicity combined with its denigration (ICTR 2003a: para. 1021).

With regard to the RTLM broadcast stating that the Tutsi 'are the ones who have all the money', the Chamber held that, although this broadcast, which did not call on listeners to take any action, did not constitute direct incitement, it demonstrated the progression from ethnic consciousness to harmful ethnic stereotyping (ICTR 2003a: para. 1021).

The Chamber opined that the context in which the statement is made to be important. A statement provoking resentment against members of an ethnic group would have a heightened impact in the context of a genocidal environment. It would be more likely to lead to violence. At the same time the environment would be an indicator that incitement to violence was the intent of the statement (ICTR 2003a: para. 1022).

Although the Chamber accepted that Hassan Ngeze had only reprinted the ten Bahutu commandments and the 19 commandments of the Tutsi, it found that the clear intent of the publication of the latter was to spread fear that the Tutsi endanger the Hutu, and of the former to tell the Hutu how to protect themselves from that danger (ICTR 2003a: para. 1022).

The Chamber noted that the positioning of the media with regard to the message indicates the real intent of the message, and to some degree the real message itself. The editor of Kangura and RTLM's broadcast journalists did not distance themselves from the message of ethnic hatred; rather they purveyed it (ICTR 2003a: para. 1024).

The Chamber also noted that the editorials and articles reviewed during the trial consistently portrayed the Tutsi as wicked and ambitious, using women and money against the vulnerable Hutu (ICTR 2003a: para. 187). The presentation of Tutsi women as femmes fatales focused particular attention on them and the danger they represented to the Hutu. This danger was explicitly associated with sexuality. By defining Tutsi women as an enemy in this way, Kangura articulated a framework that made the sexual attack of Tutsi women a foreseeable consequence of the role attributed to them (ICTR 2003a: para. 188).

Causation

The Chamber reaffirmed the Akayesu decision that incitement was a crime regardless of whether it has the effect it intends to have. In determining whether communications represent intent to cause genocide and thereby constitute incitement, the Chamber considered it significant that in fact genocide occurred. That the media intended to have this effect is evidenced in part by the fact that it did have this effect (ICTR 2003a: para. 1039).

In considering whether particular expression constituted a form of incitement on which restrictions would be justified, the Chamber noted that the international jurisprudence does not include any specific causation requirement linking the expression at issue with the demonstration of a direct effect. In the Streicher case, for example there was no allegation that the publication Der Stürmer was tied to any particular violence. Much more generally, it was found to have 'injected into the minds of thousands of Germans' a 'poison' that caused them to support the National Socialist policy of Jewish persecution and extermination (ICTR 2003a: para. 1007).

After the Genocide and the way Forward

Intervening to Prevent Genocidal Violence: the Role of the Media

The media of mass communications today include traditional printed newspapers, magazines and journals, as well as the twentieth century's core electronic resources: radio, television and the Internet. In wealthy nations, the print media, television and the Internet predominate, while in poorer states, often marked by low rates of literacy, the medium of choice for shaping and reinforcing public opinion is radio.

In utilitarian genocides, largely motivated by the desire to create, expand and preserve formal states and empires, the perpetrator calls directly on the professional armed forces of the state to facilitate the acquisition of wealth, eliminate a perceived threat or spread terror. But in genocides motivated by the search for a perfect future inspired by a utopian ideology, the state demonizes the victim group and its members, excluding them from the universe of mutual human obligations. This process usually requires intensive, sustained propaganda to mobilize violence on a grand scale. Crimes against humanity, and especially genocide, require the spread of hate propaganda and disinformation throughout the general population to reinforce key motivating beliefs. Other motives - acquisition of wealth, elimination of a perceived threat and spread of terror - often play a role in ideologically motivated genocides, but largely among the ordinary killers who operate at a social and political level below that of the key architects of the genocide.

Acute Current Questions Regarding the Role of the Media

The media do not make ideologically motivated genocide happen, but they facilitate and legitimate it. Low-level Hutu perpetrators of the Rwanda genocide affirm that broadcasts by radio station RTLM affected their thinking in key ways. Even before the death of President Habyarimana, RTLM reinforced their fear of a Tutsi conspiracy to commit genocide against them, a fear amplified by reports of killings of Hutu civilians by the Rwandan Patriotic Front (RPF) as it advanced into northern Rwanda. Following the death of the president, RTLM created an atmosphere legitimating the elimination of Tutsi through interviews with government officials and eminent Rwandans who identified all Tutsi as subversive supporters of the RPF and its alleged plan to commit genocide against the Hutu. And RTLM created a background of pervasive, overwhelming hatred toward the Tutsi, which discouraged ordinary Hutu from refusing orders to serve in well-organized patrols to hunt down and kill Tutsi.

For many of the ordinary Hutu perpetrators interviewed by Aaron Karnell (2003), RTLM's broadcasts made it appear as if all the authorities in the country urging the killing of Tutsi spoke with one voice. And while Karnell found that direct contact with local authorities rather than listening to RTLM was what immediately precipitated anti-Tutsi killing, he concludes that 'RTLM played a critical reinforcing role in the effort of authorities to mobilize Hutu for violence'.

After interviewing a very large sample of ordinary Hutu killers, Scott Strauss (2004) reached similar conclusions.

The interviews I conducted suggest that the main effect of the radio broadcasts was to help establish killing Tutsis as the new order of the day - as the new 'law,' as the new basis for authority - after Habyarimana's assassination and after the civil war resumed. [Thus, he concludes,] The radio broadcasts did not create that experience of insecurity, but likely contributed to it. (Strauss 2004: 281)

Most of the ordinary killers interviewed by Strauss cited face-to-face mobilization as 'a greater factor in their decision to take part in the killing than were radio broadcasts', but, he found, 'the radio broadcasts shaped the overall atmosphere in which the mobilization occurred and empowered the most violent killers' (Strauss, 2004: chapter 7 and 387).

Current field research in Rwanda makes it evident that broadcasts by RTLM facilitated and legitimated the Rwanda genocide of 1994. Preventing or stopping RTLM's messages of hate would have seriously undermined the ability of its high-level planners to carry out the mass mobilization required for the systematic annihilation of Rwanda's Tutsi.

Real conflicts over territorial boundaries and scarce resources are frequent occurrences in history, but they rarely require the intensive, sustained, eliminationist propaganda that one finds in cases of ideologically motivated genocide. When ethno-nationalist, utopian and racist goals become paramount, perpetrators work most intensively to persuade their subjects of the danger to their security and the need to eliminate whole groups of people portrayed as threatening their very survival. Propaganda and ideology interact synergistically to create panic - fear that allows ordinary people to believe that they are killing to preserve traditional rights imperiled by threatening groups. In such situations, the media's role is to engender fear, hatred and violence, inciting and legitimating the destruction of cultures and groups of innocent human beings as the only possible solution to the threatened loss of life, rights and property.

As William Schabas (2000) reminds us, 'Genocide is prepared with propaganda, a bombardment of lies and hatred directed against the targeted group, and aimed at preparing the "willing executioners" for the atrocious tasks they will be asked to perform.' And it is precisely this open mass mobilization of the population by the media through public encouragement of the people to endorse and join in state-supported crimes against humanity and genocide that aids us in predicting and recognizing early warnings of ideologically motivated genocide.

The newspaper Kangura, edited by Hassan Ngeze, was a private publication. Radio station RTLM was a private media outlet. Yet both played major roles in inciting Rwandans to commit genocide.

Kangura and RTLM were closely connected to the Hutu Power wing of the Rwandan government and the Coalition for the Defence of the Republic (CDR) political party through stock ownership, seats on the board of directors, cross consultation, and even the broadcasting of editorials from Kangura on radio programmes offered to the largely illiterate public by RTLM. While Kangura ceased publication before the genocide, throughout the genocide RTLM urged the killers on to greater zeal and efficiency, even furnishing listeners with the names, addresses and automobile licence plate numbers of those who still needed to be killed.

Before rendering judgement in the Nahimana media case, the judges of the International Criminal Tribunal for Rwanda (ICTR) had to examine once more the meaning of incitement as an element of the crime of genocide as defined in the United Nations genocide convention (UN 1951). And they had to do so in the context of an earlier case, the Akayesu case, in which the court had concluded, 'The prosecution must prove a definite causation between the act characterized as incitement or provocation in this case, and a specific offence' (ICTR 1998: para. 557).

A number of important principles have emerged from the ICTR's decision in the Nahimana media case. The judges set key boundaries defining legitimate expression and elaborated principles for interpreting their guidelines. In summary, the major points of the decision are:

- Incitement to commit genocide is a crime in its own right and the incitement need not have succeeded to be considered a crime.
- Because incitement is a crime in its own right, no causal relationship between the incitement and the acts of the perpetrators of genocide need be demonstrated to prove the accused is guilty of incitement.
- Incitement of ethnic hatred can be distinguished from the legitimate use of the media by focusing on three factors: the tone and not just the content of a communication; the context in which a media statement is made; whether the media distanced itself appropriately when reporting stories incorporating the messages of those who advocated ethnic hatred.
- The media play a legitimate role in a nation's self-defence, but that role requires that the media characterize as threats those individuals who are armed and dangerous rather than entire ethnic groups.
- Ethnic expressions by the media should receive more rather than less scrutiny 'to ensure that minorities without equal means of defence are not endangered' (ICTR 2003: para. 1008).
- International law rather than domestic law should be the point of reference when making determinations of freedom from discrimination and freedom of expression.

Recent history makes us aware that the effective use of the media in preventing genocide requires assessing the stage that the genocidal situation has reached and devising a response strategy appropriate to that stage.

Poor, economically developing societies struggling to move from authoritarian, arbitrary rule to establish the democratic foundations of civil society are particularly vulnerable to genocide. Such societies have few competing media outlets, possess no tradition of independent media, lack deeply rooted professional standards for journalism and endure a violent media culture that exhibits no sense of responsibility to society as a whole.

Journalists in such societies are frequently manipulated and bribed by the dominant political faction ('envelope journalism'), are dependent on stereotyping and sensationalism for the themes of their news stories and are oblivious to potential news stories that would diminish ethnic and political hatred.

Good, highly trained journalists with professional standards are frequently subjected to threats and, in the wake of assassinations and beatings, may surrender to manipulation and intimidation by the purveyors of fear (Frohardt and Temin 2003).

RECOMMENDATIONS FOR INTERVENTION

- Early-stage interventions - in conflict situations where mass killing has not begun - include domestic and foreign monitoring of the media, training programmes and codes of conduct to raise the skills and standards of local editors and journalists and strengthening of the local independent media. In such situations, local and foreign broadcasts of serial drama programmes addressed to children and soap operas for adults emphasizing the benefits of interethnic cooperation, the real benefits of compromise and peaceful solutions to problems are useful methods for lessening conflict. Local, multi-ethnic production teams have proved to be especially effective and credible originators of such productions (Frohardt and Temin 2003).

- Middle-stage intervention - in societies just beginning to suffer genocidal massacres - must be swift and aggressive. When government-sanctioned threats and intimidation make it impossible for local journalists, domestic nongovernmental organizations (NGOs) and government ministers to intervene effectively against media promoters of ethnic, religious and racial hatred, foreign governments and NGOs, regional associations of states and international organizations like the United Nations and the European Union must place the disseminators of hate propaganda on notice that their threatening messages are being monitored, recorded and transcribed to enable the prosecution and punishment of culpable media owners, editors and journalists. Foreign broadcasters should broadcast accurate, targeted news in local languages to counter the disinformation and distortions of domestic information providers and to supplement whatever material domestic anti-hate broadcasters are able to beam to their listeners. Electronic jamming of hate transmitters should be initiated.
- Late-stage intervention - launched when genocide is underway - may require actually destroying the transmitters and printing presses of the hate mongers. Foreign broadcasters should supplement their news broadcasts with frequently repeated warnings that a genocide is underway, report credible threats designed to deter the perpetrators from further killing, provide accurate information to discourage potential victims from congregating in perpetrator-targeted locations, like the churches which became killing-grounds in Rwanda, and appeal to ordinary citizens to conceal and protect members of the victim group. Future rewards should be promised for citizens who can document after the defeat of the genocidal regime that they hid potential victims and refused to participate in the killing. Whenever feasible, routes to safety and practical suggestions for survival should be announced.

Many of these recommendations have already been field-tested in countries such as Afghanistan, Bosnia-Herzegovina, Burundi, Cambodia, Kosovo, Liberia, Macedonia and Sierra Leone by international organizations, governments and NGOs including the United Nations, the European Union, the Organization for Security and Co-operation in Europe (OSCE), the BBC World Service, the BBC Trust, the British Department for International Development (Britain 2000), the United States Agency for International Development's Center for Democracy and Governance, the Internews Network, the Canadian Institute for Media, Policy and Civil Society, Search for Common Ground, the Hirondelle Foundation, the Open Media Research Institute, the Radio Partnership, the Center for War, Peace and the News Media and Lifeline Media.

Still needed is an international code of conduct that recognizes the dual-use possibilities of television and AM, FM, and satellite radio transmitters and subjects those countries already under international arms embargoes initiated by the United Nations Security Council, the OSCE and the European Union (EU 1998) to the same or even tighter export control policies as those for military equipment.

Following European Union and other international guidelines, the new code of conduct would prohibit exports of transmitters to countries:

- Not respecting sanctions decreed by the UN Security Council.
- Violating their human rights obligations, including the United Nations Convention on the Prevention and Punishment of the Crime of Genocide (UN 1951), the International Covenant on Civil and Political Rights (UN 1966) and the Universal Declaration on Human Rights (UN 1948).
- Likely to use the equipment to provoke or prolong armed conflicts or aggravate existing tensions in the country of final destination.
- Endangering regional peace, security and stability.
- Threatening the national security of the states

subscribing to the code of conduct and of territories whose security is a responsibility of member states, as well as that of friendly and allied countries.

- Demonstrating disrespect for international law, alliances and the need to contain terrorism.
- Likely to divert the equipment within the buyer country or re-export it under undesirable conditions.

To refine and further develop measures to prevent the use of hate radio in inciting genocidal violence, the Montreal Institute for Genocide and Human Rights Studies is organizing an international conference to be held in spring 2007. Specialist scholars, representatives of NGOs, government agencies and manufacturers of radio transmission equipment will convene to discuss the next stage - bringing relevant mobile and stationary radio transmitters under the jurisdiction of the existing dual-use controls for arms exports.

Once established, the new regime in radio export controls will ensure that hate-radio transmitters can be legitimately targeted for destruction if and when their operators violate the terms of the revised code of conduct. In this respect, the new code will constructively embody the fateful encounter with hate radio in Rwanda and stand as one of the many memorials to the victims of the Rwanda genocide.

Part I. The Reporter At Work

1. On the Job

Part II. The Basics

2. Components of the Story

Part III. Writing the Story

3. What Is News?
4. The Internet and Other Tools of the Trade
5. The Lead
6. Story Structure
7. The Writer's Art
8. Features, Long Stories and Series

9. Broadcast Newswriting
10. Writing News Releases
Part IV. Reporting Principles
11. Digging for Information
12. Making Sound Observations
13. Building and Using Background
14. Finding, Cultivating and Using Sources
15. Interviewing Principles and Practices
16. Speeches, Meetings and News Conferences
17. Hunches, Feelings and Stereotypes
Part V. From Accidents to Education
18. Accidents and Disasters
19. Obituaries
20. The Police Beat
21. The Courts
22. Sports
23. Business Reporting
24. Local Government and Education
Part VI. Laws, Taste and Taboos, Codes and Ethics
25. Reporters and the Law
26. Taste-Defining the Appropriate
27. The Morality of Journalism

Prewriting

To be a successful reporter

The best reporters I know are bright, persistent, honest, personable, curious and courageous. If you asked them to explain their success, this is what they might say:

1. A good reporter is a generalist, able to deal with a number of topics and talk with a variety of people. He or she can see the unusual, the ironic, in the everyday. She can think through all the possibilities and organize

a large amount of information to find the important parts.

2. A good reporter is quick. Once he is assigned a story, he goes after it. He makes the calls and keeps trying if he doesn't make contact. He remembers the sign that once hung in the Los Angeles Times newsroom: GOYA/KOD. Get off your ass/knock on doors.
3. A good reporter is curious. He or she takes pleasure in the new, and in the old, in the history or precedent that got us where we are. He enjoys reading and appreciates the details.
4. A good reporter is pleasant. She adopts a friendly nature with those she meets. She is a grateful guest, with a belief in the basic goodness of people. She conveys to those she meets that she is tolerant of them and their ideas, even though she does not like them or what they stand for. She subordinates her ego and is a good listener.
5. A good reporter is honest. He seeks the truth and acts independently. He does what he says he's going to do, and doesn't do something he promised to avoid. He returns his calls, and he's willing to say no. He's obsessed with accuracy and double checks his facts with call-backs. He sees both sides to every issue. He doesn't treat people as a means to an end.
6. The good reporter is courageous. She approaches strangers. She takes pleasure in being good, in being first. She develops a skin to deflect the inevitable criticism. She is willing to make a mistake and willing to write something that may hurt someone. She has a capacity for tempered outrage.
7. As Jon Franklin, reporter, author and teacher, said: "Back when I first started, I thought intelligence was the most important attribute a reporter could have. I have since changed my mind. You do have to be intelligent, but the big thing is courage. Courage to open your mind and let the whole damned confusing world in. Courage to always be the ignorant one, on

somebody else's turf. Courage to stand corrected. Courage to take criticism. Courage to grow with your experiences. Courage to accept what you don't understand. Most of all, courage to see what is there and not what you want to think is there."

There are three ways to gather information for your story-research, observation and interviewing. Of these, interviewing is clearly the most important. It can be done in person, over the phone, and now even by e-mail. It can be extensive or just a few questions. In whatever form, it is the key to the stories you write. Your ability to talk to people is the difference between being a mediocre reporter and a good one.

1. An interviewer once asked Vivian Leigh what part she played in the movie, Gone With the Wind. Leigh ended the interview before it started. Contrast that with the interview A.J. Liebling had with jockey Eddie Arcaro. Liebling began the interview by asking Arcaro why his left stirrup was longer than his right. One got a good interview, the other didn't. One was prepared, the other wasn't.
2. Preparation allows you to ask good questions and signals your subject that you are not to be dismissed lightly. Read all that is available. Talk to those who know the subject. As writer Tom Rosenstiel said, "A common ingredient of the superb interview is a knowledge of the subject so thorough that it creates a kind of intimacy between the journalist and the interviewee."
3. What is the tentative theme for your story and how will this interview fit that theme? When you have answered those questions, prepare a list of questions. The best way to have a spontaneous conversation is to have questions ready. That way you can relax, knowing that you will not miss an important topic.
4. Phrase your questions in a neutral way. Not: Don't you agree that this speaker should be banned from campus? Mix open-ended questions, such as, "Tell me about your love for antique cars," with closed-ended ones, such as,

"How old are you?" The closed-ended ones elicit basic information; the open-ended allow the interviewee to reveal information or feelings that you did not anticipate.

5. Decide how you will dress. You would dress differently for a hockey player than for the mayor. Ask yourself, how will my subject be dressed? Avoid anything in your dress or grooming that could be considered impertinent, flashy, sloppy or rebellious.
6. Think of your meeting with the subject as a structured but friendly conversation, not an interview. As writer Studs Terkel said, "I realized quite early in this adventure that interviews conventionally conducted were meaningless. The question-and-answer technique may be of value in determining favored detergent, but not in the discovery of men and women. It was simply a case of making conversation and listening."
7. Try to establish a rapport with the person early on. You may want to wait a bit before pulling your notebook out. This meeting stage may determine how the rest of the interview will go. Do you share a common interest or friend? If so, mention that.
8. Look the subject in the eye and listen carefully to his/her answers. Be sure to smile. A smile, they say, is lubrication for the words and collaborator of the eyes in contact. A smile helps both you and your subject relax.
9. When the source is speaking, nod or make some verbal remark to show you are listening and understand. Sit on the edge of your chair and lean forward. This is a posture that projects an eager, positive attitude.
10. Observe and record the person's body language, mannerisms, dress, physical features, distinctive characteristics and interactions with others. These allow you to paint a word picture for your reader and may reveal something that is not being said. Observe and record the sights and sounds of the surroundings. Take good notes during the interview in a handwriting you

will be able to read later. Take too many notes rather than too few.

11. Focus on what the source is saying, not on what you will ask next. Your next question will be better if you heard the answer to the last one. Listen critically. Do you understand what the source is saying. If not, ask the source to repeat or explain. Listen for what isn't said. Is the source avoiding a topic?
12. Don't interrupt, don't ask long questions, don't talk too much, don't challenge too early in the conversation. You're there to hear opinions, not offer them. Nevertheless, it can help to build rapport if you reveal something of yourself. Offer your own thoughts or observations, but sprinkle lightly.
13. Control your physical actions and mental attitude. If the subject senses that you disapprove of him or his opinions, the interview is doomed. If the subject wants to take you on a tour of her home, office, factory, garden, etc., accept the offer and record what you see.
14. Begin with easy questions, perhaps biographical ones. Ask for examples or anecdotes. Use the list of questions you have prepared and return to it frequently. As Anthony deCurtis, former editor of Rolling Stone, said, "Interviewing is a lot like talking, but you have to guide the conversation. You have to know what you want and go about getting it."
15. If the subject takes the interview in an unexpected direction, go with her/him. But remember, you are in charge of the interview. Make sure you accomplish your goals and be assertive if necessary. Stop after one hour. Be alert to the fact that the best material sometimes comes when you have reached the end and thanked the subject for their cooperation. Be sure to ask what the future holds.
16. Make accuracy your goal. Be sure your quotes are accurate. If not, paraphrase. Ask for correct spellings. Don't pretend to know something that you don't.

Summarize for the subject in your own words some of his main points. For example, you might say, "Let's see if I understand you. You mean..."

17. Tell the subject you will be calling back later to check facts (not quotes) and do so. Make the call when you are almost finished with the story. Use it as a second interview. Ask about areas you did not understand, or about areas that will be a part of the story but were not covered well during the original interview.
18. Tape record the conversation if time permits and the story demands. Is this a profile? Does your subject have a distinctive way of speaking? Is this a controversial topic?

    Willthe presence of a recorder put a chill on the conversation? If you decide to use a recorder, ask permission of the subject. Place it off to the side, but where it can be seen. Make sure it is in good working order with good batteries. Use it as a backup to your regular note taking.
19. Assume that the conversation is "on the record." If the subject asks for parts of it to be "off the record," try to convince him/her otherwise. If unsuccessful, make sure you and the subject understand the ground rules. Does "off the record" mean you can use the material, but not with her name attached to it? Can you go to someone else and get the information on the record? Or does "off the record" mean you cannot use the information, even without his name attached, and you can't go to someone else to get the information?
20. Direct quotes from your subject are essential for your story. They allow your reader to "hear" the person you are writing about. They also create the impression of objectivity, that you, the reporter, are simply telling the world about something that happened. But quotes must be 100 percent accurate. If you are not certain of every word of the quote, remove the quote marks and paraphrase. However, it is permissible to "clean up" bad grammar within a quote.

21. Make sure the quote is revealing of your subject. Avoid direct quotes if the material is boring, if the information is factual and indisputable or if the quote is unclear. Make sure the quote advances the story and does not repeat the material above it.
22. Often the advice given for interviewing makes it sound like a game of wits with your subject. They've got something you want, and they won't give it to you. You are advised to "flatter them," "make them feel comfortable," "lead up to the tough questions with easy ones," "don't take no for an answer." What's implicit here is that there are several realities that you can report. A good reporter reports at one level. A great reporter reports at another level, closer to what I call "actual reality." Strive to discover during the interview the "actual reality."
23. Figure that there is material that your subject knows, will tell you and will let you report. That is the "reportable reality." There is another reality that the subject knows, will tell you, but will not let you report. This is the "private reality." There is a third reality that the subject knows but will not tell you, much less let you report. Strive to discover through every legal and ethical means this "actual reality" and report it. Remember, journalism is what somebody doesn't want you to print. Everything else is publicity.

News reporters gather information in three ways: by interviewing people, by researching the written record and by observation. The better you are at these, the better your stories will be. This newsgathering triad underlies all good reporting and good writing. In fact, good information, even poorly written, is better than soufflé writing, or writing with no substance.

1. The more ways you gather information, and the more information you gather, the better your story will be. You will move closer to the "actual reality" of the event. Remember your goal is to use any legal and ethical means to learn what's really going on.

2. Let's start with the simplest type of news gathering, the story gathered in only one of the three ways. It is based on what you are told, rather than what you discover for yourself. This is source-controlled, source-originated journalism. Let's call it level 1 journalism.
3. Level 1 stories result from handouts, press releases, press conferences, speeches and statements. They result from what someone tells you. It is surface journalism. It is the work of a clerk, not a reporter. This type of reporting doesn't have to be bad. It can be information from the city as to when the trash will be picked up, or when to register to vote.
4. But level 1 journalism has its problems. The material can be one-sided. It can be offered by the source for personal, political or economic gain. If the newspaper is filled with this kind of material, the reading public becomes apathetic and distrustful.
5. Worse than being one-sided, level 1 journalism can be wrong. Frequently, people don't know what they are talking about, and sometimes they lie. So, what's a reporter to do? Be skeptical. Good reporters question what they are told. They check and double check. They rely on what they are told, but they improve upon it by talking to more than one person, by searching the written record, by trying to see for themselves. As President Reagan said of the Russians, "Trust but verify."
6. A word of caution: There is a difference between skepticism and cynicism. A skeptic is one who wants proof, but he or she is not prejudiced against face-value explanations. A cynic, on the other hand, refuses to believe face-value explanations and is ready to ascribe almost evil motives to those he or she covers. A good reporter is skeptical but not cynical.
7. When you take what someone tells you, and supplement it with information from your own research, your own observations, or with what others tells you, you move to level 2 journalism. You shed "air and light" on the subject, to use Lincoln Steffens' phrase. You "climb the

stairs," according to A.J. Liebling. Remember the sign in the Los Angeles Times office: GOYA/KOD, Get off your ass, knock on doors.

8. By operating on the information you have been told, you move from level 1 journalism closer to the "actual reality." You provide background, details, reaction from others, and your own observations as verification for what has been provided.
9. Suppose you were sent to cover a speech by the director of a university writing center on the subject of student writing. If you went to the speech and reported strictly what the speaker said, that's level 1 reporting. If you talked with tutors, students, professors, other writing centers, if you visited there yourself, if you provided a history of the center, then that's level 2 reporting.
10. If you take it one step further, if you attempt to answer the so what? question, if you provide some information on the causes and consequences of the issue, then that is level 3 reporting. Level 3 reporting tells the reader why things are as they are, why they work or don't work.

A good reporter makes regular contact with his or her sources. She goes to the well when she's thirsty, but she also goes to the well when she's not thirsty. There is no substitute for actually being there, for personal contact. See your sources, speak to them when you need something from them, but more importantly, when you don't need anything.

1. One of the most important qualities that a reporter must have is an ease around strangers. Always be alert to the common ground that you share with the people you deal with. Mention these topics in your conversations with them. Familiarity doesn't breed contempt. It lowers barriers.
2. A reporter has to answer the question, "What's up?" with more than, "Not much." Put sources on the receiving end of information. The FBI approach-"We ask the questions, mister"-does not work for a reporter. A

reporter is an information broker. Share information when you can.

3. With this said, you also have to be careful. You must learn to walk a fine line between getting close but not too close. As Walter Lippmann said, "There has to be a certain distance between a reporter and the source, not a wall or a fence but an air space." You serve the reader, not the source.
4. After months on a beat, working with the same sources, you will begin to think like them and talk like them. You will be sympathetic to their point of view. Be wary of this and of their efforts to use you. It is likely and legitimate that they will try to persuade you of the merit of their views, to sell you on their programs. You will have little contact with your readers, but it is them you represent.
5. The language of your source is probably not the language of your readers. Bureaucrats, scientists, educators and lawyers have their own jargon. Learn this jargon but translate it into standard English for your readers.
6. If you have obtained information from a source on the understanding that it is off the record, then it is. Remember, a source is a source for life. You may change beats, newspapers, even cities, yet your reputation will follow you. The only way to be a successful reporter over the long haul is to operate honestly. If you don't, you will be without that most valuable of all commodities, good sources.
7. Make one more call. Ask your source, "Who else can help me?" "Who holds an opposite view?" Work down the organization chart. If possible, talk to the policeman who made the arrest, not the supervisor; the teacher rather than the principal.
8. Be polite but persistent with your sources. Insist on a responsive answer to your question. Follow slow-developing stories by checking periodically with your sources. If the event or issue is still on their agenda, it probably should be on yours as well.

WRITING

Writing is probably why you became a newspaper reporter. But beware. Writing is the source of most of your pleasure, but it is also the cause of the pain. It is a frustrating task, for you will often feel incompetent, like a novice, even after years of effort. But don't let that stop you. The journey is wonderful.

THE WRITING PROCESS

Writing is a process, a logical sequence of steps. You follow a pattern in getting dressed each day, in baking a cake or in changing a flat tire. In the same way, your writing should be the product of a logical process. The successful writer gathers, focuses, orders, drafts and revises. These are the same basic steps upon which this Web site is built: prewriting, writing and rewriting.

1. The first step in the process is gathering. Good writing begins with good reporting. The writer must find the details that reveal meaning. You can't write writing; you have to have facts.
2. Once you have the facts, decide on a focus or theme. Each news story should have one dominant idea. That is the focus or reason for writing the story. Without a focus, stories wander and confuse the reader. To find the focus, ask yourself, what's the point? Imagine that you had to write a six-word headline for the story. What one sentence tells the meaning of the story?
3. Next, decide which of your facts are most important and place them in a logical order. Discard all facts that don't flow from your focus statement. Like a blueprint, each story needs a plan. Each point should grow from the previous point and lead to the next one. Poor organization loses more readers than anything else. For the reader, the easiest thing is to stop reading.
4. Write quickly from beginning to end so that you can spend time with the middle of your story and with the ending.
5. After you have written, edit your story to make it more powerful. Make sure that you have written what you

intended to write. Read it aloud to someone. Take a break, then come back to it and revise. Be merciless in removing anything that doesn't belong.

6. This process is not necessarily a straight line from gathering to revising. The writer will go back and forth, including other facts as she is revising, or changing the order as she gathers. A key point to remember is that much of the work in writing a news story is done before the first words are put to paper.

That you have gathered the material for your story, take a minute to organize it. A minute spent in planning the story will prevent countless problems later on.

1. Look through your notes and background material. Mark the best of it, the key points and strongest quotes.
2. Decide on a focus. What is the core idea for the story? You should be able to express this theme in a sentence or two.
3. What are the main points that will support this theme? Place these main points in a logical sequence. A jot outline is helpful for this. It will help you decide how to tell the story. How will the story begin? What will the middle sections look like? How will it end?
4. It is very tempting to return from an interview and immediately begin writing a lead. But your story will suffer if you do.You will omit material you want to include. Your story will be repetitious. And you run the risk of front-loading the story: good stuff at the start, followed by increasingly weaker material. Take a moment to plan the story from beginning to end.
5. As Jack Hart, writing coach at the (Portland) Oregonian, has said, "Writing is thinking. That's all there is to it. Simple as it is, it still works wonders. The act of writing a theme statement and a few main topics imposes order on the chaos of detail you often face when reporting ends."

Now that you have gathered the material for your story, take a minute to organize it. A minute spent in planning the story will prevent countless problems later on.

1. Look through your notes and background material. Mark the best of it, the key points and strongest quotes.
2. Decide on a focus. What is the core idea for the story? You should be able to express this theme in a sentence or two.
3. What are the main points that will support this theme? Place these main points in a logical sequence. A jot outline is helpful for this. It will help you decide how to tell the story. How will the story begin? What will the middle sections look like? How will it end?
4. It is very tempting to return from an interview and immediately begin writing a lead. But your story will suffer if you do.You will omit material you want to include. Your story will be repetitious. And you run the risk of front-loading the story: good stuff at the start, followed by increasingly weaker material. Take a moment to plan the story from beginning to end.
5. As Jack Hart, writing coach at the (Portland) Oregonian, has said, "Writing is thinking. That's all there is to it. Simple as it is, it still works wonders. The act of writing a theme statement and a few main topics imposes order on the chaos of detail you often face when reporting ends."

The News Lead-part I

A good news story, unlike the novel or play, is based on one main idea. That is why it is so important to decide on a focus and stick to it. A well-focused article tells your reader that you worked from a plan. It gives the reader a sense of completeness, a sense that you know what you are doing.

1. In deciding on this focus, you also are working on your lead. By asking yourself about the main theme for your story, you are deciding how to begin, for often the two-a statement of theme and a lead-are one and the same.
2. To help you decide on this theme, sometimes it helps to try the "tell-a-friend" technique. Imagine your friend asking, "What's your story about?" Answer that question

in one sentence that captures the essence of the entire story.

3. Now try to refine your answer so it can do two things. It should capture the essence of your story and do so in a way that encourages the reader to continue. It is your promise to the reader of what is to come. It is your lead.
4. After reading the lead, your reader makes a critical decision: Shall I read on? You have little time, according to Donald Murray, author of Writing for Readers. "Three seconds and the reader decides to read or move on to the next story," Murray said. "That's all the time you have to catch the reader's glance and hold it; all the time you have to entice and inform."
5. Think of the lead as a baited hook that lures the reader into the story. Think economy. Imagine you are writing the lead while seated on a hot stove, or carving it into a block of oak. Make each word count and include no extra words. One writer said she writes a lead as if each word cost her $10.
6. There are two main types of leads: direct or delayed. The direct lead reveals immediately what the story is about. It is the summary or statement of the most important events contained in the story. It is the climax, the result of the investigation, the theme. If you told a joke as you wrote a direct lead, you would place the punch line first.
7. The direct lead-also called the summary lead-is usually one sentence, but sometimes two. It answers immediately, in 25 words or less, the main questions of who, what, when and where. It is the workhorse of daily journalism, used at the top of most stories.
8. The best direct leads start with a compelling noun and a strong verb, not with a prepositional phrase. William Caldwell, a Pulitzer Prize-winning reporter, recalled the best lead he ever heard. The year was 1922. "I was on my way home from school and my stint at the local

weekly. My little brother came running to meet me at the foot of the street. He was white and crying. A telegram had come to my mother. 'Pa drowned this morning in Lake George,' my brother gasped. l was ashamed to admit my inner response. Before I could begin to sense sorrow, despair, horror, loneliness and anger, before all the desolation of an abandoned child could well up in me, I found myself observing that the sentence my brother had just uttered was the perfect lead. Noun, verb, period, and who-what-when-where to boot."

9. There is a second type of lead that is used mostly on feature stories. It is the delayed or feature lead. It usually sets a scene or evokes a mood with an incident, anecdote or example. The writer may foreshadow events to come or create a sense of foreboding or anticipated surprise. Essential information is temporarily withheld. The writer teases before she pleases.
10. The delayed lead can be short, perhaps two sentences, or it can be longer, up to four paragraphs. The delayed lead still must fulfill the two roles of the lead: It must capture the essence of the story and do it in a way that encourages the reader to continue. Like the direct lead, it leads the reader straight to the heart of the story. Good leads are like good titles: they shine a flashlight down into the story.
11. When the lead is delayed and does not immediately explain the main point of the story, it is important to include the theme statement somewhere high in the story, usually within the first four paragraphs. If you ask the reader to wait before he learns what the story is about, be sure to reward him with a clear statement of purpose, also known as a nut graph.
12. Leads must be honest. They should never promise what does not follow in the story. Don't begin with a startling or sensational anecdote if it is not organically related to the theme. As writer John McPhee said, "A lead should not be cheap, flashy, meretricious, blaring a great fanfare of trumpets, and then a mouse comes out of its hole."

The Rest of the Story

We've talked about the lead. Now let's talk about the rest of the story-the middle and end.

1. The real strength of your story will come from the details that back up the promise of the lead. This is the background material, the examples and quotes, the things you have observed, the explanations and definitions and the sense of history. These are the parts that lend meaning and significance to the event or person you are writing about.
2. You can build strength and interest in the middle of the story in a number of ways. Some of them are:
   a. Raise a question or a dilemma in one paragraph and answer it in the next. Elaborate on this cause and effect by using examples or quotes.
   b. Introduce background with phrases such as "previously," "in the past" or "two months ago." Put this information in several sections rather than one big block.
   c. Repeat a word or phrase from one paragraph to the next.
   d. Use parallel structure. Use the same grammatical order in succeeding sentences or place the same number of sentences in succeeding paragraphs.
   e. Vary sentence length. Follow a long sentence with a short one.
   f. Use anecdotes. You used one in the lead, try it in the middle of the story. An anecdote within the story creates momentum, pulling the reader through the copy.
   g. Use dialogue. Let your readers hear two of your characters talking to one another.
   h. Use a list to highlight the key points. For example, a court decision or the findings of a scientific study could be summarized in a list.
3. Finally, we have come to the end of the story. Think of it as the lasting impression, the last song you heard on

the radio. The ending is often what the reader remembers most about the story, so end strong. The ending is so important that you should know how you are going to end before you start.

4. Many writers save a good morsel for the end, perhaps their second-best quote. (The best quote would be used near the top of the story.) Roger Simon, a columnist for The Baltimore Sun, switches his leads and endings to see which works best in which spot.
5. The most common type of ending is the quote ending. Look for a quote that sums up the main idea of the story. Another favorite is the circle end. In the circle end, you return to an idea expressed in the lead.

The Tools of the Trade

When I first started as a reporter, I thought that the skills and structures used in writing a novel or play would apply to writing a news story. I have since changed my mind. Now I believe, as Roy Peter Clark of The Poynter Institute for Media Studies teaches, that there is a "language of journalism." News writing is unique in the following ways:

1. News writing is concrete and specific. At the St. Petersburg Times, they ask reporters to get "the name of the dog, the brand of the beer, and the color and make of the sports car." The task of the writer, said Joseph Conrad, "is by the power of the written word, to make you hear, to make you feel, to make you see."
2. News writing is front-loaded or top-heavy. The news writer makes meaning early with sentences that begin with subjects and verbs. Subordinating elements follow in what scholars call "right-branching" sentences. Many writers, John McPhee and Ernie Pyle come to mind, create page after page of right-branching sentences, but with such variety in length and subordination that the effect is almost invisible.
3. News writing is plain. It is tough and muscular and free of clutter. "Good prose is like a window pane," said

George Orwell. The reader notices not the writing but the world. "We are a society strangling in unnecessary words, circular constructions, pompous frills and meaningless jargon," said William Zinsser. The good writer avoids this clutter with a meanness of attitude. "By meanness I don't refer to a harsh quality in my copy," said William Blundell. "I refer to an attitude toward myself as I work. The mean storyteller becomes two people, acting alternately as he works. The first is the sensitive artist-creator, the second the savage critic who eradicates every weakness in his creation. He is cruel and hoots at affectations and pretty turns of phrase, passive constructions and wordiness. He is a rotten S.O.B., worse than any editor who ever drew a breath, and he is an artist's best friend."

REWRITING

Getting it Right-part

You've spent hours gathering material and writing your story. Now it is time for the third step in the process-rewriting. To illustrate the value of rewriting, imagine that you are suddenly asked to play third base for the Baltimore Orioles. You have no training or experience in baseball, so the experiment is likely to be a disaster. But suppose you have expert instruction and one month to prepare. Suppose someone hits you 1,000 grounders a day for that month. No doubt, after this kind of practice, you will be much more successful.

1. So it is with writing. Writing takes practice. Your first draft will never be as good as your second draft, and the second will never be as good as the third. Remember, there is no such thing as good writing, only good rewriting. Or, as Roscoe Born, former Wall Street Journal editor, said, "What you have written is only preparation for what you are going to write." Here are some ways to improve your first draft:
2. Read your story aloud. Reading aloud is a great way to test for clarity and grace. Are your sentences too long?

Is a paragraph confusing? Is your work conversational or stilted? "I read aloud so I can hear every word, can discover where the little words bump into each other and destroy the rhythm," said Don Murray of The Boston Globe. Or as historian Barbara Tuchman said, "After seven years' apprenticeship in journalism, I have discovered that an essential element for good writing is a good ear. One must listen to one's own prose."

3. Check to make sure your sentences are not too long. Sentence length should vary, but the average should be below 25 words. Reader comprehension decreases as sentence length increases. Paula LaRocque of The Dallas Morning News said, "The period is one of the clear writer's best friends." And Robert Gunning wrote, "I know of no author addressing a general audience today who averages much more than 20 words per sentence and still succeeds in getting published."
4. Check your writing for clutter. Is your work full of twisted phrases, jargon, redundancies, long words where short ones will do, unnecessary qualifiers and modifiers? The disease of American writing is clutter, said William Zinsser. Strip every sentence to its cleanest components. The gardener knows that he must thin his plants after the first seedlings appear. Otherwise, his entire crop will suffer. The same holds true for writing.
5. Make sure that you have used the subject-verb-object construction in most of your sentences. Avoid backing into sentences with long dependent clauses, especially introductory ones. Roy Peter Clark calls this "throat-clearing." Get to it.

The careful writer is precise. As Mark Twain said, "The difference between the right word and the nearly right word is the same as that between lightning and the lightning bug."

A mechanic uses a 9/16-inch wrench because no other will do. A writer must be just as selective with her words. Ask yourself these questions to make sure you have been precise:

1. Are my sentences simple and strong? Write simple sentences, where the subject is close to the verb. Rely on strong nouns and verbs, not adjectives and adverbs. As Strunk and White said, "The adjective hasn't been built that can pull a weak or inaccurate noun out of a tight place." They have their place, but "it is nouns and verbs, not their assistants, that give good writing its toughness and color."
2. Have I been concise? Prefer the short word to the long, the familiar to the fancy, the specific to the abstract. As Strunk and White said, "Don't be tempted by the $20 word when there is a 10-center handy, ready and able." Or as English poet Robert Southey wrote, "If you would be pungent, be brief; for it is with words as with sunbeams-the more they are condensed, the deeper they burn."
3. Is my writing correct? Your work must conform to the basic conventions of grammar, spelling and punctuation. These are the grease that lubricates the wheels of communication. Without them, communication becomes difficult, if not impossible.
4. Do my sentence lengths vary? If you want to convey a sense of action, tension or movement, use short sentences. A series of long sentences slows down the reader and conveys a more relaxed mood. A good writer uses a variety of sentences-long ones, short ones and those in between.
5. Have I used transitions? Lead the reader from one section to the next with transitions. They are your bridges. They assure the reader that you have a plan. Repeat key words or phrases. Use words like: now, but, and, however, since. These are the links that tie a story together.
6. Have I been sensual? Appeal to as many senses as possible: sight, sound, smell, taste and touch. Let your reader see what you saw and heard what you heard. You did note the sounds, smells and textures while you

were reporting, didn't you? "We must put all our senses to work," said James Kilpatrick.

7. Have I used comparisons? Compare and contrast your subject to something familiar. Do this with a simile or its first cousin, the metaphor. With these devices, the writer draws a word picture.
8. Have I provided examples and dialogue? Tell the story through the words and actions of your characters. This allows your reader to be an eyewitness. "An ounce of example is worth a ton of generalization," said Henry James. And from Tom Wolfe: "Realistic dialogue involves the reader and defines character more completely than any other single device."
9. Have I written about people? Write about people, not programs, policies or procedures. The latter are worthy subjects, but only as they apply to people.

Libel

In writing the news, a reporter handles a valuable and fragile possession, a person's reputation. In reviewing your writing, make sure you have not injured someone's reputation unnecessarily. Have you libeled them? Here are some things to look for:

1. First a definition: Libel is the injury to reputation that occurs when a false, published report charges criminal conduct, immorality or incompetence in one's business, profession or office.
2. The key word in that definition is "false." Truth is the best defense against libel, but knowing it and proving it are two things. Off-the-record sources may refuse to testify for you in court. Be certain you can prove what you publish.
3. You will not be guilty of libel if your false report is privileged. It can be privileged if it was a full, fair and accurate report from a judicial, legislative or other public proceeding or from a public record, and if it was done without malice.

4. If you repeat a libelous statement, you can be held liable, even though it is attributed. Disclaimers such as "it is alleged" or "it is reported" won't save you.
5. Reporters enjoy great protection when they cover public officials. The Supreme Court has defined these public officials as those "who have substantial responsibility for, or control over, the conduct of public affairs."
6. To successfully recover damages for a defamatory falsehood, a public official must prove "actual malice." In other words, the reporter knew the facts were false, or had a reckless disregard of whether the facts were false-he or she did not check their accuracy using normal reporting practices.
7. The same standards apply to public figures. These are prominent private citizens, some celebrities or those who have thrust themselves into a public controversy.
8. However, private citizens enjoy a different standard than public officials or public figures. They must prove only negligence or carelessness to successfully sue for libel.
9. At least 90 percent of all libel suits arise from run-of-the-mill stories. A Harvard study concluded: "The gee-whiz, slam-bang stories usually aren't the ones that generate libel, but innocent appearing, potentially treacherous minor yarns from police court, traffic cases, from routine meetings and from business reports."
10. Libel usually results from carelessness, exaggerated writing, statements of officials made outside privileged situations, inadequate verification or failure by the reporter to talk with the subject of the defamation.

Ethics

A doctor who prescribes an illegal medicine could lose his license. A lawyer who misleads a client, or an accountant who knowingly misrepresents a company's financial statement, may be guilty of violating a code of ethics. But a reporter who poses as a policeman to get private phone records may win a Pulitzer

Prize. The doctor, lawyer and accountant must pass exams to be licensed, and they have regulatory bodies to enforce proper conduct.

Journalism does not, for these are seen as contrary to a free press. The power to license or regulate is the power to censor. So it is crucial as you are revising your writing to reflect on how it came to be. Have your behaved ethically?

1. Two of the defining characteristics of a profession are its mandatory code of behavior and the enforcement of that code. Journalism has neither. You become a journalist when you declare that you are one, and you remain one as long as you keep declaring it.
2. Reporters may feel responsible to the public, but they are not. Their readers do not elect them and cannot fire them. The government does not license them or set standards for behavior. They are not responsible to other reporters. They are responsible only to themselves and their employers. Reporters are self-regulated.
3. Because of this, newspaper work has been described as a "swampland where eerie mists of judgment hang low over a boggy terrain." It is, but there are standards to light the way. Some of them are:
   a. Seek truth and report it fully. Inform yourself continually. Be honest, fair and courageous in gathering and reporting the news. Give voice to the voiceless, and hold the powerful accountable.
   b. Seek out and disseminate competing perspectives without being unduly influenced by those who would use their power counter to public interest. Remain free of associations and activities that may compromise your integrity or damage your credibility.
   c. Minimize harm. Be compassionate of those affected by your actions. Treat sources, subjects and colleagues with respect, not as means to an end. Do not lie, pose or misrepresent yourself.

d. Don't report on any group or organization to which you belong. Avoid active involvement in partisan causes, politics, community affairs, social actions or demonstrations. Avoid service on governmental, quasi-governmental or community-wide boards, commissions or committees.

e. Don't write about someone related by blood or marriage, or someone with whom you have a personal or financial relationship. Don't use your position to seek benefit or advantage in business, financial or commercial transactions. Don't take freebies.

2

REPORTS REGARDING SUICIDES

The media plays an important role as a mass communication channel in the society, through which, news stories exert powerful influence on the construction of social norms and values. In recent years, the number of suicide cases in Hong Kong has shown a drastic increase. How our media report suicide has drawn great concern from the public, there are strict criticisms on the breach of code of ethics. The general public worries that detailed media accounts of suicidal acts may encourage vulnerable people or youngsters to imitate them.

We understand the difficulties the media face with when reporting any suicide story. In fact, the causes of action are usually complicated. The deceased's identity, mental condition and problems encountered are closely related to his/her fatal attempt; it is a great task to clarify all information under the time strain. However, due to the keen market competition, journalists might have to report unconfirmed materials to meet deadlines. From various studies, we have reason to recognize the association between portrayal of suicide and subsequent actual suicides is causal1. The detailed description of suicide methods, the dramatized death, the deceased's photo being shown and the big font headline may cause great impact. And youngsters seem to be the most vulnerable to the influence.

For this reason, countries such as USA, UK, New Zealand and Australia have issued guidelines for media reporting suicide. The World Health Organization (WHO) has listed "toning down reports in the media" as one of its six key strategies on suicide prevention. The Hong Kong News Executives' Association

(HKNEA) and the Hong Kong Journalists Association (HKJA) have established codes of ethics including guidelines about suicide reporting.

This booklet aims to assist frontline journalists to be more aware of the potential positive and negative influences that may incur. To supplement the existing guidelines, the booklet will provide relevant research results and experiences from other countries. We encourage self-disciplines. Our aim is to minimize the "copycat effects" on the vulnerable group but in the meantime to preserve the freedom of the press.

Suicide in Hong Kong at a Glance

Based on the data from the Coroners' Court and analysis of our center, about 1,238 people committed suicide in 2003, at a ratio of 18.2 to 100,000 people, which is over 11% higher than the suicide rate in 2002. This figure is higher than the world's average rate of 15.0. Suicide has become the 6th killer in Hong Kong, and 3 to 4 people commit suicide everyday.

Middle aged people have become a high-risk group. Their suicide rate was 18.9 in 2002, 16% higher than the average suicide rate in Hong Kong. Not to neglect the young group of age 15 to 24, where the rate increase from 9.0 in 2001 to 12.7 in 2002 has alarmed the public. Moreover, charcoal-burning has become a prevalent method since 1998, and the situation is getting worsen these days. Among all suicide methods, the rate of charcoal-burning increased from 3% in 1998 to 26.4% in 2003, it is now the second most common method of suicide.

Suicide Reporting in Hong Kong

In Hong Kong, media coverage of suicide or attempted suicide is very common. However, it is controversial how the media report the story. According to the Hong Kong Press Council's web page, the Council denounced certain newspapers' way of reporting three students who burned charcoal to commit suicide on 2nd May 2002 and denounced several newspapers for publishing photos of two deceased, a mother and her son, who died after falling from a building on 9th October 2002. Our centre analyzed how five major local Chinese newspapers reported suicide stories in 2007-8. About 6% of the suicide cases appeared on the front page, 87% with photos or diagrams, and 93% mentioned the suicide methods in the headlines.

From the preliminary result of our center's Prevalence Study 2004, 36.9% of the respondents were disturbed, from a little disturbed to very disturbed, by celebrity suicide. 2.4% of the respondents changed the way they saw suicide, and found it to be more acceptable and thought about suicide after the celebrity's suicide. In additions, 68.3% of the respondents were dissatisfied and very dissatisfied with how the media reported the suicide news. 20% of the respondents were influenced by the suicide news reported by the mass media.

Copycat Effect of Media Reporting

The first known "copycat" case occurred in 1774, when Gother's "The Sorrows of the Young Werther" was published. Many youngsters imitated the character of the book to commit suicide. This behaviour was coined as "Werther effect" by the academy.

According to the social learning theory, high-risk suicidal people may learn from news stories or books written about suicide. When they find similarities with the object, they tend to follow the same action to "solve the problem". The impact would be 10 times or more if the story is about a celebrity or any person known by the public.

In November 1998, the first charcoal-burning case in Hong Kong was widely publicized with detailed illustrations by the media. In the following month, there were 9 more suicides by the same means. Charcoalburning became one of the most prevalent methods in 1998. In 2003, it even accounted for 26.4% of the total suicide cases in Hong Kong. There are people in our neighborhood areas such as Japan, Macau and Taiwan who also adopted this method to end their lives.

In October 1999, there were several suicide incidents involving school kids. Six young students killed themselves within 11 days and shocked the community. As of November 2003, 4 students had committed suicide in the same school of

Tin Shui Wai in two and half years. Voices from our community blamed this as the copycat effect. In April 2003, famous artiste Leslie Cheung died of falling from a building; in the following 9 hours there were 5 more suicides committed by the same means.

Effects of Mass Media

Research studies have indicated the correlation between media reports and the subsequent suicide cases. The more the media mention, on front pages or intensively dramatized, the higher suicide rate to follow.

Suicidal or mentally distressed people are more sensitive to suicide reporting. How detailed the story is can have a great impact on these people, as they may have atendency to copy or follow the act.

Newspapers

Researches indicated a higher suicide rate when more suicide news was seen. In 1984, US study revealed that after a celebrity's death by suicide, which was followed by intensive reports and news headlines, there was a remarkable increase in the suicide rate. When the media repeatedly mentioned certain suicide method, similar incidents will follow in increased numbers.

Television

Studies indicated youngsters' suicidal thought is closely related to how often they watch television. Experts advised that suicidal youths pay more attention to such news on television. These reports may deepen their mind, and they have more exposures to watch and imitate. Researchers also found a substantial increase of suicide cases within 10 days after the television broadcast certain suicide news.

Drama and Plays

WHO pointed out there is no obvious association between drama or plays and suicidal acts. However, analysis indicated that after a railway suicide drama was seen on TV, there were

60 similar cases occurred in the following 70 days. And the suicides were of same age as the character in the drama.

Internet

The popularity of the Internet has shown great impact on our daily life. Some websites mentioning various suicide methods draw the public's attention, as these may have adverse influences on youngsters. However, systematic studies on the topic are still limited, and the relation between Internet influences and suicide is not ascertained as of this day. In October 2004, there was a great public concern on the "suicide pact" through Internet. Japanese police had found the bodies of nine people who apparently committed suicide after meeting via special suicide sites on the Internet and then some people in Taiwan adopted the same way to attempt suicide.

Suspected Cases: News Story Triggered Suicide Acts

The famous Hong Kong artiste Leslie Cheung fell from a building and died on 1st April 2003. There were extensive media reports. According to the data from the Coroners' Court and analysis from our centre, the number of suicides increased drastically in the first half of April 2003. Analyzing the demographic of these suicide victims, they were mostly aged from 25 to 39, and chose the same means, jumping, as Cheung did.

As Leslie Cheung's incident occurred during the SARS epidemic, it is not certain to what extent the increase of suicides could be attributed to contagion. However, the suicide rates during SARS period March, May and June 2003 did not increase significantly. On the other hand, study showed that the outbreak of SARS has enhanced social networking and solidarity , which might be a protective factor of suicide. Therefore, it is reasonable to assert that the copycat effect is related to the increase of suicide rate.

The copycat effect may trigger a certain age group to attempt suicide by the same means. Therefore media professionals should be more cautious when reporting suicide cases.

Japanese case: Okada Yukiko

On 8th April 1986, the young Japanese singer Okada Yukiko jumped out from her company's building and died. She was only 20 at that time. According to Yoshitomo Takahashi, a Japanese scholar specialized in suicide study, the Japanese media reported the case extensively and sensationally with photos and detailed descriptions. As a result, suicide rate in 1986 increased drastically, and most were youngsters under 20.

Media as a Proactive Role

The above reporting examples indicated the adverse effects of media reporting. However, media can play a proactive role in helping to prevent suicides. According to the media resource issued by WHO, "Reporting of suicide in an appropriate, accurate and potentially helpful manner by enlightened media can prevent tragic loss of lives by suicide."

This booklet aims to assist journalists reporting suicide with more concern and to release any information in a more caring attitude.

Success Stories of Appropriate Media Reporting

Case 1

After the Viennese media extensively reported subway suicides, the number increased since 1983. There were 7 cases in 1984, 13 and in 1986. 9 cases were reported in the first half of 1987. In mid 1987, an organization preventing suicides alerted the public by promulgating the media guidelines. Subway suicides dropped to 2 by the end of 1987, 80% less than the first half of the year. (Afterward, there were 3 cases in 1989 and 4 in 1990). Moreover, the overall suicide rate in Vienna also dropped.

Case 2

In 1994, the suicide death of the famous singer Kurt Cobain did not trigger any substantial increase of similar attempts in his hometown Seattle. The media did not simply glorify his achievements, but also emphasized his death was a wasteful act of giving up life. The news lines also discussed about the risk of committing suicide and ways to seek help.

Case 3

In the early 1990s, suicide reporting in Switzerland raised the public concern. Scholars and medical practitioners held a conference with the media and set up guidelines. A comparative study of suicides being reported in 1991 and 1994 showed that front pages coverage dropped from 20% (of all news reported) to 4%, photos published reduced from 43% to 8%, and sensational headlines decreased from 62% to 25%. Even though the number of suicide stories increased, the overall suicide rate had a small decrease. This indicated that reporting with caution helps to prevent suicides.

Professional Media Reporting

The Hong Kong Journalists Association has established guideline on suicide reporting. This passage and the following passage of "Issues on suicide" are extracted from the codes of ethics of WHO30, USA31, suicide prevention organization, Canada and Australia.

Professional journalists should prevent reporting suicide in a way that could have potential negative effect on the vulnerable group of suicide or youth readers. Media professional can play a role in publicizing the warning signs and to convey the message of help seeking. Their emphasis could include educational purpose and provide only necessary information to the readers. The following principles should be followed by media professionals:

Appropriate Reporting

3Placement and Headline

Avoid publishing the suicide news on the front page unless the reporting involves public interest;

Avoid using large font headline;

Avoid mentioning the suicide method or suspected cause such as "jumping" or "charcoal burning" in the headline.

Contents

Wordings

Avoid phrases like: "successful suicide", "unsuccessful suicide" or "suicide-prone person"; Use "suicide rate" instead of "spread/epidemic of suicide"; Don't sensationalize the reporting (especially of the celebrity).

Minimize the coverage to only necessary content; the wordings should not be exaggerated; Don't glorify or romanticize suicide; Don't criticize, condemn or sympathize suicide;

If the report mentions the full name or other personal information of the deceased or attempter, it may has a wrong signal that suicide people can draw the public attention. The reporting should pay special attention.

Suicide Method

Don't report specific details of the suicide method and its procedures, especially the venue of suicide, the tools used, the amount of pills taken, etc.

Cause of Death

Suicide is never caused by a single reason. Don't over-simplify the explanations for suicide; Suicide should not be reported as unexplainable or a "mystery"; The personal history of mental health or drug abuse record should be mentioned.

Description

The news report should not attribute suicide as a choice of solution to any problem (such as bankruptcy or study problem); The sorrow or guilt of the surviving relatives and friends should not be focused, which may be a wrong signal that suicide can draw other people's attention.

Others

The way of presentation should consider the feeling of the surviving relatives and friends. If the photo of the deceased or the surviving relatives and friends is published, this may hurt the survivor deeply.

Pictorial and Graphic Presentation

If the media publishes the photo of the deceased, this may give the false impression to the vulnerable people that committing suicide can make them famous. The reporting should pay special attention to this; Don't illustrate the suicide method or venue of suicide in graphic presentation.

Seek Help Information

Provide solutions, such as information of mental health, hotline numbers and the warning signs of suicidal behaviour; Present the examples of successful counseling; Provide Hotline numbers which help the surviving relatives and friends; Advocate the message "depression is a highly treatable illness".

TV Reporting

Avoid presenting suicide cases as the headline TV news unless the reporting involves public interest; Use precise and accurate wordings; Don't report specific details of the suicide method. Presenting any personal information of the deceased or attempter should pay special attention; Don't romanticize suicide.

Issues on Suicide

(i) Suicide Rate and Statistical Data

Suicide rate is usually presented as a number of suicide cases per 100,000 people. If the population is too small, the interpretation of suicide rate should be paid special attention. If the population is less than 250,000, it is recommended to present the exact number of cases; When comparing the statistics of different countries, it should be bear in mind that the research methods may vary among countries; If the suicide rate is reported, it is recommended to seek comments from suicide researchers. (Please refer to "Talk to the experts")

(ii) Celebrity Suicide

Undoubtedly, celebrity suicide has great news value, but it can also influence the vulnerable and suicidal people. Media professionals should be very cautious, and should evaluate whether the substance of reporting is essential; Don't glorify the death of celebrity. The news reporting should be just mourning but not romanticize or sensationalize; Suicide is never caused by a single reason. Don't over-simplify the explanations for suicide; Mental illness or drug abuse record of the celebrity should be mentioned clearly.

(iii) Interviewing Surviving Relatives and Friends

The surviving relatives and friends usually cannot accept the fact right after the incident. Therefore the media should be considerate and avoid disturbing them; The grieving survivors may have emotional fluctuation or even have suicidal thoughts. Media professional should refer the case to social worker, psychiatrists or healthcare professional; The journalists should bear in mind that the accounts based on the initial reaction of surviving relatives and friends are often unreliable.

(iv) Interviewing Suicide Attempter

It is not recommended to interview youngsters about their suicide attempt history, which may have adverse effect to other high risk youngsters; For adult attempters, it is recommended to ask their mind change during counseling, and deliver positive messages to the audiences.

(v) Homicide-Suicide

The media should be cautious to this kind of cases. Media professional should be aware that the tragedy of the homicide can mask the suicidal aspect of act. Follow the rules of this recommendation.

(vi) Suicide Pact

Suicide pacts are mutual arrangements between two people who kill themselves at the same time. This is uncommon. Media should not simplify the reason as the act of loving individuals who do not wish to be separated.

Responsible Reporting

The New York Times: Grim Reminder on Mental Illness Comment: Reporting the death of a successful businessman does not need to be sensational, but it is good to point out his depression when he was alive. Mental health professional was also interviewed to inform the public about the suicidal risk of depression. Also, the passage analyzed the reasons why many executives were reluctant to seek help, which can enlighten the public.

The Buffalo News: The Specter of Suicide

People take their lives not over an isolated incident, but usually during a significant psychiatric illness, experts say. Comment: This passage emphasized the relationship between suicide and the mental health rather than the suicide methods or other background information. The passage even pointed out that suicide is not resulted from a single incident, and often related to emotional distress. The journalist did not link up all incidents together unthoughtfully, but emphasized that the story behind was not that simple.

Inappropriate Reporting: Case 1

Violating the WHO guidelines: Don't report specific details of the method used/Don't publish photographs or suicide notes Comment: When the first case of charcoal-burning suicide happened in Hong Kong, the media report extensively. Some coverage even used pictorial presentation to illustrate the method of suicide. According to the Archives of General Psychiatry, there were 9 more cases in the following month and charcoal-burning became one of the most prevalent methods of suicide. In 2003, charcoal-burning even accounted for 26.4% of all the overall suicide cases. Some people in our neighbourhood areas like Macau and Taiwan imitated the acts.

Inappropriate Reporting: Case 2

Violating WHO guideline: Don't report specific details of the method used Comment: It is highly inappropriate to have red arrows indication of the falling direction of the suicide people.

This would act as certain "guidance" to the vulnerable people. In addition, for the same venue where both two incidents took place, the paper mentioned "The 8/F of Times Square" in the headline, which may trigger the suicide ideation of vulnerable people especially when they pass by. The two cases may be relevant to the result of copycat effect.

Inappropriate Reporting: Case 3

Violating WHO guidelines: Don't give simplistic reasons Comment: The passage claimed that the deceased was "addicted to soccer betting" and "left a large sum of loan". However, the surviving relatives revealed to the interviewer of CSRP that the victim just borrowed $7000 from other relatives, such should not be "a large sum of loan", and a large part of it was for living expenses rather than soccer betting. The relatives also claimed that the deceased had started to engage in soccer betting for a short period of time, and our centre could not find evidence to support that the deceased was a pathological gambler.

The newspaper just simplified the cause of death to be the debt problem from gambling, which was unfair to the deceased and his family. It also has a wrong signal to the other people in debt that suicide is a way to solve the problem.

1. Can interviewing people who have attempted suicide help the prevention of suicide?

   It depends on who is telling the story and how it is told. If an adult suicide attempter is interviewed, it may be helpful if he/she shares the emotional change and talks about the negative consequence of suicide and the way of seeking help. Interviewing youngsters may be harmful. It may be a wrong signal to them that suicide can draw public attention.

2. Would people become suicidal just by reading about suicide?

   There is no reason to believe that someone who is not suicidal can become so by reading a news story. Our concern is that someone who is suicidal may be stimulated to act by the nature of what is read. Those who work for the media might feel that the press should report suicide. What the recommendations convey is that there are responsible and helpful ways of doing so that minimize risk.

3. If someone is going to commit suicide, can media reporting change their mind?

   In fact, the majority of people who consider suicide are ambivalent. They are not sure that they want to die. They are just discontent with the reality. If some people can offer them help and counseling, their suicidal thoughts may be altered.

4. Many people just claim to commit suicide but do not actually try to do it?

   In fact, people who have attempted suicide would have greater chance to retry than any ordinary people. Accordiı.g to different studies, about 30-60% of suicide attempters have tried it before. About 15-25% of them would commit suicide again in one year time, and about 40% of deaths by suicide have attempted suicide in the past. Therefore we should not overlook their claims and but refer them to seek help.

5. If we stop reporting about specific methods used to commit suicide, won't they just find another way to kill themselves?

   There is research evidence that media recommendations have an impact on the overall suicide rate, not just the rate for a specific method. For example, the overall suicide rate in Vienna decreased steadily after the promulgation of recommendations, which dramatically stopped the reporting of subway suicides. While the sharpest decrease was for subway suicides, there was no increase in other methods of suicide, indicating no substitution effect of suicide method.

6. Would the recommendations conflict with the press freedom? Freedom of the press and the above suggestions are both based on the public interest. While the media has their freedom, at the same time they should be responsible to the public. When we learn that media coverage of suicide may exert adverse impacts on some readers, the media should pay special attention to the issue.

7. The causes of suicide are complicated. Why should the media bear the burden? In fact, causes of suicide are complicated and never resulted from a single factor. Therefore the responsibility does never lie on any single party. Suicide prevention is the responsibility of everyone. When we learn that media coverage of suicide may exert adverse impacts on some readers, the media should pay special attention to the issue. On the other hand, media can also play an active and positive role in suicide prevention.
8. Where can I find the information about suicide in Hong Kong? Who can I interview on this issue? The Hong Kong Jockey Club Centre for Suicide Research and Prevention is specialized on the evidence-based research on Hong Kong's suicide problem. Our monitoring and surveillance system gathers all local suicide statistics. Our staff can help any journalists to work on their reports.
9. What is depression? How does it relate to suicide? It is noted that a large proportion of people who committed suicide had certain mental illnesses when they were alive. Depression is one of the most common mental illnesses.

If you experience any five of the following symptoms, and the symptoms persist for more than two weeks, which significantly affect your study, work and/or relation with others, you should consult with professional or seek help.

Irritability
Low mood
Loss of interest in all activities
Insomnia or hypersomnia
Rapid loss/gain in appetite
Dramatic weight loss/gain
Constant feelings of fatigue
Difficulty in concentrating
Feelings of hopelessness about the future
Feelings of worthlessness
Frequent thoughts of death or suicide

What to Do & What Not to Do

"Reporting of suicide in an appropriate, accurate and potentially helpful manner by enlightened media can prevent tragic loss of lives by suicide."

Preventing Suicide: A Resource for Media Professionals, World Health Organization (2000)

It is reasonable to recognize the association between portrayal of suicide and subsequent actual suicides is causal. People with suicidal ideation seem to be most vulnerable to the influence of the media; Media professionals can play an important and positive role in helping to prevent suicide;

The following suggestions can act as reference to media professionals to minimize the adverse impacts on vulnerable people.

What to Do

1. Work closely with health authorities in presenting the facts.
2. Refer to suicide as a completed suicide, not a successful one.
3. Present only relevant data, and on the inside pages.
4. Highlight alternatives to suicide.
5. Provide information on helplines and community resources.
6. Publicize risk indicators and warning signs.

What Not to Do

1. Don't publish photographs or suicide notes.
2. Don't report specific details of the method used.
3. Don't give simplistic reasons.
4. Don't glorify or sensationalize suicide.
5. Don't use religious or cultural stereotypes.
6. Don't apportion blame.

3

Conflicts in Media

In the wake of the deadly and destructive civil conflicts so prominent in the 1990s, academics and practitioners have increasingly focused on predicting and preventing civil conflict, rather than on responding to and recovering from it. Accordingly, various methods have been developed to identify societies in which violent conflict is likely to occur, and significant research has been conducted into the root causes of civil conflict. That work has focused on identifying and understanding such causal factors as economic decline, long-standing grievances between groups and the ethnic and religious make-up of society. But insufficient attention has been devoted to the use of the media to promote violent conflict.

In this paper, we focus on the role of media in vulnerable societies, which are defined as societies highly susceptible to movement toward civil conflict or repressive rule. This often describes societies in developing countries and countries in transition, almost always those struggling to make the transition from authoritarian to democratic government. It frequently describes multi-ethnic societies as well, which, over the past decade, have proved more likely to fall victim to conflict than societies with greater ethnic homogeneity.

Although media outlets can be actively used to promote conflict, media can also contribute to conflict involuntarily. Such passive incitement to violence most frequently occurs when journalists have poor professional skills, when the media culture is underdeveloped or when there is little or no history of independent media. Under such circumstances, journalists can inflame grievances and promote stereotypes by virtue of the manner in which they report, even though their intentions are not necessarily malicious and they are not being manipulated by an outside entity.

Perhaps media have generally been overlooked in analyses of conflict because, on their own, they are rarely a direct cause. Nonetheless, as part of a larger matrix of factors, media can be extremely powerful tools for promoting violence, as witnessed in Rwanda, the former Republic of Yugoslavia, the former Soviet republic of Georgia and elsewhere. As Jamie Metzl (1997) observes, 'mass media reach not only people's homes, but also their minds, shaping their thoughts and sometimes their behavior.' Media behaviour can also provide indicators of impending conflict, as certain characteristics of media structure and media behaviour tend to precede conflict; some are evident early enough that an intervention may be feasible. If preventing conflict is the goal, then influential tools such as media must be closely examined, their pernicious effects mitigated and positive output magnified.

The various approaches to precluding or stopping the use of media as a tool to promote division and conflict range from training journalists to advising legislators on drafting media legislation. But for such training or advising to be effective, the role of media in moving societies toward or away from conflict needs to be clearly understood.

CLUES TO CONFLICT

Using a series of indicators, it is possible to identify societies in which media outlets are especially susceptible to abuse or that may be in the early stages of manipulation.

These indicators are divided between those dealing with media structure (the way the media sector is set up) and those dealing with media content (the articles and programming that media outlets produce). None of these indicators constitutes either sufficient or necessary conditions for media manipulation to occur, but when a significant portion of them are evident media outlets are especially vulnerable to abuse.

Structural Indicators

Structural indicators can be divided into three categories: indicators concerning the media outlets themselves; indicators concerning the professionals - journalists, editors, managers and owners - associated with the outlets; and indicators concerning the structure of government institutions dealing with the media.

Media Outlets

These indicators concern the configuration of the media landscape in a particular country and the influence that media outlets exert over society. They include reach, accessibility and plurality.

The reach enjoyed by media outlets is critical for obvious reasons: if the reach of an outlet is minimal, then its capacity to influence a society will also be limited. Factors affecting reach include the strength of radio and television signals and the breadth of newspaper distribution.

Media accessibility is equally important. Even if media are widely available, people still need to have access if they are to be influential (recognizing this fact, the Rwandan government handed out free radios before the 1994 genocide). For newspapers this means that people must be literate in the language of the newspaper and have the means to acquire a newspaper, whether that means purchasing one, borrowing one from a friend or other means. For radio and television, it means owning or having access to a radio or television and understanding the language of the programming. In developed countries, media access is taken for granted, but in many developing countries it is not easily achieved.

The degree of media plurality is critical because with greater competition, one or a small number of media outlets are less likely to have the capacity to dominate. Plurality applies not only to the number of outlets but also to the number of divergent voices emanating from those outlets. In other words, a multitude of private stations all playing music, or all espousing similar messages, does not constitute plurality. The society in which media can exert the most influence, both positive and negative, is one in which media outlets enjoy wide exposure but have relatively few competitors.

An important variable here concerns whether the media scene is dominated by either state-owned or private outlets or if there is a balanced mixture of the two. Particularly where the media scene is dominated by the state, there is often little or no check on media behaviour.

Another important variable is the receptivity of the population to diversified independent media. This is often taken for granted in developed countries, but in many societies there is little or no history of media diversity and independence. Under these circumstances, when media diversification does occurs, one of the consequences can be the type of situation that developed in the former Soviet republic of Georgia, where suddenly vacant media space was filled by outlets operating from distinctly nationalist and ethnic perspectives.

Media Professionals

The second set of indicators concerns media professionals. This includes not only journalists, but also the people behind the scenes, such as editors, station managers and owners. The indicators are journalist capacity; journalist isolation; the political, ethnic, religious and regional composition of the media corps; and the degree of diversity in the ownership of media outlets.

Journalist capacity refers to journalists' ability to carry out their charge with a reasonable degree of professional integrity and skill. More capable journalists tend to make media outlets less susceptible to abuse. Journalism training is an important variable. Questions that should be asked in any society that may be vulnerable to conflict include: Is there a school of journalism or communications in which journalists are trained? Do journalists enter the profession with the skills needed to report responsibly?

The degree of fact checking in place is also important: Do journalists write unsubstantiated stories filled with rumours? Or are the origins of most stories clear and are they attributed to credible sources? The answers to these questions go a long way toward determining the susceptibility of journalists to abuse.

The second indicator is the degree to which journalists are isolated, physically and metaphorically, from their domestic and international colleagues. An awareness of international standards of professional journalism provides a basis from which journalists may feel justified, beyond their own personal conviction, to resist manipulation, because they enjoy a network of support and feel part of a larger community of journalists who adhere to a common standard. Not only are they emboldened by that support, but they may also be able to use the network to communicate with the outside world if media freedom comes under attack. Consequently, those who intend to manipulate the media may be more hesitant if every time they apply pressure behind the scenes their actions are made public by the local or international media.

Particularly in traditional societies where ethnic bonds are strong, simple peer pressure and an emphasis on the importance of responsibility to clan or group can facilitate media manipulation. In such societies, it may be relatively easy for individuals holding revered positions in their groups to manipulate members of the same group who work as journalists. They can sometimes do so using threats or bribes, without having to revert to overt coercion.

Along the same lines, diversity in the ownership of media outlets is critical because, ultimately, it is the owners who exert the most control over content. A society is especially vulnerable to media abuse when all or a significant portion of media outlets are owned by one or a small number of people, particularly if those people are of the same ethnicity or religion, support the same political party or are from the same region.

Even a balanced mix of state-owned and independent media outlets may not be sufficient to guard against abuse, because the 'independent' outlets may have strong ties to the government. It is also important to determine whether more subtle links exist between influential members of particular groups and media outlets, such as discrete financial relationships.

Government Institutions Concerned with Media

Perhaps as important as the structure of media outlets and the people involved in them are the independence and effectiveness of government institutions concerned with the media, particularly the legislature and judiciary. The degree of media independence and freedom established in a country's laws and the degree to which those laws are enforced define the space in which media are allowed to operate. The relevant indicators here are media's legal environment and changes in media controls.

Two very different types of legislation are critical to maintaining a healthy legal environment for media: legislation protecting journalists and media outlets from abuse and guaranteeing their freedom to operate without government interference; and legislation, such as libel and slander laws, protecting private individuals from being the subject of unjustified insult or falsehoods appearing in the media. The former allows journalists to operate without fear of government coercion, unwarranted prosecution or personal harm.

If such legislation is in place and consistently enforced, then journalists and media outlets are not likely to be very susceptible to abuse. But if such legislation is absent, journalists and media outlets are essentially 'fair game' for the government, meaning that the state is free to attempt to manipulate them however it chooses. Journalists, in turn, have few options for recourse.

If private individuals have no effective avenue for registering complaints against the media, then few options are available to people or groups who may be unfairly criticized or demonized in the media. The absence of the possibility of punishment emboldens those associated with hate media outlets and may encourage the formation of such outlets, because the risks involved are reduced. To counteract this effect, mechanisms for punishment, such as libel or hate speech legislaion that protects both individuals and groups, can be beneficial.

Recent research into the causes of civil conflict suggests that societies in transition (those that are in the process of liberalizing and moving toward a more open, democratic dispensation) are more vulnerable to conflict than societies that have already gone through a transition or those awaiting one. In other words, it is societies 'on the way up' that tend to experience civil conflict. A common characteristic of liberalization is relaxation of controls on the media and, although this is generally a positive development, dangers accompany it. Newly opened media space can quickly be filled by media outlets that mirror political or ethnic centrifugal forces promoting conflict. Thus, a relaxation of media controls can sometimes actually lay the groundwork for future conflict.

On the other hand, a tightening of media controls can also be a precursor to conflict, as it can be indicative of a government's intentions: for example, the Zimbabwean government-imposed tight restrictions on media toward the beginning of its violent land-seizure initiative and its effort to ensure Robert Mugabe's victory in the 2002 presidential elections. By forcing these measures through parliament, Zimbabwean authorities telegraphed their intentions.

CONTENT INDICATORS

Content is critical to the overall analysis because media content helps shape an individual's view of the world and helps form the lens through which all issues are viewed. The content indicators presented here can be evident early in the manipulation process, at a point where intervention may still be feasible. However, once media manipulation is widely apparent it may be too late, and interventions may yield little or no benefit.

Content Creating Fear

The construction of fear is likely to be a component of any effort to use media to promote conflict. In Rwanda before the genocide, a private radio station tried to instil fear of an imminent attack on Hutus by a Tutsi militia. These efforts were at least partly successful, as many people subscribed to the 'imminent' threat, although only flimsy evidence was provided to support it. When such reporting creates widespread fear, people are more amenable to taking preemptive action, which is how the actions taken in Rwanda were characterized. Media were used to make people believe that 'we must strike first in order to save ourselves.' Creating fear laid the foundation for taking violent action through 'self-defence'. In assessing the construction of fear, one must be circumspect, however, because there is an important distinction between content that criticizes a person or group in a manner that is simply degrading (as seen in many Western tabloids) and printing or broadcasting information that is clearly intended to create a fearful reaction. Although the former can lay the groundwork for the latter, it is most often the latter that increases the likelihood of conflict. Four strategies commonly used to create fear are:

1. Focus on past conflicts and on a history of ethnic animosity. By highlighting the fact that violent conflict has occurred in the past and that the same groups behind violent acts then are suspected of planning them now, the potential for future conflict can appear much greater to media consumers than it actually is, and the means and capacity for carrying out such atrocities more attainable. Media can be used to make the point that 'they did it before, they can do it again'.
2. Manipulation of myths, stereotypes and identities. This often occurs through the dehumanization of members of the 'other' group. Frequent references to Tutsis as 'cockroaches' in the Rwandan media are an example of this phenomenon. As soon as people in the other group are perceived as 'less than human', engaging in conflict with them and killing them becomes easier to justify. A related strategy is to portray members of a particular group as 'irrational' or 'unpredictable', providing additional justification for pre-emptive action.
3. Overemphasis on certain grievances, inequities, or atrocities. This tactic can create the impression that circumstances are worse than they really are and that a particular group is more victimized than it actually is. If the overemphasized grievance or inequity is particularly sensitive, such as a religious issue or an

issue concerning the use of natural resources, excessively negative reporting can be particularly inflammatory. Overemphasis adds fuel to the fire by creating the impression that a group is being intentionally discriminated against and that the situation is particularly dire, even though neither of these impressions may be accurate. Discrimination may be present, but the size and scope of the discrimination may be exaggerated in the media; thus, the 'victimized' group is given added incentive and justification for reprisal, regardless of whether their grievances are actually legitimate.

4. Shift toward consistently negative reporting. The critical element here is change; if the situation has been bad from the start and consistently negative reporting is the norm, then it is not likely to be inflammatory. But a significant shift in reporting toward a decidedly negative and pessimistic tone creates the impression that the country's situation is worsening considerably and provides justification for people or groups to stop and reverse that slide by taking decisive action, including violence.

Content Creating Inevitability and Resignation

Just as media outlets have been used to create a pervasive sense of fear, they have also been used to convince people that conflict is inevitable. This leaves media consumers resigned to the notion that conflict will happen, and when such resignation is prevalent, efforts to prevent conflict tend to be seen as futile, which makes them increasingly unlikely to succeed.

Portraying conflict as part of an 'eternal' process is a strategy frequently used to create the impression that conflict is inevitable. This often occurs when media promote 'primordial identities' that suggest that people of different ethnicities have, since the beginning of time, been in conflict with one another, have never coexisted peacefully and are somehow preordained to be in perpetual conflict. Rarely, if ever, is this actually the case, as virtually every ethnic conflict involves groups that have lived together peacefully at one stage or another. A similar strategy for promoting the inevitability of conflict is to use media to discredit alternatives to conflict. For example, Alison Des Forges (2002: 241) observes that Rwandan radio 'seized the opportunity to impress upon Hutu that Tutsi could never be trusted and that any form of power-sharing, such as that specified in the Arusha Accords, could never work'.

Opportunities for Intervention

The term 'intervention', as it is used here, does not denote any sort of military or armed initiative (with one exception in the segment on 'aggressive interventions'). Rather, the term refers to support for the development of diverse, pluralistic independent media outlets giving voice to a variety of views and opinions. Such interventions are not carried out by soldiers or peacekeepers, but by journalists, professional media trainers and nongovernmental organization (NGO) workers.

Structural Interventions

The most effective strategy for strengthening a professional media sector and protecting its content from biased influence is through reforms in media structure. Structural reforms have many advantages over interventions that target only content. If carried out early enough they can prevent media abuse from taking place. Structural reforms can also go a long way toward obviating future attempts to manipulate the media during periods of social stress. Once in place, these reforms are no longer dependent on foreign assistance, so they tend to maintain legitimacy and build popular support. Eight types of structural interventions are detailed below.

1. Strengthening independent media. Enhancing the ability of independent media outlets to resist unwanted influence from the government or elsewhere is critical to developing their ability to avoid abuse and manipulation. This strengthening is often a product of media plurality and longevity, both of which make using media to incite violence increasingly difficult. Plurality creates strength in numbers; with a variety of diverse

independent media outlets in place, if one or even several are co-opted the effect is mitigated. Through media expansion and diversification, hate media can be marginalized; for example, in the United States, hate media exist but are virtually irrelevant. Longevity contributes to the strength of independent media because the longer independent outlets are in place, the more ingrained in society they become. Consequently, if such ingrained outlets are abused, or shut down, the public outcry is likely to be substantial.

One of the most prominent examples of independent media thwarting government attempts to manipulate information comes from Serbia under Slobodan Milosevic, where the independent radio station B92 is credited with playing an instrumental role in informing and mobilizing the population.

2. Developing journalist competence. This intervention involves two basic objectives: enhancing the physical resources available to journalists (such as computers and vehicles) and enhancing human resources (such as writing ability, editing skills and contextual knowledge). If journalists lack physical resources, they are likely to be more susceptible to co-optation and corruption. Human resource needs are more difficult to define and to provide because they are not tangible goods. The principal method of enhancing human resources is through training, often through peer-to-peer training conducted by journalists. Although the results of such training are often difficult to quantify, the benefits accrued by journalists can be substantial.

   Even with the latest technology, ultimately it is the quality of the journalist that determines the quality of the journalism. Improving the technical or material components of the medium does not, in itself, improve the message. Consequently, addressing human resource needs must be a top priority. An added benefit of developing journalist competence is that more competent journalists are more likely to investigate and report on actors attempting to abuse the media and to expose their intentions, which can deter or thwart their efforts. Investigative journalism can be critical to blocking efforts to incite conflict and can debunk some of the inflammatory myths and stereotypes propagated in the media.

3. Another type of structural intervention involves working with the legislature and judiciary, the government institutions responsible for protecting citizen's rights, including the rights to free speech and independent media. Particular attention should be paid to the legislature because of its capacity to make and modify legislation. In many societies susceptible to media abuse, the legislation necessary to prosecute media abuse - including laws that protect the independence of private media outlets and that address hateful and antagonistic media content, such as slander and libel laws - is absent, ineffective or poorly designed. Thus it is important for experts in comparative media to work with legislatures to aid them in crafting such legislation.

   Once the necessary legislation is in place, it is equally important that the judiciary has the capacity to enforce the laws. If it is effective and impervious to corruption, the judiciary can provide an important check on media abuse because it can punish actors attempting to use the media maliciously. But in so many of the societies recently succumbing to conflict and in those vulnerable to doing so, rule of law is weak and the legal system is riddled with bribery and corruption. Among the recommendations by the NGO Article 19 following the Rwanda genocide was that government 'should seek to strengthen the judiciary to ensure that the necessary steps can be taken within the domestic legal system to prevent the broadcasting of incitement to violence' (Article 19 1996: 171). But often the government is poorly equipped to do this, and assistance from the NGO community can make a significant difference. NGOs should focus on strengthening the mechanics of the judiciary and on reducing the susceptibility of judges to corruption.

4. Promoting diversity in the journalist corps and media ownership. If there is little diversity among journalists and owners of media outlets, they are more vulnerable to abuse by members of the dominant group or groups in society. The way to combat this effect is clear - promote diversity - but strategies for doing so are not as obvious. One way to promote diversity among journalists is to impress on managers and owners of media outlets the importance of diversity and how they can benefit from it, both commercially and through content improvements that result from employing more diverse personnel.

   Another strategy is to work with members of certain political, ethnic, religious or regional groups to help them become involved with media (though this involves the risk of appearing to favour one group over another). A third strategy is to create incentives for outlets to promote diversity in their hiring, for example by having donor organizations provide more support, financial or otherwise, to outlets that are more diverse. Promoting diversity in media ownership is even more complex, because in a market economy it would be difficult and ill-advised to set quotas concerning the demographics of media ownership. Worse yet, in a non-market society, the government controls the media outlets and is unlikely to be convinced of the merits of diversity in ownership. Nonetheless, there are ways both to aid individuals to create new private media outlets and to encourage governments to allow for such outlets. One route is through bilateral aid, particularly aid channelled from development banks through national financial institutions via leasing and other financial support, intended for developing small- and mediumsized businesses.

5. Licensing and regulation of media outlets. A balance must be struck in the media regulatory environment so that starting a media outlet is not an overly complex,

time-consuming, bureaucratic task, but regulation is not so lax that almost anybody can have a radio station or newspaper. Complete state control over media is not the solution, but neither is the total absence of regulation. Some type of government oversight of the licensing process is often in order, but one that is shielded, to the extent possible, from heavily political or corrupt influences. Again, it may be difficult for governments, particularly in developing countries still building and consolidating their democracies, to design and implement such regulations effectively. Assistance and encouragement from the domestic and international NGO communities can provide a strong impetus for establishing regulations, and international assistance can provide a blueprint for how to implement such regulation. Bilateral relations between donor and developing countries are also important, as they often involve assistance to government institutions and advice on the overhaul of bureaucratic processes, which can strongly affect the domestic regulatory environment.

6. Strengthening domestic and international networks. Because journalists in vulnerable societies are often isolated from both domestic and international colleagues, establishing and strengthening journalist networks can be an effective way to combat media abuse. Domestically, this can be accomplished through journalist organizations or unions. When effective, they serve various purposes - providing journalists with information and ideas on how to report in a particular context (especially when there are personal safety issues involved), defending journalists' rights and freedoms and providing journalists with legal counsel. All of these services are critical, particularly in a society where the state is wary of independent media and eager to crack down on independent journalists.

International journalist networks can be just as important. Such networks can help journalists operating in difficult circumstances feel part of a larger community of colleagues around the world, which can strengthen their resolve. These networks can also inform journalists on what may be considered international standards of journalism.

A more programmatic form of international networking involves making international media, such as CNN or the BBC, accessible to journalists in vulnerable societies. The benefits of this are twofold: sometimes journalists use the content verbatim, but even if they do not, they are better informed and are exposed to a different perspective, which helps them in their own reporting.

7. 'Demand-side' intervention. Too often the 'supply side' of the media equation (meaning the news and information that is supplied by media outlets) is closely scrutinized at the expense of attention to the 'demand side' (the demand by individuals for that news and information). A problem often found in societies in which media abuse occurs and in societies with underdeveloped media in general is that media consumers - everyday citizens - rarely consider and question the source and credibility of their news. Instead, they take for granted that what they hear on the radio and read in the newspapers is accurate and unbiased. For example, Des Forges (2002: 246) observes that in Rwanda before and during the genocide, 'most ordinary people saw no reason to call into question their practice of taking the radio as the voice of authority'.

   Part of the reason for the absence of critical analysis of the media was that, prior to the genocide, most Rwandans had never been exposed to alternatives to state-owned media, so they were conditioned to believe everything they heard from the few state-controlled outlets to which they had access. It was also due to the fact that most Rwandans had little understanding of the bias inherent in all media outlets.

   The prescription is increased public education and enhanced awareness of how media outlets operate. People need to understand that media outlets report from a particular perspective, one that may represent interests contrary to their own. B92 in Serbia tried to create such an understanding. 'The idea was to provoke the public to start thinking about the information that they were receiving,' according to one of the station's managers. 'So don't be just a passive recipient of this information, think about it and decide, do you believe it or not?' (Glyn-Pickett 1999).

8. Media monitoring. The final structural intervention is quite broad: monitoring media behaviour in an effort to identify the indicators described above so that the interventions detailed here can occur. It is imperative that someone keep watch over the media and, just as critical, over forces influencing the media. Such oversight is accomplished most effectively through media monitoring initiatives, organized efforts to monitor for specific characteristics. Some monitoring of broadcasts in various countries already occurs - the United States government runs the Foreign Broadcast Information Service and the BBC has a monitoring service - but it is not broad enough and does not cover media outlets in some of the most vulnerable societies.

Monitoring for the indicators presented above can inform policymakers about societies at risk of media manipulation. In doing such monitoring, it is important to work with local NGOs to develop a local monitoring capacity.

Content-specific Interventions

Content-specific interventions are often based on observations of the content indicators detailed above, which tend to appear at a relatively late stage. But content-specific interventions can also be pre-emptive.

The interventions described here can occur before the appearance of the indicators, to ensure that they do not appear. Content-specific interventions are most effective when media abuse is involuntary due to a lack of training and competence, rather than calculated.

If the media abuse is intentional, content-specific interventions are unlikely to succeed because journalists are fully aware of the consequences of their actions. But when media abuse is involuntary, such interventions offer alternatives to structural interventions; in circumstances where structural interventions are ineffective, content-specific interventions may be more successful. They may also serve as short-term remedies for some forms of media abuse, allowing more time for structural interventions, which tend to take longer to implement and yield results.

1. 'Repersonalization'. As described above, one of the strategies for using media to instigate conflict involves the 'dehumanization' and 'depersonalization' of individuals. Through this process, people are portrayed in the media as members of a stigmatized group rather than as individuals. Training on how journalists can move beyond the political, ethnic, religious or regional factors to identify the true source of a grievance (be it an economic grievance or another concern) and how they can portray people first and foremost as individuals can ease tensions and move a society away from conflict. These strategies concern not only mitigating the negative effects of media abuse but also using media as a positive tool for reconciliation and conflict prevention.
2. Issue-oriented training. Journalists can be trained in reporting issues that tend to be particularly sensitive and possibly explosive. Reports on economic issues and environmental resources, in particular, can be distorted and twisted into tales of ethnic hatred and animosity because they are issues that affect people's livelihood, as they can have a dramatic effect on both personal economic viability and general stability. Thus it is particularly important that they are reported on in a professional manner, and issue-oriented training focusing on how journalists can frame these issues helps ensure that they are.
3. Entertainment-oriented programming. Entertainment-oriented programming offers another way to use media

as positive tools for preventing and resolving conflict. The work of the NGO Search for Common Ground provides several impressive examples of such programming. Among other projects, they have co-produced a dramatic television series for Macedonian children intended to facilitate cross-ethnic understanding; and they have established radio studios in Burundi, Liberia and Sierra Leone that produce, in addition to other programming, soap operas designed to encourage dialogue and discourage violence. Entertainment-oriented programming can have a direct effect and may be significantly more influential than news programming.

Aggressive Interventions

Finally, the third group of strategies for combating media abuse and manipulation involves what may be considered 'aggressive interventions'. Such interventions tend to be a last resort and usually occur after media abuse and manipulation is widely apparent, often after violent conflict has begun. They are more reactive than proactive.

They are also externally imposed and some forms are unlikely to be effective if not accompanied by other forms of intervention, such as military intervention. Such aggressive interventions do not usually change media structure or content, although some forms do disable physical infrastructure. Clearly, earlier intervention that stands a chance of preventing media abuse and manipulation before it proliferates is preferable.

1. Alternative information. A prominent strategy for aggressive intervention is for foreign entities, including governments, NGOs and political parties to offer sources of information other than those available domestically. In several instances, alternative information has played an important role in mobilizing a population and injecting new ideas into society. Among them are Democratic Voices of Burma, a station broadcasting into Burma out of Norway, and Radio Freedom and Capital Radio in South Africa. Radio Freedom was

broadcast by the African National Congress into South Africa from several southern African states in the 1970s, and Capital Radio broadcast from the 'homeland' of Transkei to the rest of South Africa in the 1980s. Both served as valuable sources of news about the realities of apartheid, winning many converts among the white population along the way.

More generally, in many countries major international radio networks, such as the BBC and Voice of America (VOA), are regularly heard on the airwaves and offer citizens reliable information that sometimes contradicts information broadcast by local media outlets.

Alternative information can be specifically designed to counter information broadcast by a single or small number of sources, such as government media or hate media outlets.

A good example of the use of alternative information is the Ring Around Serbia, a multilateral project spearheaded by the United States in 1999. It involved assembling a ring of radio transmitters in countries neighbouring Serbia and broadcasting programming from the BBC, VOA, Deutsche Welle, Radio France International and Radio Free Europe into Serbia. Such an intervention is reactive and occurs late in the manipulation process. It is also expensive, difficult to organize and of questionable legality. Broadcasts prepared specially for transmission into 'hostile territory' are often perceived as propaganda and thus discounted by the intended audience. But if all other opportunities for media intervention have been missed, broadcasting alternative information may merit consideration.

2. Radio and television jamming. Perhaps the most frequently discussed strategy for countering hate media is jamming radio and television signals. In looking back at Rwanda, several scholars and practitioners, foremost among them Roméo Dallaire, the UN commander in Rwanda during the genocide, have suggested that jamming Rwandan radio would have made carrying out

the genocide significantly more difficult and would have been worth the effort and cost (to his credit, Dallaire proposed radio jamming before the genocide as well). But jamming is a blunt instrument that comes with substantial legal concerns and would only be seriously considered once violence is already widespread. The more effective and less costly alternative to radio jamming is removing media from the 'toolkit' belonging to actors intent on inciting conflict, which is what the structural and content-specific interventions detailed above are designed to do.

Recommendations

As this analysis demonstrates, media can be extremely powerful tools used by those intent on instigating conflict. Media are multipliers: they amplify and disseminate messages and opinions. Media spread information and misinformation, shape individuals' views of others and can heighten tensions or promote understanding.

This makes controlling media and their messages an important goal for anyone intent on promoting conflict. This analysis concludes with four recommendations to the international community for addressing the use and abuse of media in vulnerable societies:

1. *Media in Vulnerable Societies should be Monitored:* Media in vulnerable societies should be monitored for the 'clues to conflict' detailed above. Special attention should be devoted to the structural indicators - including, in particular, journalist competence, media variety and plurality and media's legal environment - as they can reveal how vulnerable or resistant media are to manipulation and point to specific interventions that might prevent media co-optation and abuse before it occurs. Attention should also be given to content indicators, such as a focus on past atrocities and a history of ethnic hatred; manipulation of myths, stereotypes and identities to 'dehumanize'; and efforts to discredit alternatives to conflict. The monitoring

should be comprehensive; put in context with political, economic and social indicators; and conducted by experienced or trained monitors.

2. *There should be greater collaboration between media organizations and conflict resolution organizations:* The role of media in fomenting conflict is seldom addressed comprehensively by either media or conflict resolution NGOs. Media organizations tend to devote limited attention to the dynamics and causes of violent conflict, while conflict resolution organizations often overlook the role of media in fomenting or tempering the conflicts they scrutinize. However, working together, these organizations can pool their knowledge and address the role of media in conflict from both sides of the issue. Particularly in efforts to develop early-warning instruments, media organizations should be consulted and media 'indicators' incorporated into the analysis, so that media are considered, along with other factors, when trying to identify societies highly susceptible to conflict. Such collaboration can enhance understanding of the relevant issues and the design and implementation of early-warning instruments and preventive interventions.

3. *Media organizations need to build a better case for monitoring and early intervention and encourage appropriate donor support:* Early, preventive media intervention, such as the structural interventions described above, can be significantly more effective and beneficial than later, reactive interventions, such as radio jamming. Early interventions are more cost-effective and can lay the foundation for the long-term institutional development necessary to combat political or ethnic instability. Media organizations need to provide donors with reliable research and reports on significant field experience to justify supporting early interventions, even before traditional conflict indicators are visible. Further collaboration and information-sharing between conflict resolution and media organizations, particularly

through common methods for identifying critical points for intervention, will contribute greatly to assuring donors that funding early intervention is worthwhile and cost-effective.

4. *A systematic review of media behaviour in vulnerable societies should be conducted:* An effective approach to gaining a better understanding of use and abuse of media in vulnerable societies would be to conduct a comprehensive study by monitoring the characteristics of media behaviour in several countries deemed close to conflict. Such a review could provide the quantitative and qualitative data needed to focus the attention of donors and media organizations on the role of media in such societies and on the importance of early, preventive intervention.

4

Reporting the News with Due Responsibility

Hands rose up from the grave to grasp each coffin, as if the dead were welcoming the remains of the genocide victims. The simple wooden boxes contained bones recovered from mass graves and pit latrines so that they could be re-interred during ceremonies marking the tenth anniversary of the Rwanda genocide. It was 7 April 2004 in Kigali, and a gaggle of television crews, reporters and photographers jostled for space around a concrete tomb where victims of the 1994 genocide were finally being given a dignified burial. Earlier, pall bearers had descended into the crypt, climbing down a ladder so they could be in place to receive the coffins. The boxes were gingerly passed one by one into their final resting place at Rwanda's national memorial to the 1994 slaughter.

Ten years after the genocide, Rwanda was still burying its dead and representatives of the international media were there, watching. Heading the dignitaries assembled to take part in the ceremony was Paul Kagame, president of Rwanda and in 1994, leader of the Tutsi-dominated Rwandan Patriotic Front, which ended the genocide and took over the country. Retired Canadian General Roméo Dallaire, who led the ill-fated United Nations mission to Rwanda during the catastrophe, joined Kagame at the ceremony.

Both Kagame and Dallaire could have been forgiven for asking a pointed question as they regarded the international media throng gathered for the ceremonies: where were the world's media a decade earlier when a campaign to exterminate the Tutsi minority and Hutu moderates resulted in the massacre of more than 800,000 innocents?

In hindsight, the media shorthand for the Rwanda genocide goes something like this: the world community failed to intervene and abandoned Rwanda while dead bodies clogged the rivers and piled up on roadsides. These events were reported by the news media, but not very prominently. When the media finally descended on the story, it was to cover the cholera epidemic in refugee camps across the border in Zaire, camps populated by Hutu who fled Rwanda at the tail end of the genocide.

Looking back, it is easy to see what the news media did wrong, both inside Rwanda and without. Many journalists within Rwanda were implicated in the killing. Hate media were instrumental in the extermination campaign. International news media misconstrued or downplayed the Rwanda story. Political figures, such as US President Bill Clinton (1998), later claimed that they did not have enough information to fully grasp what was going on in Rwanda. More likely, because the public was not very engaged by the Rwanda story, there was little pressure for leaders to do anything.

This collection of papers set out to examine the role of the news media in the 1994 catastrophe, inside and outside Rwanda. More than a decade later, are we any wiser? What has changed and what have we learned from what went wrong? In part, the answer lies in Darfur, the region in western Sudan widely acknowledged in early 2006 to be a humanitarian and human rights tragedy of the first order. By some accounts, as many as 5,000 people continued to die each month in a deteriorating situation of massive atrocities against civilians, blamed primarily on the government and its allied Janjaweed militias.

In the face of reliable accounts of what is at best ethnic cleansing and at worst genocide - a situation that some have described as Rwanda in slow motion - the world community did little. By most accounts, North American media have drastically underplayed the situation in western Sudan, just as they did in Rwanda, despite evidence of massive violations of human rights and a government supporting forces wreaking havoc on innocent civilians. Perhaps, just perhaps, content analysis would demonstrate that Darfur has registered on the media radar screen to a greater degree than did Rwanda. But it has not become a mega-story, or a media sensation. It has not captured our imaginations. And that signals, once again, a media failure.

For what it's worth, the international community has shown a measure of contrition with regard to the events of 1994. Rwanda is now a synonym for the world community's failure to intervene in the face of gross violations of human rights, a genocide. Rwanda is invoked repeatedly, often in sentences that contain the phrase 'never again.' Key figures in the Rwandan drama have apologized, or at least expressed regret, for their failure to act to the best of their abilities. And in large part because of Rwanda, a new paradigm emerged and eventually won formal recognition on the world stage.

The Canadian-inspired doctrine called The Responsibility to Protect (ICISS 2001) was formally adopted by the United Nations in September 2005. (Whether it is ever put into force is another matter.) The doctrine was set out in the December 2001 report of the International Commission on Intervention and State Sovereignty.

It overturns the notion of absolute national sovereignty when it comes to massive violations of human rights and genocide, marking the first time that state sovereignty and non-interference in internal affairs have been qualified. In effect, the UN declaration enshrines in international law the notion that the world community has a right to intervene - a responsibility to protect - to stop a government from massive violation of the human rights of its citizens.

But the document is virtually silent on the role of the news media, and there is little discussion of the part journalists and news organizations could or should play in the face of the kind of atrocities witnessed in Rwanda. All these years later, we don't yet seem to have figured out that part of the puzzle. Perhaps it is time to advance a new paradigm for journalists: the responsibility to report. If we cannot adequately address the kind of structural constraints that handicapped the media in the case of Rwanda, at least we can deal with the behavioural aspects of the media - the way individual journalists conduct themselves.

In the years since 1994, Rwanda has become a case study in hate media, a textbook example of how journalism and particularly the broadcast media can be perverted in the name of hate. And, since Rwanda, considerable attention has been devoted to defining how monitoring the media in zones of actual or potential conflict can help policymakers to grasp more accurately what is going on and to use that information to frame responses with the best chance of preventing or mitigating violence. In Britain, the Foreign and Commonwealth Office (FCO) and BBC Monitoring (BBCM) have established a specialized 'tension and hate speech monitoring' project. BBCM aims to track the world's media for its clients (four main stakeholders: the BBC World Service, the FCO, the Ministry of Defence and the Cabinet Office). BBCM also has a 50-year old partnership with the Foreign Broadcast Information Service in the United States. In August 2002, BBCM began intensively monitoring media in 15 countries of interest, then providing monthly transcripts. A small-scale project, begun in September 2003, involved a focus on media and hate speech and incitement in the former Soviet Union, Israel-Palestine, Kosovo, Albania and Côte d'Ivoire.

Clearly, media monitoring for hate speech has taken on a high profile because of Rwanda. As one observer quipped, we are all now well prepared to stop the Rwanda genocide - ten years too late.3 And yet, what are the chances of once again coming across such a textbook example of hate media and incitement as Rwanda? We should probably be focused on media interventions that come much earlier in the trajectory that culminates in hate media. In fact, rather than using monitoring reports to try and shut down media outlets, a more useful exercise would be to use the material to design programmes to improve media standards, conduct media training and develop codes of conduct for journalists - behavioural rather than structural solutions.

More than a decade after the genocide, the media sector in Rwanda is still in need of this kind of assistance with training and development. There was no school of journalism in Rwanda until the late 1990s. Before the genocide, Rwanda's journalists were either professionally trained outside the country or trained 'on the job', in some cases with seminars and workshops to improve their skills. The School of Journalism and Communication was founded in 1996 at the National University of Rwanda in Butare. In early 2006, Carleton University's School of Journalism and Communication launched a collaborative effort with its counterpart in Butare to work together on staffing and curriculum development through a project called The Rwanda Initiative.

But efforts to foster a more professional media sector in Rwanda come at a time when respect for human rights and press freedom in the country is a genuine cause for concern. Major human rights organizations, such as Amnesty International and Human Rights Watch, have been highly critical of the Kagame government's treatment of human rights organizations and the news media. The government has been accused of an intimidation campaign that prompted Rwanda's primary human rights organization, LIPRODHOR, to close its doors in early 2005 (AI 2005). Amnesty International accused the Rwandan government of 'inappropriately manipulating the concept of genocide to silence not only organizations and individuals critical of the government but organizations who have a close relationship with the Rwandese people and whose loyalty the government questions' (AI 2004a). And in November 2004, Amnesty International urged the government of Rwanda to do its utmost to foster the independence of the press and to refrain from using the law to repress journalistic activities (AI 2004b). Reporters Without Borders went so far as to label President Kagame an enemy of press freedom. More than a decade after a genocide that deeply implicated the news media, there are still lessons to be learned in Rwanda.

What lessons have the international media drawn from the debacle of Rwanda? Like other international actors, the news media have been slow to acknowledge their failures during the genocide. Journalists tend to look forward, not back. For that reason, it took nearly 60 years for The New York Times to come to terms with the impact of its coverage of the Nazi Holocaust. In a 14 November 2001 feature headed 'Turning Away From the Holocaust,' former Times executive editor Max Frankel described the influential newspaper's 'staggering, stunning failure' to properly depict Hitler's methodical extermination of the Jews of Europe. Frankel noted that only six times in nearly six years did the front page of the Times mention Jews as Hitler's unique target for total annihilation. Sound familiar? The belated media mea culpa about coverage of the Holocaust has not been replicated when it comes to Rwanda, despite all the evidence of an abysmal media failure.

Instead, history continues to repeat itself. Stories like Rwanda continue to be downplayed. Year after year, the international news media devote less and less attention to foreign affairs, with the exception of the 'big' stories, such as the war in Iraq, the war on terror or the disaster du jour. Claude Moisy, former chairman and general manager of Agence France-Presse, described an inescapable paradox that 'the amazing increase in the capacity to produce and distribute news from distant lands has been met by an obvious decrease in its consumption' (Moisy 1997). Writing in the late 1990s, Moisy described a clear pattern: with the exception of a surge of international coverage in 1990 and 1991 due to the first Gulf War, the number and length of foreign topics covered in the evening news had declined far below Cold War levels. In early 2006, chances are that a rigorous content analysis would show, pound for pound, a significant up-tick in media coverage of foreign affairs. But factor out the overwhelming focus on Iraq and we are almost certainly looking at a continuation of the trend away from media coverage of international affairs.

Once again, journalists and critics cite a number of factors affecting the limited coverage of Darfur: the difficulty of getting into the region, tight budgets, the news focus on the war in Iraq and the presumed lack of audience interest in Africa (Ricchiardi 2005). For example, one researcher calculated that the nightly newscasts of ABC, CBS and NBC devote a total of roughly 24,900 minutes to news each year - an average of 20 minutes of news in each of these newscasts every night. In 2004, all three networks combined aired a total of only 26 minutes on fighting in Sudan, which has been described by some as genocide. (ABC devoted 18 minutes to Darfur coverage, NBC 5 and CBS only 3.) By contrast, houseware maven Martha Stewart's legal woes garnered 130 minutes of nightly news coverage (Tyndall Report 2004).

More recently, a quantitative monitoring of all news segments aired in June 2005 on ABC, CBS, NBC, CNN, FoxNews and MSNBC demonstrated that coverage of Darfur was overshadowed by reporting on the so-called 'runaway bride' (the Georgia woman who drove across the country and concocted a fake kidnapping to escape her wedding in April 2005), the Michael Jackson trial and Tom Cruise's new movie and relationship with actress Katie Holmes.

The shocking thing about these findings is that they no longer shock us. They haven't shocked us for a long time. In fact, we now take this kind of media coverage for granted. There is a vast academic literature on media coverage of international affairs and more specifically, coverage of Africa and the developing world. Some go at this empirically, with an eye to figuring out what the news media are actually doing. Others take a normative approach, prescribing what the media and journalists should do. We need more of both lines of enquiry.

But the problem with media prescriptions is that they are often so general that they are beyond implementation. In essence, the prescriptions end up being variants on the symptoms: news organizations should devote more resources to coverage of Africa and the developing world; the media should train more professionals in coverage of conflict and development issues; news from the developing world should be given more prominence on news pages and in broadcasts; news organizations should deploy more full-time foreign correspondents; rather than just covering wars, the media should pay more attention before a conflict erupts and after the fact, examine efforts at conflict resolution and ways the news media could actually support reconciliation and peace (for examples of this prescriptive approach, see Carnegie Commission 1997: 121-3 and Manoff 1997).

All of these prescriptions are really just reworded descriptions of the problem. Clearly, we need more information and more first-hand, eyewitness reporting from places like Darfur. We need to hear more and different voices. But how can we make that happen? Who moves the media? And what is 'the media' anyway? How can we talk coherently about such a disparate, diverse group of commercial and state enterprises that differ vastly across continents? Media organizations are populated by individual journalists, editors, media executives and others. More broadly speaking, 'the media' includes anyone who can apply some code of professional standards and disseminate news and information. So is it even realistic to look for discernible patterns of coverage in the media with an eye to recommending a different course of action?

And yet, some simple truths seem to be borne out by the evidence, and one of those truths is that media coverage does matter. There is a vast literature on how media coverage influences or is interwoven with foreign policy decisions: either directly through the provision of information that ignites public opinion (the so-called 'CNN effect') or indirectly through what Bernard Cohen (1963) described as the media's remarkable agenda-setting power to instruct people as to what they should be thinking about. Others have suggested that media influence is most likely to occur when policy is uncertain and media coverage is critically framed and empathizes with suffering people. But when policymakers have made up their minds and a policy track has been chosen, the news media can have much less influence (Robinson 2000: 614). We probably can't resolve the debate over whether media reports prod decision-makers into action or simply manufacture consent, but there can be no disagreement about the fact that more coverage of an issue or a region is more likely to generate policy action than less coverage (for more on this, consult Robinson 2002 and Wanta et al. 2004).

Media coverage, or lack of it, also matters in the inverse. The media glare of the big story casts a deep shadow on its fringes. Some argue that rather than seeking to measure the impact of media coverage, we should pay more attention to the 'nether world of absence of news' (Sonwalkar 2004: 207) and what happens when the news media methodically downplay or ignore a story.

The crux of the Rwanda piece is that more extensive media coverage might have made a difference, might have pushed international actors to do something in the spring of 1994. Roméo Dallaire argues that media coverage of Rwanda never gained momentum during the genocide, never reached the kind of critical mass needed to move leaders. That momentum only emerged in July 1994, when media descended in droves to cover the plight of those living in the refugee camps in Goma and sparked an international response.

We keep asking ourselves, why did the news media clamber to cover Biafra in 1968, Ethiopia in 1984, Somalia in 1992-93, but not the Rwanda genocide? And why have news media systematically downplayed events in Sudan for the past two decades and virtually ignored other locales (Livingston 1996)?

Could the answer be that 'the media', writ large, the 'cyclops' as some have called it (Bierbauer 1994), can only focus its gaze on one major story at a time? And in choosing such stories, are journalists more likely to seize on a simple, dramatic storyline, featuring good and evil, without the complexities of ethnicity and power politics to clutter the narrative?

According to analysis of 200 English-language newspapers worldwide, the 2004 tsunami in South East Asia generated more column inches in six weeks than the world's top ten 'forgotten' emergencies combined over the previous year (IFRC 2005). The media blitz prompted unprecedented generosity. By February 2005, the international community had donated US$ 500 for every person affected by the tsunami, compared with just 50 cents for each person affected by Uganda's 18-year war (IFRC 2005). Why did the tsunami and the subsequent relief efforts generate so many headlines? There was a simple storyline - a natural disaster. There were no complex political relationships to explain. And even though events were unfolding on the other side of the world, the tsunami met some 'proximity' criteria for Western news editors because many Western tourists were involved.

In World Disasters Report 2005, the International Federation of Red Cross and Red Crescent Societies put it bluntly: 'Editors sort stories by death tolls. Disasters that are unusual yet explicable, and that cause considerable death or destruction in accessible places which the audience is believed to care about, get covered. Baffling stories get less attention' (IFRC 2005). Rwanda was a baffling story, as is Darfur. As the Red Cross points out, news can be driven by ratings and circulation. So TV news is part news and part entertainment. No surprise then that 'sudden, dramatic disasters like volcanoes or tsunamis are intensely newsworthy, whereas long-drawn-out crises (difficult to describe, let alone film) are not.' By that score, the estimated 3.8 million deaths in the Democratic Republic of Congo since 1998 from war, disease and malnutrition have generated scant media coverage. But the dramatic eruption of the Nyiragongo volcano near Goma in early 2002 sparked an influx of journalists, even though it killed fewer than 100 people.

But when the cyclops turns its 'monocular gaze', the news media can become a major humanitarian actor, particularly, as Piers Robinson (2000) points out, when decision-makers are uncertain how to proceed. But that media role is very ill-defined and hard to predict with any degree of certainty. That is in part because the media are no less complex as an institution than government or humanitarian organizations. And yet, most studies treat the news media as a monolithic actor (Minear et al. 1994: 31).

As Minear and colleagues suggest, rather than seeing the media as an actor with a purpose, it is probably more instructive to see the media as an institution with a process. And that process is inclined toward gatekeeping principles regarding what is news and what is not, what warrants the cost of news coverage and is likely to garner the interest of the audience (Chang and Lee 1992). And often, media attention to one emergency comes at the expense of another. The devastating earthquake in Pakistan in the autumn of 2005 overshadowed coverage of the hurricane and mudslides in Guatemala, just as, in some ways, Michael Jackson overshadowed Darfur.

And ironically, the 24-hour news cycle, rather than leading to more in-depth, comprehensive reporting, has arguably driven coverage in the other direction - toward fleeting, episodic encounters with events outside our daily lives. That makes the news media a bad early warning system. As journalists, we seem to be best at recording and reporting conflict once it has reached a certain pitch, by acting as witnesses to genocide and other atrocities. The economics of the news business is a key factor here. Although it would seem to make sense to go where the news is about to happen, to get ahead of the story, we are more likely to go where the news is happening, where conflict has broken out. It is a sure bet; you're not going to buy a plane ticket and end up with no story. Not much preventive value there. Journalists react to the same impulses as political decision-makers, and conflicts often show up on journalists' radar screen at about the same time as that of the decision-makers and diplomats - or more likely much later.

Not surprisingly, journalists largely reflect the societies in which they live and share the same ambivalence toward what is going on outside their borders, the same focus on domestic issues and selected international issues that are deemed to be relevant. In my view, it is up to individual journalists to crawl outside their skin, to get beyond that domestic focus and to exercise their role fully. Just as nation states have begrudgingly acknowledged the Responsibility to Protect - driven by the simple realization that we have a responsibility to others - I think journalists, as individuals, must accept the responsibility to report.

I suppose my simple point is that we've been lamenting for three decades how 'the media' fail to cover stories like Rwanda and Darfur. I echo the lament, which is backed up by a stream of qualitative and quantitative research. But normative prescriptions for what 'the media' should be doing differently have little application. Could it be that everyone is going about it the wrong way, looking top-down at the media, which is an amorphous, disparate beast anyway, when they should be looking from the ground up, at individual journalists and the role they can play?

British journalist-cum-politician Martin Bell (1998) has spoken about the 'journalism of attachment', a call for empathy with humanity among journalists, something that some regard as an affront to the classical notion of journalistic objectivity and neutrality. But surely journalists can talk about an ethic of responsibility, a responsibility to report on people, places and events that have been excluded from the agenda of news organizations for a myriad of reasons. Surely individual journalists can try to make a difference, even if news organizations and the media are unable or unwilling to fully exercise their role.

Journalists such as Nicholas Kristof of The New York Times and Sudarsan Raghavan - now with the Washington Post and formerly Africa correspondent for Knight Ridder - have made it their mission to keep the Darfur story on the world's radar screen. They have demonstrated that individual journalists can make a difference. Canadian journalist Stephanie Nolen, Africa correspondent for the Globe and Mail newspaper, has single-handedly kept the issue of HIV/AIDS on the Canadian agenda through dogged, persistent reporting on a scourge that is decimating Africa in its own kind of genocide. In my own way, during 17 years as a reporter with the Toronto Star - Canada's largest circulation daily newspaper - I made every effort to use my position to interest the newspaper's powerful editors in stories that were not immediately on their radar screen, stories that took me on assignment to such places as Rwanda, Somalia, Sierra Leone and Kazakhstan. My personal interest and sense of responsibility as a journalist were shaped by a seminal experience in the early 1990s, when a development organization saw fit to invest in me and financed a media internship that took me to Africa for an extended period.

Since then, at every opportunity I have urged development assistance agencies, government and nongovernmental organizations, and advocates interested in media coverage of the developing world to invest in individual journalists - those new to the profession and also veterans - by endowing research grants, fellowships and awards that make it possible for journalists to visit the developing world or to explore areas that otherwise fall into that nether world of media absence. In my experience, journalists exposed to the developing world want to go back again and again. And their reporting can make a difference.

In the carnage in Rwanda in 1994, individual journalists tried to fulfil their mandate, even though they were constrained by the chaos and the world's indifference. Thomas Kamilindi, who quit his job at Radio Rwanda on the eve of the genocide, wrote in this collection of his attempts to reach the outside world from his hiding place in the Milles Collines Hotel. Kamilindi kept trying the phone lines until he could get on the air and describe what was happening on the streets of Kigali. One of the attempts on Kamilindi's life came after he managed to get through to radio colleagues in France and describe the atrocities in Rwanda. Imagine the impact if journalists of good conscience, like Kamilindi, had been able to publish blogs in 1994, to circumvent the media inertia of budgets, racism and competing news interests.

Another Rwandan journalist, whose identity remains unknown, managed to capture on videotape some of the atrocities in the streets of Kigali. The journalist, believed to have been a camera operator with Rwandan television at the time, travelled with a group of Interahamwe through the streets of Kigali at some point in April 1994. According to one report, the camera operator had apparently befriended members of the death squads, even though he was opposed to the killing. As a journalist, he took considerable risk to gain permission to ride with the death squads through the streets of Kigali, filming some of the scenes and capturing rare footage that has become the mainstay of later documentary accounts of the genocide and a key part of the historical record (Hughes 1998). The world needs more journalists like Kamilindi and the unknown Rwandan TV camera operator.

The concept of media intervention to foster a more highly professional cadre of journalists in the developing world flourished in the decade after the Rwanda genocide. In 2003, Ross Howard, an associate at the Vancouver-based Institute for Media, Policy and Civil Society (IMPACS) estimated that in the previous ten years, US$ 1 billion had been invested in media-related interventions in conflict-stressed societies. Howard (2003) pointed to the emerging belief that news media may well be the most effective means of preventing war and conflict. Such media interventions abound. The Washington-based Search for Common Ground and its European counterpart operate radio studios in Burundi, Liberia and Sierra Leone, producing news, features, drama, music and speciality soap operas for social change as well as television productions. The organization also supports media training workshops in Africa, the Middle East and the Aegean region. The Panos network of organizations works to stimulate debate around key development issues, in part through a media programme. The network includes offices in the Caribbean, Eastern Africa, London, Paris, South Asia, Southern Africa, Washington DC and West Africa, with a combined staff of well over 100 people. Vancouver-based IMPACS supports programmes to foster free, responsible, independent media in emerging democracies by enhancing the contribution of the media to democratic development, good governance and public sector accountability. The Soros Foundation's Open Society Institute, the London-based Institute for War and Peace Reporting and others are also active in vital media training.

We need more voices, more first-hand accounts of events from journalists in the North and the South. Technology makes the arguments about newsroom budgets increasingly less relevant. Simply put, it is much, much cheaper to travel to the developing world and do journalism than it used to be. And why not use more locally based correspondents as well? Isn't it about time that Western news organizations re-examined their assumption that visiting foreign correspondents are of more value than locally based journalists?

One need look no further than the body of work of journalists like Sorious Samura, the documentary film-maker originally from Sierra Leone who has made it his mission to tell African stories. Samura's very personal and engaged form of journalism has resulted in documentaries broadcast widely in North America and Europe on such topics as the atrocities of Sierra Leone's civil war, the real stories of people living with hunger in Ethiopia, the plight of refugees in Darfur, the exodus of migrants through North Africa and the scourge of HIV/AIDS in a country like Zambia. Samura's work is powerful and emotional stuff. But it also far exceeds the professional threshold for broadcast to an international audience. Surely he is not the only journalist in Africa capable of producing top-quality material for a Northern audience.

And Africans don't just need to tell their stories to the outside world. They need to tell them to each other. For decades, London-based Gemini News Service pioneered the notion of South-South journalism, maintaining a network of journalists in the developing world. These local correspondents filed their copy to Gemini's London office, where it was edited, packaged and transmitted through Gemini to be published elsewhere in the developing world. Gemini broke the cycle of dependence that previously forced many Southern news outlets to see themselves through stories written by reporters from the North. And in turn, Gemini News Service provided some news organizations in the developed world - such as The Toronto Star and Southam News Service in Canada - with a steady stream of quality news features written by authors based in the developing world. One of Gemini's most innovative projects was a village reporting exercise that saw more than 15 reporters from such countries as India, Sri Lanka, Fiji and Lesotho head off to spend two months living in a village to report on daily life.

Gemini was truly a pioneer in recruiting and cultivating homegrown journalists and using them as correspondents to report on matters of interest to developing countries. Gemini's founder, former Daily Mail journalist Derek Ingram, always objected to the notion that he was running an alternative news agency. He wanted Gemini to be regarded as a mainstream source of copy that would also appeal to newspapers in the developed world (for an excellent history of Gemini News Service, see Bourne 1995). Along the way, Gemini served as a springboard for legions of promising young journalists from the developing world as well as a generation of young Canadians who worked at the news agency through fellowships funded by the International Development Research Centre.6 Sadly, Gemini struggled for years to be financially viable and finally closed its doors in 2003 after nearly 30 years in operation. Perhaps it is time for an agency like Gemini News Service to be reborn. Other individual journalists are joining forces to try to make innovative use of new technology and web-based information platforms to bring the stories of the developing world to a wider audience. Early in this century, news consumers were introduced to the 'blog', short for weblog. These online journals by individual writers usually consist of frequently updated commentaries, posted to a World Wide Web address. Now, millions of bloggers are sharing their opinions with a global audience in postings that combine content drawn from mainstream media and the web. As Daniel Drezner and Henry Farrell (2004) suggest in a recent paper, 'What began as a hobby is evolving into a new medium that is changing the landscape for journalists and policymakers alike.'

Drezner and Farrell argue that blogs are gaining more influence over the content of international media coverage, primarily through their agenda-setting function and by focusing on new or neglected issues. 'Increasingly, journalists and pundits take their cues about "what matters" in the world from weblogs. For salient topics in global affairs, the blogosphere functions as a rare combination of distributed expertise, real-time collective response to breaking news, and public-opinion barometer,' they write.

And television networks, with their notoriously top-heavy news operations, have begun to deploy 'video journalists', or VJs, individual journalists who carry small hand-held cameras and shoot and edit their own material. The work of some of these VJs is akin to a televised blog, with a mainstream connection. In Canada, the national broadcaster, CBC-Television, has deployed video journalist Saša Petricic in this way. The group proposes a new programme concept for international news, an approach designed to bypass current distribution systems and build a new audience. The project aims to produce a new international news series using small teams of video journalists to explore an array of political, economic, health and cultural issues in a given country each month. The plan is to produce content for multiple platforms - including television, the Internet, DVDs, print and radio - and to promote it aggressively. For its part, Carleton University has expanded its Rwanda Initiative to include a media internship programme for Canadian journalism students who want to do work terms with a news organization in Africa. The initiative is also helping student journalists in Rwanda to produce freelance material for an outside audience.

It is difficult to fashion a strategy to deal with the structural flaws in the news media that resulted in the failure to provide adequate coverage of the Rwanda genocide or the crisis in Darfur. But surely that difficulty should not prevent us from trying to change the structure one small piece at a time, through the work of individual journalists. This is a rallying cry to those who call themselves journalists, who practise this profession. Rwandan journalist Thomas Kamilindi recounts an encounter he had in Côte d'Ivoire with a group of young reporters who wondered how to avoid being drawn into the hate media in their country. Kamilindi's admonition was simple: stand up and be reporters, do your job. He is echoed by Roméo Dallaire, who reminds journalists that they can be powerful individually and collectively and must stay dynamic in the search for truth.

As Maxwell McCombs notes in a recent review of the literature on media agendasetting, the space on the media agenda and public attention to that agenda are both rare commodities. 'Setting the agenda is an awesome responsibility,' McCombs (2005: 556) concludes. 'Arguably the most fundamental, overarching ethical question for journalists concerns their stewardship of these resources.' This collection of papers ends on a simple note, a plea to journalists: do your job, use the power that this profession affords and take up your responsibilities, starting with the responsibility to report.

THE MEDIA DICHOTOMY

The news media - both domestic and international - played a crucial role in the 1994 Rwanda genocide. From my vantage point as commander of the United Nations Assistance Mission for Rwanda (UNAMIR), I was able to watch the strange dichotomy of local media, on one side, fuelling the killing while international media, on the other side, virtually ignored or misunderstood what was happening.

The local media, particularly the extremist radio station Radio-Télévision Libre des Milles Collines (RTLM), were literally part of the genocide. The genocidaires used the media like a weapon. The haunting image of killers with a machete in one hand and a radio in the other never leaves you.

The international media initially affected events by their absence. A tree was falling in the forest and no one was there to hear it. Only those of us in Rwanda, it seemed, could hear the sound, because the international media were not there in any appreciable numbers at the outset.

And my mission, especially in those early days, was ill equipped to monitor what was being broadcast in the local media or to counteract it with strong messages of our own about the UN and its role in Rwanda.

To step back for a moment, it is important to set the scene in Rwanda in 1993-94, then to look at the ways in which the media were involved, both locally and internationally. This was a time when Rwanda had, in theory, finished a civil war. Enemies had signed a peace agreement, some of them under duress. In the course of a year, the country moved from a peace agreement through political stagnation to assassinations, massacres, civil war and, ultimately, genocide. In the end, the Tutsi minority actually won the war, gained control of the whole country and is now on a different path.

In my view, 1993-94 was an era in the 'new world disorder', not the 'new world order', as George Bush, Sr, called it. No new military thinking, no new diplomatic thinking was coming to the fore.

We were entering an era of conflict into which many diplomats, politicians, soldiers and humanitarian relief workers stumbled. They did a lot of on-the-job training, a lot of crisis management. In some cases they applied too many resources, at a terrible cost of life. In Rwanda, they didn't want to get involved at all, creating an orphan nation, where the people simply didn't count.

The American experience in Mogadishu in October 1993 significantly changed the will of the Western world to commit itself to the betterment of the developing world. Eighteen American soldiers were killed. They were professional soldiers who knew that every day when they woke up, they risked their lives. It was part of their way of life, their professional commitment. But after 18 military deaths in Somalia, the imperial power turned tail and ran.

The Americans had entered Somalia, along with Canadians and soldiers from many other countries, because hundreds of thousands of Somalis were dying of thirst and lack of food and medical supplies. When the Americans eventually pulled out - and pulled the heart out of the mission leaving it in the hands of Pakistanis, Italians, Canadians and the UN - there were still hundreds of thousands of Somalis dying. But for the United States, the price had become too high. The price of 18 soldiers was too high for the American government to continue with its stated aim of helping Somalia.

In Rwanda, in the first 24 hours of the genocide, the death of ten Belgian soldiers was too much for Belgium, the ex-colonial power, to sustain. It was a massive shock, I agree, and the Belgians pulled out and tried to convince everybody else that we should leave. They said we would all be massacred and nobody wanted to get involved in another African escapade where the risk of soldiers' lives was too high.

A representative of one major power came to me within the first weeks of the genocide and said quite clearly that, after doing an assessment, they had decided that they were not going to come and stop the carnage. There were bodies all over. We were already burning bodies with diesel fuel, because of the fear of disease, the smell and the wild dogs. This representative said, 'You know, this country is of no strategic value. Geographically, it provides us nothing. It's not even worth putting a radar station here. Economically it's nothing, because there's no strategic resources, only tea and coffee, and the bottom is falling out of those markets.' This person said, 'In fact what there's too much of here is people. Well, we're not going to come because of people.' In quantifying that, he went on to say that his government could only reconsider its decision not to intervene if for every one if its soldiers either killed or injured, there would be an equivalent of 85,000 dead Rwandans.

Are all humans human or are some more human than others? Do some count more than others? Millions of dollars were pouring into Yugoslavia in 1994 along with tens of thousands of troops. Everybody was looking at Yugoslavia. Nobody came to Rwanda. They pulled everything out and abandoned us in the field. There were more people killed, injured, internally displaced and turned into refugees in 100 days in Rwanda than during the six years of the Yugoslav campaign. And yet, the powers that be ripped the heart out of the possibility of stopping, or at least curtailing, the killing or saving of black Africans. It was as if those people didn't count.

In Yugoslavia, the problems were portrayed as long-standing divisions that educated people had debated. It was religious and ethnic conflict, something studied and analyzed. As such, we brought in new terms, like 'ethnic cleansing' to describe Yugoslavia. In Rwanda, it was just a bunch of tribes going at each other, like they always do. Rwanda was black. Yugoslavia was white European.

And where were the media? Where were the media in that debate? How many were taken in or set up? In terms of humanity, the real crisis at that time was in a small country in black Africa that nobody was interested in. The media for the most part travelled down the road of the mainstream thinking of the world powers- it was Yugoslavia that mattered, not Rwanda.

While the killing raged on in Rwanda, the O.J. Simpson case dominated the airwaves. Tonya Harding's kneecapping of her figure skating competitor was there as well. You had Nelson Mandela's election in South Africa. You had Yugoslavia. And. oh yes, somewhere in there, a bunch of black tribesmen in Africa were killing each other. During the 100 days of the Rwanda genocide, there was more coverage of Tonya Harding by ABC, CBS and NBC than of the genocide itself. Was that because of a love of pathos? Was it because of the excitement? Was it because the Harding story was on CNN's radar screen? Or was it the hand of someone above, guiding the media and getting across the subtle message, 'Listen, we have absolutely no interest in going into another hellhole in Africa. We do not want to get involved in Rwanda. So don't get us involved.'

The media, like so many others in Rwanda, failed. The world powers failed. Individually we failed.

Major news agencies devote fewer resources to Africa to begin with and virtually ignore small countries like Rwanda, which are deemed to be of little strategic value. There is no context, no general understanding of situations like the one that evolved in Rwanda. As I say in my book, when I was asked to go and serve as commander of the mission in Rwanda, I had to ask, 'Rwanda, that's in Africa isn't it?'

Before the genocide, the media scene in Rwanda was essentially internal with some local stringers, who were responding more often than not to the international journalists based in Nairobi. Until the start of the war, international media involvement amounted to: 'Is there an event? Do we go or do we just get the stringer?'

Months before the genocide, when we opened our mission headquarters with President Habyarimana in attendance, a number of journalists from international agencies were there. When the president was sworn in as part of the new government, there was international media coverage. When there was a massacre in the northwest of the country, there was international coverage.

But in essence, the international press were neophytes when it came to Rwanda. In fact, one international media organization was using a Rwandan stringer in Kigali who was part of the extremist movement. I had a call from a London journalist, who asked questions that were clearly based on false information. Thank God a person like Mark Doyle of the BBC spent considerable time on the ground and worked to set the record straight.

In my view, most of the journalists who came into Rwanda after the war started knew little or nothing of the country. Those who did know a lot were not necessarily listened to. Many stories were simply gruesome accounts of killings. There was little analysis of why we let a potential peace process fall into disarray.

After years of ignoring the place, after 6 April, all of a sudden every journalist wanted to jump on whatever aircraft or truck was available to get to Kigali. They didn't know what they were looking for, but there was excitement and it had reached the CNN radar screen. So, in the first days, a number of journalists did appear; within the first week, more than 200 were sitting in Nairobi.

They came to report that people were being slaughtered. Platoons of journalists would come in for three or four days, then leave so I could bring more in. We guaranteed their safety and provided them with transport, food and lodging. To me it was absolutely essential that they get their story. I put the lives of my troops on the line to guarantee that people got their daily story. Not only to get to the places where the catastrophe was evolving, but also to get their stories out. I had officers and soldiers run the gauntlet to get television tapes to my headquarters in Uganda, then to Kampala and then Nairobi where the technology existed to transmit images.

It took some time before the big media outfits arrived and set up their international capabilities. Within the third week of the genocide, when the UN had buckled under and decided that it was not only not going to reinforce the mission, but that it was also going to abandon Rwanda, the only voice, the only weapon that I had, was the media. If, through the media, I could shame the international community into acting, then I would have achieved my aim. But despite the courageous work done by reporters in the field, the stories often didn't get past the editor's desk. The story never really got told and that's why O.J. Simpson and Tonya Harding got a lot more press than 800,000 human beings being slaughtered.

The media can be a two-way street. I tried to give journalists what they required and some of them were instrumental in providing me with information. Many journalists were courageous enough to go between the lines. I opened my headquarters to them. The only time I didn't want them there was when we were planning operations. At other times, I would see journalists standing at the big map boards with my operations duty officers. They would be marking the map and saying, 'Yes, I've been through there and, yeah, there is a massacre site there and, yes, there are about 50,000 people on the side of that hill over there.' The exchange was transparent.

But after the initial flurry of attention in the first few days of April, most international media representatives were evacuated with the other expatriates and it seemed like there was no one left, like no one cared.

When news reaches the general population, it shapes public opinion. When there is a lack of statesmanship, public opinion can force a government to make decisions. Getting information out to the general population and holding decision-makers accountable - by continuously berating them about what is going on and what they are doing or not doing - is more crucial than a few talk shows and a couple of newscasts. In the case of Rwanda, that's where the process broke down. The events in Rwanda simply did not break through to such an extent as to create momentum.

From mid-April into the beginning of May, only a handful of international reporters were on the ground to witness the genocide. I went to great lengths during that period to attract international media attention. I wanted journalists to get their stories and, as I said, I used UNAMIR resources to get tapes up to the Ugandan border, so that they could eventually reach Europe. The BBC's Mark Doyle used my satellite phone from time to time. I felt that one good journalist on the ground was worth a battalion of troops, because I realized they could bring pressure to bear.

I had a policy of taking all media calls in the evening and gave instructions to my staff to facilitate those interviews. I had frequent conversations with Michael Enright on the Canadian Broadcasting Corporation's radio programme 'As it Happens'. But the media coverage wasn't enough to create an outcry in the international community. The ambivalence of the great powers toward Rwanda was too imbedded; they had reason to be disinterested, to turn away, because of 'Somalia fatigue'.

Ironically, the news media finally descended in hordes once the genocide was over and the 'refugee crisis' occurred in Goma. A clouded picture of the suffering appeared, as genocidaires were among those who fled and were now getting ten times the media attention given to the genocide itself.

I have been asked why I didn't leak the famous 11 January cable, with its warning about Interahamwe militia training to kill thousands, making lists and hiding weapons. There has been much debate about my message to the UN in New York, about an informant who provided information about arms caches and the preparation of lists of people to be exterminated. I informed New York of my intention to raid some of the arms caches, but was ordered not to intervene. Once it was clear the UN system was not going to act on those warnings, should I have leaked the information to The New York Times or the Washington Post?

If the media had come and asked me what was going on, if they had come and queried me about the stagnation and the political and security process and asked me what we were doing, they would have got the answer. And they could have reported what was happening. But I was not going to leak that document. You cannot be ethical and fiddle with the media.

Within the country, Rwandan media played an exceptionally important role in the genocide. The country is known as a radio country. In some villages, radio was like the voice of God. At the height of the killing, in the camps for the displaced and refugees, you could still find people with portable radios. I wondered where they got the batteries. We couldn't even get batteries for our flashlights.

RTLM was created specifically as a tool of the genocidaires to demonize the Tutsi, lay the groundwork, then literally drive on the killing once the genocide started. A great handicap for UNAMIR (in effect the representative on the ground of the world community) was our initial ignorance of what was really happening and of the mixed media messages. We had so little capacity to monitor broadcasts, particularly those in the local language, Kinyarwanda. For a long time, we didn't notice the difference in tone between RTLM broadcasts in French and those in Kinyarwanda. We missed this vital early-warning sign of what was to come because, in effect, we weren't listening properly to local media and what it was telling people in January, February and March 1994.

I still believe it would have made a significant difference if we had had the capacity to monitor local media comprehensively from the outset. This was one of the lessons learned from Rwanda - that part of the role of an international force is to get the whole picture, to realize the importance of media messaging.

In the first few days after 6 April, it was Rwanda's prime minister designate, Faustin Twagiramungu, who was in hiding in my headquarters, who acted as my media monitor, listening to RTLM and translating from Kinyarwanda. Later, we hired a young man who could speak English and French and trained him to perform the same task.

Missions such as ours need people with media and linguistic skills. You ignore the local media at your peril. And there was another lesson in this volatile situation: UNAMIR desperately needed its own media outlet, its own radio station. We were unarmed in the media war that was going on and had virtually no capacity to explain ourselves to the local community to whom radio was so important.

People were turning to the extremist RTLM, the state-run Radio Rwanda and the rebel-controlled Radio Muhaburu. In Cambodia, for example, the UN's use of radio was essential. But in our case, the equipment was unavailable, so it was dropped from the budget for our mission. In January and February, when it became apparent that we needed a media outlet to explain ourselves, we begged the UN for that facility. We knew that equipment from the UN station in Cambodia was in storage in Italy, but although we pleaded for it, we didn't receive the gear until well after the genocide. We did not have a radio station to take part in the debate or to sell our 'product'. It became clear to me that none of the radio stations in Rwanda actually told people why we were there. No information from us was being passed on. People saw a white vehicle with a blue flag going by at 70 kilometres an hour, but many Rwandans had no idea why we were there. Those who did know were led to believe that we could do much more than our mandate actually permitted.

In fairness, before 6 April, at the behest of Jean-Marie Higiro, then the director of Radio Rwanda, we were allowed 30 minutes a week on the air. But we discovered that no one in our small mission had the skill to do 30 minutes of programming. In fact, some weeks we didn't even go on the air. Without interpreters or media analysts, we didn't even have the ability to present a lucid programme.

Once the killing started, I would meet displaced people and Rwandans would always have this sort of look of astonishment with regard to the Blue Berets. They believed that the UNAMIR mandate was to protect and defend the Rwandans, whereas, in fact, the Security Council limited it to assisting in establishing an atmosphere of security. The limitations of our mandate were never really explained to the whole of the nation, and that is one of the great tragedies of the mission.

Another tragedy was our failure to intervene early to shut down RTLM, which had become the voice of the devil in Rwanda. Through January, February and March 1994, before the genocide began, the radio station stepped up its campaign, delivering the message that there were people who should not live in Rwanda. It even described ways to eliminate them. Failing all else, we should have shut down RTLM. I repeatedly asked for the capability to jam RTLM, but the request was denied. The argument was that this would amount to a violation of state sovereignty and that there was also a very high cost attached to maintaining jamming equipment.

In my view, it was time to question the absolute of state sovereignty and to ask whether it was becoming an impediment to humanity. When RTLM started to attack not only the mission, but also myself, when RTLM was launching its descriptions of how to kill, it was obvious to everyone that RTLM was operating without any rules. It was beyond rules. It was beyond limits. And it was an overt instrument of genocide. I went to the UN and the big powers, and said, 'I need two things. One is a radio station and, second, I need somebody to find that RTLM emitter and close her down, either by jamming it or ultimately destroying it.' At the height of the genocide, the response was that Rwanda is a sovereign state, the airwaves belong to that sovereign state and we cannot intervene. Sovereignty became an instrument for not doing something.

In fact, on 25 May 1994 in a convocation speech at the US Naval Academy in Annapolis, Maryland, President Clinton said the US could not be the policeman of the world and would only participate in and fully support UN peacekeeping operations that were deemed to be in the vital interests of the US. 'We cannot solve every such outburst of civil strife or militant nationalism simply by sending in our forces,' Clinton said. 'We cannot turn away from them. But our interests are not sufficiently at stake in so many of them to justify a commitment of our folks.'

This doctrine was spelled out in Presidential Decision Directive 25, unveiled that same month, even as the killing went on unabated across Rwanda. That directive codified and complicated US participation in peacekeeping operations. Indeed, it is my understanding that weeks earlier, on 7 April, in the working room of the Security Council, Madeleine Albright and her colleagues said bluntly about Rwanda, 'The Americans are not going to intervene, and they're not going to help anybody who wants to.'

The world failed utterly to deal with one of the century's most clear-cut examples of abuse of the media. Sadly, we dealt with it only in hindsight through the 'Media Trial', the important prosecution at the International Criminal Tribunal for Rwanda.

As for the international media, I think we need to ask ourselves, did the lack of attention and understanding by the international media actually contribute to the genocide? Did the decision to ignore Rwanda border on complicity by letting this atrocity go unreported?

The media can be both a weapon and a conscience to humanity. Journalists can be powerful, individually and collectively. But they can also be manipulated very easily if the depth of the subject is not there. For future journalists, my advice is get yourselves a lot more cultured, learn some geography, some anthropology, some sociology and maybe even some philosophy. Bring more depth to your questions and to your analysis. And stay dynamic in the search for the truth, for you are an instrument of the absolute called 'justice'. If you abdicate or if you are perfunctory, then we will all be weakened.

PG - PARENTAL GUIDANCE OR PORTRAYAL OF GENOCIDE: THE COMPARATIVE DEPICTION OF MASS MURDER IN CONTEMPORARY CINEMA

In the hour of brief interviews with film stars preceding the 2005 Oscars, Don Cheadle, nominated for best actor for his role as Paul Rusesabagina, the courageous hotel manager in Hotel Rwanda, stated that he was honoured to be associated with a film that told the story of 'a little known genocide' (CTV 2005). Cheadle's remarks indicate a problem relating to the filmic, and often fictionalized, depiction of genocides generally. Whether in Rwanda in the 1990s, Cambodia in the 1970s or Nazi-occupied Poland of the 1940s, genocides are always seemingly, and remain often decades after the fact, 'little known'.

Genocides always take place off-screen, so to speak. There are no images from within the Nazi gas chambers to establish once and for all (if such proof were still required) that the Holocaust happened. There are very few images of the mass slaughter with clubs and machetes of the approximately 800,000 Tutsis killed in Rwanda. There are, however, images of numerous bodies after the slaughter and of cleaned skulls in rows and rows at memorial sites in Rwanda, as in Cambodia, that show that mass killings did occur.

There are also the mental images imprinted in the minds of those who witnessed or survived such events, in the form of flashbacks or related associations reactivated by location, smell, etc. These internalized images are, of course, impossible to show and so become the source of acute personal suffering labelled 'post-traumatic stress disorder'. Such dilemmas of representation leave the actual perpetration of genocide open to doubt, most notably in the case of Holocaust deniers (see, for example, Shermer and Grobman 2000).

Curiously, regarding the genocide of non-Jewish populations (the Armenian case being something of an exception), doubts about the actual occurrence of the slaughter seldom arise, although generalized ignorance at the time, or worse impotent indifference, serve a somewhat equivalent function. This may have to do with the fact that we live in a post-Holocaust era, in the sense that the Holocaust set new standards for the acceptability of mass murder on a scale never previously known to humankind.4 Either way, the actual killings remain off-screen. This is both a problem and a challenge for film-makers, as much for documentary film-makers as for those who have opted to deal fictionally with these issues. (It is equally a problem for historians, philosophers, theologians and the like, different again for novelists, although these will not concern us here.)

What will concern us is some of the problems encountered by certain film-makers who have attempted to represent genocide. For reasons of space, this will be a selective analysis, focusing on differences between 'Holocaust films' and 'genocide films', in which the victims are non-Jews.

THE G WORD

A first step must involve some definitional discussion of the problematic term 'genocide'.

One of the 'diplomatic' issues surrounding the lack of intervention in the Rwandan case was the Western powers' inability to agree on when a genocide actually is one, as opposed to, for example, 'an "acceptable" (if tragic) round of ethnic murder' (Power 2002: 346). Coined by the refugee Polish lawyer Rafael Lemkin, 'genocide' - from the Greek geno (race or tribe) and the Latin caedere (killing) - meant 'a coordinated plan of different actions aiming at the destruction of the essential foundations of the life of national groups, with the aim of annihilating the groups themselves' (Lemkin 1944).

He did not intend the term to capture or communicate the Nazi 'Final Solution'; rather 'genocide' was meant as an 'ideal-typical' concept in international law, a standard by which 'civilization' could begin to come to grips with the novel twentieth century problem of unprecedented mass murder (Power 2002: 43). Through Lemkin's own tireless personal efforts, combined with the legal problems posed by the (equally unprecedented) Nuremberg Trials, the term genocide rapidly did become not only widely accepted (if in other ways unclear) but also entrenched in international law in the 1948 United Nations Convention on the Prevention and Punishment of the Crime of Genocide (as specified acts 'committed with intent to destroy, in whole or in part, a national, ethnical, racial or religious group' (UN 1951)).

If not intended to be conflated with the Nazi Judeocide, in fact it was. Genocide and the Holocaust soon became equivalent ideas, if not in international law, then in the broader post-Holocaust culture. Paradoxically, this conflation would make it harder to reach agreement on genocides that did not involve the extermination of millions (by implication, of Jews; this being the standard). One of the difficulties, then, in the case of the 'diplomatic' debate attempting to come to grips with what was going on in Rwanda in 1993, was the following, in Roméo Dallaire's words:

I was self-conscious about saying the killings were 'genocidal' because to us in the West, genocide was the equivalent of the Holocaust or the killing fields of Cambodia - I mean millions of people. 'Ethnic cleansing' seemed to involve hundreds of thousands of people. 'Genocide' was the highest scale of crimes against humanity imaginable. It was so far up there, so far off the charts, that it was not easy to recognize that we could be in such a situation. (Power 2002: 358)

Note that Dallaire's reference to Cambodia indicates a shifting downward of the scale of 'acceptable' genocidal killing from the canonical figure of six million to a mere 1.7 million in Cambodia.5 If the conflation of genocide with the Holocaust compounded the difficulty of rating a mass killing for diplomats and generals, how much more difficult would the issue be for the non-specialist, popular culture at large?

The Holocaust Film

As Barbie Zelizer (1998) remarked in her important study of Holocaust memory through the camera's eye, Remembering to Forget, the initial dissemination of newsreels of British army bulldozers plowing thousands of emaciated cadavers into the lime pits of Bergen-Belsen raised some of the many problems relating to the depiction of the Holocaust. The main one concerns the problematic status of 'the image' in mass media cultures. The paradox here is that for all the proliferation of mediated images that we have lived with since the mass dissemination of first the movies and then television, we still do not fully understand, scientifically, philosophically and otherwise, how human beings respond to images individually and collectively.

The naïve belief that 'a picture is worth a thousand words' is a highly dubious proposition, especially if the picture depicts something never seen before; just consider modern art's scandalous reception since the beginning of the twentieth century. Thus, the unleashing of images of the Nazi concentration camps, after their liberation by the allied armies in the spring of 1945, of mountains of dead or near-dead staggering survivors, a dissemination widely encouraged by the highest authorities of the Supreme Headquarters Allied Expeditionary Force, posed whole new problems.

As Zelizer notes, these images had no 'framing' - they were just suddenly there. She notes as well that this was in a context of a rising professional rivalry between print journalists and photographers, as attested to by Life magazine, which, during World War II and the Pacific War in particular, had become increasingly 'realistic' in its photographs of dead American soldiers.

Similarly, it was the showing of the same footage of the bulldozing of murdered concentration camp inmates that caused the uproar at the Nuremberg Trials of the major Nazi war criminals, rather than the massive documentary, textual evidence assembled by the prosecution that journalists covering the trials found so 'boring' (Douglas 2001).

In his feature film Judgment At Nuremberg, director Stanley Kramer (1961) recaptures precisely the shock of the showing of these same images within the film's depiction of one of the smaller trials involving lesser figures of the Nazi leadership. It was all so shocking and incomprehensible that the most widespread collective response was to repress the whole business for several decades.

'Holocaust' TV Series

Hot on the heels of ABC's enormously successful mini-series Roots in 1977, NBC responded the year after with the 9.5-hour mini-series Holocaust. As historian Peter Novick (1999: 209) writes, 'more information about the Holocaust was imparted to more Americans over those four nights than over all the preceding thirty years.' Nearly 100 million Americans watched all or part of the mini-series, written by screenwriter Gerald Green who also wrote the subsequent novelization (Green 1978).

Although both teleplay and novelization have been criticized for their stereotypical characterizations, wooden dialogue and patronization of Holocaust victims (Schartz 1999: 162),9 the critical reception of Holocaust was 'rhapsodic' (Novick 1999: 211). Novick describes the millions of copies of special inserts, study guides and other promotional and educational materials about the Holocaust prepared around the mini-series by American Jewish organizations in an attempt to sensitize gentiles as well as a developing (American) Jewish identity. As for the lasting effects of this first depiction of the Holocaust before a mass audience, Novick is less sanguine. His 'guess is that it hasn't mattered that much' (Novick 1999: 212).

The notable exception concerns the showing of the mini-series in West Germany in January 1979. Not only is Holocaust credited with helping persuade the Bundestag later that year to abolish the statute of limitations on war crimes, but as one German journalist wrote: 'It is absolutely fantastic ... Holocaust has shaken up post-Hitler Germany in a way that German intellectuals have been unable to do. No other film has ever made the Jews' road to suffering leading to the gas chambers so vivid' (Herf 1986: 214). If Holocaust incontestably acted as a turning point in the German popular culture's reluctance to confront the Nazi Final Solution (in part perhaps because the mini-series was a major American production and so a perspective from outside), in America itself, the effect was less clear. Despite many subsequent attempts to bring the Holocaust to American television (Shandler 1999), none would turn out to have the fanfare and audience that Holocaust first garnered until the release, 15 years later, of Steven Spielberg's 197-minute feature film Schindler's List.

Thus, the representation of the Holocaust by the mass media entailed a gamut of responses, from initial celebration of a medium's ability to partly, if fictionally, depict events drawn from the historical record - technically speaking, what Barbara Foley (1982) terms the 'pseudofactual' in the sense that it replaces literary effects with some form of engagement with the historical - to the posing of such problems as the representability of the Holocaust itself. But these would be issues taken up, in the interim, by film-maker intellectuals, most notably Claude Lanzmann.

Lanzmann's Shoah

The fact that the first documentary images of the Holocaust appeared 'out of the blue' posed a range of problems, particularly concerning the place of the image not only in contemporary culture, but also in respect to the making of collective memory. There is arguably a demand for understanding history and especially our human relation to it, but there are two contradictory responses to this.

On the one hand, there is a popular demand for understanding history that is greater than the kind of history produced by professional, academic historians; for example, the contemporary fascination with biography both in book form and television documentaries (indeed, entire television channels!). On the other hand, and precisely because of the surrounding proliferation of images, there is also an equivalent sense of fragmentation and of conflicting representations of the past, a problem that is only enhanced by the increased technical capacity to turn black-and-white images (formerly signifiers of 'pastness') into colour as well as to redigitize images such that they no longer have any basis in any reality outside of their own.

Thus the debate over the representability of the Holocaust - denounced by Elie Wiesel (1978) as a sacrilege at the time of the airing of Holocaust - was the starting-point for Claude Lanzmann's (1985a) nine and a half hour 'documentary' Shoah in which there is not a single shot of what we conventionally understand as documentary archival footage. Indeed, Lanzmann has claimed repeatedly that no such images of the Holocaust exist - and even if he had found such images, he would have destroyed them. Arguably they do not exist, just as no document, blueprint or written order of any kind stating 'Now the Jews will be killed' exists either (Lanzmann 1985b: 72). Shoah does include footage of present-day Sobibor, Chelmno, Treblinka and Auschwitz, or what remains of these major killings centres. As Simon Srebnik says, when taken back to the present-day site of Chelmno of which nothing remains except the forest,

It's hard to recognize, but it was here. They burned people here ... Yes, this is the place ... I can't believe I'm here ... It was always this peaceful here. Always. When they burned two thousand people - Jews -every day, it was just as peaceful. (Lanzmann 1985b: 6)

The film's only access to the past is through the voices, expressions and memories of those speaking, the survivors of the Holocaust, the 'technicians' of the Final Solution, the contemporary Polish bystanders. As Ilan Avisar (1997: 38-58) writes,

the principal channel to the past is ultimately memory. The avoidance of any archival footage further enhances the reliance on personal memories as the sources of knowledge, while the camera documents the ongoing dramatic processes of painful recollection ... Indeed, Lanzmann's 'Shoah' conveys the painful recognition that memory is the only cognitive avenue to the unimaginable.

Seeing and hearing the tormented workings of memory in the testimonies of the survivors, compounded by the sheer length of the film, its long takes and pauses, not to mention Lanzmann's presence urging his witnesses to remember no matter how painful it is to do so, makes Shoah a living (not re-living) present, in which the past is abolished because it is still here, 40 years later - thus the force of the film and its justly celebrated status as the masterpiece of Holocaust film. Not only did Shoah single-handedly entail the abandonment of the use of the word 'Holocaust' in France for the more accurate Hebrew term, but one of the reasons that motivated the making of the film was a furious response to the kind of depictions that Holocaust, the mini-series, had evoked in Lanzmann as how not to make a film about the Judeocide. Still, for all the controversy and debate that Shoah sparked - not least a colloquium at Oxford over Lanzmann's unflattering depiction of the Poles - it remained, like much of the extensive academic scholarship on the Shoah itself, confined within specialist film or intellectual circles. The biggest Holocaust film of them all was still to come.

'Schindler's List'

Steven Spielberg's Schindler's List has been compared to both D.W. Griffith's Birth of a Nation and Orson Welles' Citizen Kane, arguably the two greatest films in the American cinema (Hansen 2001: 127-51). Released to a torrent of publicity preceded by the director's not inconsiderable reputation for such films as E.T. and Jurassic Park, it would sweep the Oscars, much as the Holocaust mini-series had swept the Emmys in 1978. Because the film's release coincided with the opening of the United States Holocaust Memorial Museum in Washington, DC, publicists for the film included no less a figure than the President of the United States (Novick 1999: 214).

If Time magazine would write that the film showed 'the greatest sequences of chaos and mass terror ever filmed' (Avisar 1997: 21), other critics such as J. Hoberman wondered whether it was 'possible to make feel-good entertainment about the ultimate feel-bad experience of the twentieth century' (Hansen 2001: 130). The issue, however, is less the critical response to what is certainly, on many levels, an extremely powerful attempt to come as close as possible to a filmed depiction of what aspects of the Holocaust may have been like. This is particularly the case with the sequences concerning the 'liquidation' of the Kraków ghetto. As for Spielberg's depiction of concentration camp 'life' as a state of relentless, unpredictable terror, he tends to personalize this, particularly through the evil character of Plazsow labour camp commander Amon Goeth (Ralph Fiennes), who enjoys pre-prandial random target shooting of prisoners. Italian writer Primo Levi (1960: 29) managed to better grasp the state of constant terror in four words spoken to him by a guard ('Hier ist kein Warum' [There is no why here]).

It is interesting that Spielberg declared his film to be 'a document', a claim apparently supported by the fact that much of it was shot in Kraków where many of the historical events depicted took place, and in black-and-white photography, which as we noted earlier serves to signify 'the real past'. Such claims seem disingenuous, to the extent that Spielberg owes his reputation to his virtuosity in manipulating the codes of Hollywood cinema.

Still, there is more involved than predictable arguments about trivialization or Americanization, as Miriam B. Hansen recognizes in elaborating the term 'popular modernism'. This concept, which she compares to Fordism, for example, is the fusion of capitalist means of production with an aesthetic, in a modern vernacular of its own. Such an approach gives her the means of situating Schindler's List as 'more sophisticated, elliptical and self-conscious ... than its critics acknowledge' in its capacity for 'reflecting upon the shocks and scars inflicted by modernization on people's lives in a generally accessible, public horizon' (Hansen 2001: 135, emphasis added).

Thus there is little question regarding the visual and aural sophistication of Schindler's List (as Hansen demonstrates in a series of frame analyses). It's certainly self-conscious, not only as Hansen argues by its references to Kane, but also by the homage it pays to Lanzmann's Shoah. In the latter, as survivor Richard Glazer talks about the train trip to Treblinka:

'[W]e'd been able to open a window - the old man in our compartment saw a boy ... cows were grazing ... and he asked the boy in signs, "Where are we?" And the kid made a funny gesture. This (draws finger across his throat).' The same gesture is also made by a farmhand. 'And he made that gesture. Like this. We didn't really pay much attention to him. We couldn't figure out what he meant' (Lanzmann 1985b: 34).

In Schindler's List, during the train trip to Auschwitz in which a group of Schindler women is accidentally embarked, Spielberg recreates the scene - two shots - described by Glazer of a small boy in a snow-covered field shown making 'that gesture' at the passing boxcars. It's a visual quote from Shoah, but we, of the after-Shoah, now know what it means.

Still, and because the idea of popular modernism doesn't exclude cheap tricks, Spielberg seemingly can't resist not showing off, this time in a perverse homage to Hitchcock's Psycho. Soon after their arrival at Auschwitz, among sweeping lights and snarling dogs, the Schindler women, their hair cut badly to the length of Janet Leigh's, are sent naked to the Bad und Disinfektion rooms of what we fear - as do they - are the gas chambers, spewing out their greasy flakes of ashened flesh that look like snow. After the door is bolted, we see them through the peephole, huddling together in dreaded anticipation. The camera tilts up to the 'showerheads'; we - and they - wait for what seems the inevitable. And then real water begins to spurt down onto the naked bodies that burst into relieved laughter. There's another shot of the showerheads, to remind us of their double function (life-giving water/death by Zyklon B gas). But we've been had, and are disgusted at our own relief. When the women, sprung by Schindler's tractations, are leaving Auschwitz, they pass a long line of people going the other way who, as we all now know, are about to shortly feel the showerheads' other function. Just to make the point crystal clear, this is followed by a shot of the smoking chimneys of the crematoria. Now that's 'Shoah' business, as the grim joke has it.

A third point, made by the Israeli critic Ilan Avisar, concerns the two endings of Schindler's List. The first is within the story when Oskar Schindler, after receiving the ring made for him by his Jews from their gold teeth fillings, bursts into tears and reproaches himself for not having saved more Jews. He launches into a bizarre calculation: his car, had he sold it, would have been worth ten more Jews; the ring two more. The second ending, as a coda to the film, which follows a dissolve as the former prisoners seem to march in a long line from Czechoslovakia to Israel singing sabra songs, shows real Schindler Jews and the actors who played them placing stones in the commemorative ritual gesture on Schindler's Jerusalem grave with its visible Christian cross. Avisar argues - not totally convincingly - that in the first ending it is 'the Christian "savior" who ends in the highest moral position.'

More important is what he writes about the second ending that links the Holocaust and the founding of the Jewish state. Avisar (1997: 52) writes that 'in Spielberg's film, ideology combines with aesthetic effect as the linkage creates a narrative closure that deemphasizes the horrors of the genocide in the context of Jewish revival and independence in Israel.'13 Hansen (2001: 129) also notes with some ambivalence the film's 'enormous success in Germany ... and the discovery of local Schindlers everywhere'. If Holocaust inadvertently helped Germany begin to cope with its repression of the Final Solution, Spielberg, by the same token, de-emphasizes the long history of Christian anti-Semitism by the good deeds of one Christian opportunist and, to be doubly safe, redeems the Judeocide since it 'caused' the founding of the Jewish State.

THE GENOCIDE FILM

The genocide film plunges us into a different set of problems, although with the occasional parallel to the Holocaust film, but steering clear of the politico-theological issues raised in the previous paragraph. As with the Holocaust film, the genocide film does not 'show' genocide, except metonymically. Instead, it deals more with questions of racism and, more important, it raises once again, although not directly, the very problem that confronted what Dallaire terms 'the failure of humanity' with respect to Rwanda; namely, what makes a genocide a genocide?

The 1948 UN convention that came into force in 1951 is not terribly helpful in defining what constitutes a genocide. Article II defines genocide as:

a. Killing members of the [national, ethnical, racial or religious] group;
b. Causing serious bodily or mental harm to members of the group;
c. Deliberately inflicting on the group conditions of life calculated to bring about its physical destruction in whole or in part;
d. Imposing measures intended to prevent births within the group;
e. Forcibly transferring children of the group to another group. (UN 1951)

Although such a definition might seem fairly encompassing, some critics have written that it is not broad enough in that it does not cover the killings of certain subgroups, for example, the Soviet killing of the Kulaks as a social class. Others have noted that it focuses on 'physical' extermination as opposed to 'cultural' destruction, linguicide and so on (Kuper 1981; Stein 1996). As Stein, for example, observes, international law until recently was of little help in clarifying the parameters of the 1948 convention, among other reasons because one state has to accuse another of genocide. As noted earlier, the conflation of the Holocaust with a normative conception of genocide has made coming to grips with genocide harder, particularly once such acts occur outside of the European context. The case of Cambodia is a useful illustration of these problems.

Cambodia

Today, it is widely assumed that '(t)he Cambodian genocide of 1975-1979, in which approximately 1.7 million people lost their lives (21 per cent of the country's population), was one of the worst human tragedies of the last century' (Yale n.d.).

However, it was not until March 2003 that the UN signed an agreement with Cambodia to try the surviving members of the Khmer Rouge leadership for crimes under Cambodian law, international law and custom and international conventions recognized by Cambodia. The latter include genocide, war crimes and breaches of the Geneva Convention. Thus, it took about a decade, since the 1993 elections that outlawed the Khmer Rouge, for the legal machinery to get itself together. A key turning point was the United States Congress' passage in 1994 of the Cambodian Genocide Justice Act. In other words, it is a complex process to try the leadership of a state for a range of crimes, of which genocide may be one.

The Cambodian case is further complicated by the fact that it is far from clear that what went on under the Khmer Rouge's radical attempt at massive social engineering between 1975 and 1979 was actually a genocide. One of the leading Western historians on Cambodia, the Australian David P. Chandler, does not use the word in his numerous books on the period.

The closest he comes to it, because the Khmer Rouge's crimes were largely committed against other Khmers, is French author Jean Lacouture's term 'autogenocide' (Chandler 1999: vii). For Chandler, what distinguishes the Cambodian case is the fusion of the (catastrophic) attempts of other Communist regimes to surpass Western economic development - the Soviet collectivization of agriculture in the 1930s, China's Great Leap Forward in industrial production of the 1950s, the Chinese Cultural Revolution of the 1960s and the Vietnamese and North Korean equivalents - but, in the Cambodian instance, pushed to unprecedented heights of Marxist and indigenous utopianism (such as in the Super Great Leap Forward of 1976).

It is something of an oversimplification to lump all these processes together under the rubric 'genocide'. In his book on the workings of the main Khmer Rouge torture centre, S-21, where some 14,000 men, women and children were interrogated, tortured and killed (only seven people emerged alive), Chandler (1999) uses the term 'crimes of obcdience'15 to explain what went on there. These distinctions, while in no means meant to minimize the far-reaching effect of what Chandler (1991) terms 'the Typhoon', do, however, blur the picture somewhat when it comes to 'genocide films' dealing with Cambodia.

The Killing Fields

'The Killing Fields' (Joffé 1984) is probably the best-known film in the West about the fall of Phnom Penh to the Khmer Rouge armies in the spring of 1975 and the almost instantaneous evacuation of the cities' populations into forced rice-growing in the countryside. Despite its title, the film is not really about the killing fields at all. Rather it is mainly about the friendship between The New York Times correspondent Sidney Schanberg and his Cambodian translator, coffee boy and apprentice journalist, Dith Pran. Second, it is about the hardships faced by the Western press corps attempting to cover civil wars in dangerous faraway places, with very strong parallels to the chaotic evacuation of Saigon by the panic-stricken Americans at the end of the Vietnam War. Third, much like Hotel Rwanda, The Killing Fields is at its most general level about the complex links between white foreigners and non-white locals and what happens to the locals once they are abandoned to a local fate.

Ultimately, the film is about the slippery notion of identity in a world or region being globalized by war. Dith Pran survives his capture by the Khmer Rouge, escapes to the Cambodia-Thai border, is reunited with Schanberg and ends up working as a photographer for the Times in New York. Dr Haing S. Ngor, who plays Dith Pran, became the first Southeast Asian - and Buddhist - to receive an academy award.

S-21: The Khmer Rouge Killing Machine

Rithy Panh's (2003) 101-minute documentary is, as critics have noted,16 more modestly the Cambodian Shoah, using similar strategies as the Lanzmann film. Panh, who fled to France in 1979, returns to Cambodia and the infamous S-21 former prison, now the Tuol Sleng Museum of Genocidal Crimes, where some of the former guards serve as guides. Panh's film documents two of the surviving former prisoners, notably the painter Vann Nath who survived by drawing official portraits of his guards and today reproduces on canvas scenes of the atrocities he witnessed. Unlike the Lanzmann film, former guards, torturers and interrogators are confronted with survivors, Nath and Chum Mey. Like the Lanzmann film, S-

21 details the tortured workings of memory; guards and torturers 'act out' in minute detail the actions committed on the job. But the strength of Panh's film is as a study of the power of affect - how expressions and body language change according to the memory - and also of the human mind's capacity for rationalizing awful deeds. Thus the guard 'explains' that they were victims too and just as terrorized as their victims. S-21 is an almost clinical analysis of the psychology of torture, and its effects 20 years later.

Back to Rwanda

Returning, then, to the case of Rwanda, we find that some of the problems raised initially have gained in contextualization. As we saw in the case of Cambodia, the slow legal process of actually trying crimes of genocide would at last see fruit in Rwanda with the establishment of the International Criminal Tribunal for Rwanda (ICTR) and the first trial as of January 1997. The Akayesu case decided by the ICTR in 1998 was the first in which an international tribunal was called upon to interpret the definition of genocide based on the 1948 convention. The subsequent conviction of former Prime Minister Jean Kambanda was the first time that an accused acknowledged guilt for the crime of genocide before an international tribunal and the first time that a head of government was convicted for the crime of genocide. As the legal process grinds on (it is expected to have completed all trials and appeals by 2010), films about the Rwanda genocide are filling in the blanks in public memory. As of this writing, three films have been released so far: Hotel Rwanda (George 2004), 100 Days (Hughes 2001)- two films that in many ways could hardly be more different - and Shake Hands with the Devil (Raymont 2004).

Several more features were released by summer 2005: the United Kingdom/Germany co-production Shooting Dogs, starring British actor John Hurt as a Catholic priest, is described as focusing on 'the human aspects of the story', as it frankly admits '(i)t can't ... say everything about the genocide' (Caton-Jones 2005). Sunday by the Pool, based on the novel A Sunday at the Pool in Kigali (Courtemanche 2004), was produced by

Montreal company Equinox Productions. Sometimes in April (Peck 2005), another Rwanda genocide feature that was a success at the recent Berlin Film Festival, was aired on HBO in March 2005 and on PBS in April. A feature film version of Dallaire's memoir Shake Hands with the Devil, co-produced by Barna-Alper Productions and Halifax Film Company, was shot on location in Rwanda and will be in theatres in 2007.

Hotel Rwanda: African Schindler?

As is by now well known, Hotel Rwanda tells the story of a good man caught in terrible times. It is the story of Mille Collines hotel's 'local', that is, African, manager, Paul Rusesabagina, and how he saved some 1,200 people from the slaughter raging outside in Kigali. Earlier, I suggest a parallel with Oskar Schindler, although one that needs qualifying. Rwanda's strategic unimportance - landlocked, no significant minerals, or for that matter of any compelling interest to any of the Western powers, except perhaps Belgium whose former colony it was17 - means that whereas Schindler was an industrialist (in enamel-work at first and then armaments), Rusesabagina is in the hospitality industry. Which doesn't mean that he can't grease local palms with Cuban cigars or Scotch in an attempt to gain the protection of high-ranking RGF officers.

Rusesabagina's adeptness is in keeping his customers happy, and his Belgian bosses in Brussels informed. His seeming servility is what allows him to be able to bend the rules and provide a refuge for threatened Rwandan Tutsis in what is, first of all, a hotel for white tourists and prominent locals. Unlike Schindler, who despite his breakdown of remorse at the end of 'Schindler's List' maintains a proprietorial relationship to 'his' Jews, Rusesabagina falls into his subversive role after French and Belgian troops, armed to the teeth, come to repatriate their white fellow nationals. And when he also realizes that his 'masters' in Brussels, whom he has loyally served, can't do very much for him at all. As he tells his wife in a powerful scene of his own coming to self-consciousness: 'I am not even a nigger, I'm an African.' Out of this realization of his own 'nothingness', however, comes altruism.

Unlike Dith Pran in The Killing Fields, who seems to bear no ill will at all to the whites who abandoned him, for Rusesabagina, the realization that no white can help him or his endangered fellow citizens is a crucial moment of utter loneliness. (The irony is that he will end up in exile in Belgium.) Similar to The Killing Fields, Hotel Rwanda is about 'identity': on the one hand, the Tutsi-Hutu identities that were a by-product of Belgian colonial anthropology mired in classical nineteenth century race science in the sense that the Tutsi were 'whiter' anthropomorphically; and the subsequent murderous frenzy of the Hutu attempt to reassert their 'threatened' identity. But on the other hand, the film is also about the illusions of 'identity' - except, of course, for the 'big other' provided by skin colour and especially the difference between being white and being black. In this sense, it is racism, both in Hotel Rwanda and in The Killing Fields that screens out the genocide; whereas in the Holocaust film, it is the 'racism' that leads inexorably to the killings.

100 Days

Oddly for a 'genocide' film, Nick Hughes' (2001) 100 Days is an astonishingly gentle film about a gentle people, some of whom are directed by state authority to suddenly begin to murder their long-time neighbours. The French word 'pudique' (discreet but in a bodily sense) is perhaps better than gentle to describe what I'm getting at. The film keeps its gaze turned away from the horrors - except for the sequence of the massacre at the Kibuye Church; and the suggestion of the rape by the priest of Josette and the other Tutsi women (that echoes the tactical use of rape in the former Yugoslavia as a means of eliminating one ethnic group by forced insemination by members of the rival group). 100 Days in its gentleness is the love story of Josette and Baptiste, and how the genocide comes to kill that love. With the exceptions mentioned, the genocide itself is at times referred back to in time, after the fact, by the memorial markers that are set up at the Church's mass grave site. Or conversely, that remains off-screen, in that for the film's Rwandan actors who had lived through the events and the film's investors and co-producers who had lost countless family members, the making of 100 Days becomes more an extra-diegetical act of 'working through' memory than what the film itself actually shows.

CONCLUSION

Like the Marxist conception of the commodity, a film is two-sided and full of metaphysical subtleties. It has use-values (aesthetics, narrative, psychology of characters, action, etc.). It also has exchange-value: a film is capital-intensive and that capital must ideally be recouped through the rental of seats by ticket sales, the selling of foreign and other distribution rights, and the like. However, these two sides of a film are hard to separate. On the contrary, they tend to blur into each other.

As various critics have remarked, conceptual entities referring to historical events such as the Holocaust or, more loosely, genocide, are themselves 'word-commodities' whose value also changes over time. Largely going from neglect, indifference, and lack of knowledge, to varying degrees of approximation to what they refer to. Both the film commodity and the word commodity are subject to fluctuations. As historians like Peter Novick have shown, the meanings attributed to the Holocaust in the American case have followed such a pattern of fluctuation, from an initial shocked high, then to low, and subsequently increasingly higher again, tied as well to the United States' changing relationship to Israel after the Six Day War, and other factors related to the American sense of Jewish identity. Norman Finkelstein's (2000) really bad book, The Holocaust Industry, attempts to make something of a similar point, if ham-fistedly: namely that 'Holocaust' is not only a word but also a veritable cultural industry.

Yet words, like films, rise and fall in currency. If the Holocaust commodity, so to speak, has had a fairly good run, it would seem these days that it has been largely replaced by the genocide commodity, perhaps because the latter better satisfies our contemporary obsession with victimhood as the signifier of historical identity - to wit, the website of Yale University's genocide studies programme: 'As in the Ottoman Empire during the Armenian genocide, the Soviet Union under

Stalin, Nazi Germany during the Holocaust, and more recently in East Timor, Guatemala, Yugoslavia and Rwanda' (Yale n.d.). Or that of Latrobe University in Australia on a 2003 conference on the topic of colonialism and genocide. The latter is viewed as an integral part of not only Australian history, but of settler societies more generally (Canada and the United States, for instance), with their Indigenocides; or the nineteenth century German colonization of Namibia that foreshadowed the Holocaust; and the very barbarism of 'civilization' itself with its many forms of cultural genocide (of languages and demographics) (Veracini 2003). World history, in a word, is one long series of genocides. As well it may be: the nineteenth century philosopher Hegel referred to world history as the butcher's block of nations. So, if the general idea is not exactly novel, having a word for it, thanks to Lemkin, seems to be. And where there is a word commodity, the film commodity will surely follow.

This is not, to be sure, a state of affairs to be lamented. On the contrary, the more we learn about the world we live in, the better, presumably. But to expect that words, or even less so, films, will significantly change the world any time soon is perhaps setting the bar too high. Because, in the words of another German philosopher (Martin Heidegger), the world 'worlds'. For all else, there's always the movies.

5

PARTICIPATORY JOURNALISM

Citizen journalism, also known as public or participatory journalism, is the act of citizens "playing an active role in the process of collecting, reporting, analyzing and disseminating news and information," according to the seminal report We Media: How Audiences are Shaping the Future of News and Information, by Shayne Bowman and Chris Willis. They say, "The intent of this participation is to provide independent, reliable, accurate, wide-ranging and relevant information that a democracy requires."[1] Citizen journalism should not be confused with civic journalism, which is practiced by professional journalists. Citizen journalism is a specific form of citizen media as well as user generated content.

In a 2003 Online Journalism Review article, J. D. Lasica classifies media for citizen journalism into the following types: 1) Audience participation (such as user comments attached to news stories, personal blogs, photos or video footage captured from personal mobile cameras, or local news written by residents of a community), 2) Independent news and information Websites (Consumer Reports, the Drudge Report), 3) Full-fledged participatory news sites (OhmyNews), 4) Collaborative and contributory media sites (Slashdot, Kuro5hin), (Newsvine), 5) Other kinds of "thin media." (mailing lists, email newsletters), and 6) Personal broadcasting sites (video broadcast sites such as (KenRadio).

Dan Gillmor, former technology columnist with the San Jose Mercury News, is one of the foremost proponents of citizen journalism, and founded a nonprofit, the Center for Citizen

Media, to help promote it. The Canadian Broadcasting Corporation's French-language television network has also organized a weekly public affairs program called, "5 sur 5", which has been organizing and promoting citizen-based journalism since 2001. On the program, viewers submit questions on a wide variety of topics, and they, accompanied by staff journalists, get to interview experts to obtain answers to their questions.

History -

The citizen journalism movement emerged after journalists themselves began to question the predictability of their coverage of such events as the 1988 U.S. presidential election. Those journalists became part of the public, or civic, journalism movement, a countermeasure against the eroding trust in the news media and widespread public disillusionment with politics and civic affairs. Jay Rosen, a journalism professor at New York University, was one of public journalism's earliest proponents. From 1993 to 1997, he directed the Project on Public Life and the Press, funded by the Knight Foundation and housed at NYU. He also currently runs the PressThink weblog. Initially, discussions of public journalism focused on promoting journalism that was "for the people" by changing the way professional reporters did their work. A study done for the Pew Center and the Associated Press Managing Editors found that "45 percent of all editors surveyed say that their newsrooms use the tools and techniques of civic journalism. Sixty-six percent say they either embrace the label or like the philosophy and tools, suggesting that there are even more practitioners." According to Leonard Witt, however, early public journalism efforts were, "often part of 'special projects' that were expensive, time-consuming and episodic. Too often these projects dealt with an issue and moved on. Professional journalists were driving the discussion. They would say, "Let's do a story on welfare-to-work (or the environment, or traffic problems, or the economy)," and then they would recruit a cross-section of citizens and chronicle their points of view. Since not all reporters and editors bought into this form of public journalism, and some outright opposed it, reaching out to the people from the newsroom was never an easy task." By 2003, in fact, the movement seemed to be petering out, with the Pew Center for Civic Journalism closing its doors.

Public participation - such as telephone calls into the running broadcasting - might also be seen as an (old-fashioned) part of it.

However, just a few years prior, new internet technologies gave birth to a new form of this movement.

Birth of Blogs and the Indymedia Movement

In 1999, activists in Seattle created a response to the WTO meeting being held there. These activists understood the only way they could get into the corporate media was by blocking the streets. And then, the scant 60 seconds of coverage would show them being carted off by the police, but without any context to explain why they were protesting. They knew they had to create an alternative media model. Since then, the Indymedia movement has experienced exponential growth, and IMCs have been created in over 200 cities all over the world.

Simultaneously, journalism that was "by the people" began to flourish, enabled in part by emerging internet and networking technologies, such as weblogs, chat rooms, message boards, wikis and mobile computing. A relatively new development is the use of convergent polls, allowing editorials and opinions to be submitted and voted on. Overtime, the poll converges on the most broadly accepted editorials and opinions. In South Korea, OhmyNews became popular and commercially successful with the motto, "Every Citizen is a Reporter." Founded by Oh Yeon-ho on February 22, 2000, it has a staff of some 40-plus traditional reporters and editors who write about 20% of its content, with the rest coming from other freelance contributors who are mostly ordinary citizens. OhmyNews has been credited with transforming South Korea's conservative political environment.

In 2001, ThemeParkInsider.com became the first online publication to win a major journalism award for a feature that was reported and written entirely by readers, earning an Online Journalism Award from the Online News Association and Columbia Graduate School of Journalism for its "Accident

Watch" section, where readers tracked injury accidents at theme parks and shared accident prevention tips.

In 2004, a citizen journalism website called Associated Content.com was launched. The "People's Media Company", as they claim to be, was the first company to offer monetary compensation for their users that publish quality content in the form of articles, videos and audio clips. A few years later, WorldVoiceNews.com was launched, claiming the tagline "Honest and Unfiltered," and paying editors and reporters a per-story fee based on the number of stories they submit and the revenue for the company each month.

During the 2004 U.S. presidential election, both the Democratic and Republican parties issued press credentials to citizen bloggers covering the convention, marking a new level of influence and credibility for nontraditional journalists. Some bloggers also began watchdogging the work of conventional journalists, monitoring their work for biases and inaccuracy. A recent trend in citizen journalism has been the emergence of what blogger Jeff Jarvis terms hyperlocal journalism, as online news sites invite contributions from local residents of their subscription areas, who often report on topics that conventional newspapers tend to ignore. "We are the traditional journalism model turned upside down," explains Mary Lou Fulton, the publisher of the Northwest Voice in Bakersfield, California. "Instead of being the gatekeeper, telling people that what's important to them 'isn't news,' we're just opening up the gates and letting people come on in. We are a better community newspaper for having thousands of readers who serve as the eyes and ears for the Voice, rather than having everything filtered through the views of a small group of reporters and editors."

What is Citizen Journalism?

There is no easy answer to this question and depending on whom you ask you are likely to get very different answers. Some have called it networked journalism, open source journalism, and citizen media. Communication has changed greatly with the advent of the Internet. The Internet has enabled citizens to contribute to journalism, without professional training. Mark Glasser, a longtime freelance journalist who frequently writes on new media issues, gets to the heart of it:

The idea behind citizen journalism is that people without professional journalism training can use the tools of modern technology and the global distribution of the Internet to create, augment or fact-check media on their own or in collaboration with others. For example, you might write about a city council meeting on your blog or in an online forum. Or you could fact-check a newspaper article from the mainstream media and point out factual errors or bias on your blog. Or you might snap a digital photo of a newsworthy event happening in your town and post it online. Or you might videotape a similar event and post it on a site such as YouTube.

This might seem radical to some, but the idea that average citizens can engage in the act of journalism has a long history in the United States. Professor Mary-Rose Papandrea, a constitutional law professor at Boston College, notes in her article, Citizen Journalism and the Reporter's Privilege, that:

[i]n many ways, the definition of journalist has now come full circle. When the First Amendment was adopted, "freedom of the press" referred quite literally to the freedom to publish using a printing press, rather than the freedom of organized entities engaged in the publishing business. The printers of 1775 did not exclusively publish newspapers; instead, in order to survive financially they dedicated most of their efforts printing materials for paying clients. The newspapers and pamphlets of the American Revolutionary era were predominantly partisan and became even more so through the turn of the century. They engaged in little newsgathering and instead were predominantly vehicles for opinion.

The passage of the term "journalism" into common usage in the 1830s occurred at roughly the same time that newspapers, using highspeed rotary steam presses, began mass circulation throughout the eastern United States. Using the printing press, newspapers could distribute exact copies to large numbers of readers at a low incremental cost. In addition, the rapidly increasing demand for advertising for brand- name products fueled the creation of publications subsidized in large part by advertising revenue. It was not until the late nineteenth century that the concept of the "press" morphed into a description of individuals and companies engaged in an often competitive commercial media enterprise.

What has changed, however, is that with today's technology, the average person can capture news and distribute it globally. As Yochai Benkler has noted, "the capacity to make meaning - to encode and decode humanly meaningful statements - and the capacity to communicate one's meaning around the world, are held by, or readily available to, at least many hundreds of millions of users around the globe."

Who does Citizen Journalism?

According to Jay Rosen, citizen journalists "the people formerly known as the audience," who "were on the receiving end of a media system that ran one way, in a broadcasting pattern, with high entry fees and a few firms competing to speak very loudly while the rest of the population listened in isolation from one another- and who today are not in a situation like that at all. ... The people formerly known as the audience are simply the public made realer, less fictional, more able, less predictable." "Doing citizen journalism right means crafting a crew of correspondents who are typically excluded from or misrepresented by local television news: low-income women, minorities and youth -- the very demographic and lifestyle groups who have little access to the media and that advertisers don't want," says Robert Huesca, an associate professor of communication at Trinity University in San Antonio, Texas.

Public Journalism is now being explored via new media such as the use of mobile phones. Mobile phones have the potential to transform reporting and places the power of reporting in the hands of the public. Mobile telephony provides low-cost options for people to set up news operations. One small organization providing mobile news and exploring public journalism is Jasmine News in Sri Lanka.

In 2004, when the 9.1-magnitude underwater earthquake caused a huge tsunami in Banda Aceh Indonesia, a footage of a person who experienced the tsunami was broadcast in almost all TV channel. It was a mark of citizen jurnalism type news in the country. In 2008 the first fully citizen jurnalism news site by the name of SwaBerita.com (swa means self, and berita means news) was established.

In 2005, the Rocky Mountain News in Denver, Colo., created a hyperlocal citizen journalism Web site called YourHub.com that allows any registered user to post news articles and photos that are published online and in community-centered weekly newspaper sections that are delivered with the News and the Denver Post. An editorial staff monitors and edits the Web sites and contributes some professional content, but the majority of content is created by citizens. In 2006, the YourHub.com branding was franchised and sold to several markets around the country.

The Pulitzer Center on Crisis Reporting has embraced citizen journalism through an essay contest on the citizen journalism website Helium.com as a way to bridge the gap between professional journalists and citizen voices. The Helium writers are asked to write on the world's so-called underreported issues.

Legal Implications in the United States of America

The growth of online participatory journalism gives rise to the legal question of whether bloggers who gather and disseminate "news" should be classified as journalists. In light of the proposed federal reporter-shield law, the resolution of this issue will have far reaching implications for the millions of people in this country who disseminate information via blogs. In other words, are bloggers the modern day equivalent of the revolutionary pamphleteer who passed out leaflets on the street corner?

Currently, 30 states and the District of Columbia have enacted shield laws that allow journalists the privilege to shield their confidential sources from disclosure. These states are Alabama, California, Colorado, Delaware, Florida, Georgia, Illinois, Indiana, Kentucky, Louisiana, Maryland, Michigan, Minnesota, Montana, Nebraska, Nevada, New Jersey, New

Mexico, New York, North Dakota, Ohio, Oklahoma, Oregon, Pennsylvania, Rhode Island, South Carolina and Tennessee. (The First Amendment and The Fourth Estate, Ninth Edition, Foundation Press, p. 542.) In its landmark decision in Branzburg v. Hayes, 408 U.S. 665 (1972), the United States Supreme Court recognized that "the administration of a constitutional newsman's privilege would present practical and conceptual difficulties of high order ... Sooner or later it would be necessary to define those categories of newsmen who qualify for the privilege, a questionable procedure in light of the traditional doctrine that liberty of the press is the right of the lonely pamphleteer who uses carbon paper or a mimeograph just as much as the larger metropolitan publisher who utilizes the latest photocomposition methods." The time is fast approaching when these legal lines will have to be drawn. In recent times, bloggers have broken too many stories of national interest that mainstream media either overlooked, or decided against reporting, not to be considered legitimate news gatherers and reporters.

Moreover, the fact that many bloggers are anonymous is of marginal importance to the question of whether they qualify as journalists. The Supreme Court has long recognized that anonymous speech is entitled to First Amendment protection. In Talley v. California, 362 U.S. 60 (1960), The Supreme Court exclaimed that "[a]nonymous pamphlets, leaflets, brochures and even books have played an important role in the progress of mankind." Indeed the Federalist Papers were published under the pseudonym "Publius." Accordingly, there are times and circumstances when the authorities may not compel those engaged in the dissemination of ideas to be publicly identified for the fear of identification and reprisal might deter perfectly lawful discussions of matters of public importance. The way the courts deal with the myriad issues that will arise from the use of this cyber-soapbox will determine the extent to which First Amendment freedoms will flourish in the age of Internet.

Criticisms

Citizen journalists may be activists within the communities they write about. This has drawn some criticism from traditional media institutions such as The New York Times, which have accused proponents of public journalism of abandoning the traditional goal of 'objectivity'. Many traditional journalists view citizen journalism with some skepticism, believing that only trained journalists can understand the exactitude and ethics involved in reporting news. See, e.g., Nicholas Lemann, Vincent Maher, and Tom Grubisich.

A paper by Vincent Maher, the head of the New Media Lab at Rhodes University, outlined several weaknesses in the claims made by citizen journalists, in terms of the "three deadly E's", referring to ethics, economics and epistemology. This paper has itself been criticized in the press and blogosphere.

An article in 2005 by Tom Grubisich reviewed ten new citizen journalism sites and found many of them lacking in quality and content. Grubisich followed up a year later with, "Potemkin Village Redux." He found that the best sites had improved editorially and were even nearing profitability, but only by not expensing editorial costs. Also according to the article, the sites with the weakest editorial content were able to aggressively expand because they had stronger financial resources.

Another article published on Pressthink examined Backfence, a citizen journalism site with initial three locations in the DC area, which reveals that the site has only attracted limited citizen contributions. The author concludes that, "in fact, clicking through Backfence's pages feels like frontier land -- remote, often lonely, zoned for people but not home to any. The site recently launched for Arlington, Virginia. However, without more settlers, Backfence may wind up creating more ghost towns."

Others criticise the formulation of the term "citizen journalism" to describe the concept, as the word "citizen" has a conterminous relation to the nation-state.

The fact that many millions of people are considered stateless and often without citizenship (such as refugees or immigrants without papers) limits the concept to those recognised only by governments. Additionally the global nature of many participatory media initiatives, such as the Independent Media Center, makes talking of journalism in relation to a particular nation-state largely redundant as its production and dissemination do not recognise national boundaries. Some additional names given to the concept based on this analysis are grassroots media, people's media, or participatory media.

MEDIA DEMOCRACY

Media democracy is a production and distribution model which promotes a mass media system that informs and empowers all members of society, and enhances democratic values. The term also refers to a modern social movement evident in countries all over the world which attempts to make mainstream media more accountable to the publics they serve and to create more democratic alternatives.

It is a concept and a social movement that has grown as a response to the increased corporate domination of mass media and the perceived shrinking of the marketplace of ideas. Its proponents advocate monitoring and reforming the mass media, strengthening public service broadcasting, and developing and participating in alternative media and citizen journalism.

Definition

Media democracy is a difficult term to define, since in addition to being a concept, it is also an advocacy movement being advanced by a number of academics and grassroots organizations, each with its own methods and goals.

It is also difficult to define because the term democracy itself is contested. Market liberals would claim that democracy is best served by the media if there is a minimalist state that allows for private media ownership, does not censor content, or require public-interest broadcasting. In this way, the market would facilitate technological innovation and provide whatever fare the consumer demands. By contrast, media democracy advocates argue that corporate ownership and commercial pressures influence media content, sharply limiting the range of news, opinions, and entertainment citizens receive. Consequently, they call for a more equal distribution of economic, social, cultural, and information capital, which would lead to a more informed citizenry, as well as a more enlightened, representative political discourse. More radical thinkers argue that media democracy remains an under-defined concept because of deliberate structural pressures that prevent individuals from questioning the connection between media and democracy. A leading proponent of this view is Noam Chomsky, who argues that The concept of "democratizing the media" has no real meaning within the terms of political discourse in the United States. In fact, the phrase has a paradoxical or even vaguely subversive ring to it. Citizen participation would be considered an infringement on freedom of the press, a blow struck against the independence of the media that would distort the mission they have undertaken to inform the public without fear or favor... this is because the general public must be reduced to its traditional apathy and obedience, and driven from the arena of political debate and action, if democracy is to survive.

Despite the difficulties in defining the term, the concept broadly encompasses the following notions: that the health of the democratic political system depends on the efficient, accurate, and complete transmission of social, political, and cultural information in society; that the media are the conduits of this information and should act in the public interest; that the mass media have increasingly been unable and uninterested in fulfilling this role due to increased concentration of ownership and commercial pressures; and that this undermines democracy as voters and citizens are unable to participate knowledgably in public policy debates. Without an informed and engaged citizenry, policy issues become defined by political and corporate elites. A related element of this concept examines the lack of representation of a diversity of voices and viewpoints, particularly of those who have traditionally been marginalized by mass media.

KEY PRINCIPLES

Media Ownership Concentration

A key idea of media democracy is that the concentration of media ownership in recent decades in the hands of a few corporations and conglomerates has led to a narrowing of the range of voices and opinions being expressed in the mass media; to an increase in the commercialization of news and information; to a hollowing out of the news media's ability to conduct investigative reporting and act as the public watchdog; and to an increase of emphasis on the bottom line, which prioritizes infotainment and celebrity news over informative discourse.

This concentration has been encouraged by government deregulation and neo-liberal trade policies. For example, the U.S. Telecommunications Act of 1996 discarded most media ownership rules that were previously in place, leading to massive consolidation in the telecommunications industry. Over 4,000 radio stations were bought out, and minority ownership of TV stations dropped to its lowest point since the federal government began tracking such data in 1990. In its review of the Telecommunication Act in 2003, the Federal Communications Commission (FCC) further reduced restrictions and allowed media corporations to grow and expand into other areas of media.

The past decade has also seen a number of media corporate mergers and takeovers in Canada. For example, in 1990, 17.3% of daily newspapers were independently owned; in 2005, 1% were. These changes, among others, caused the Senate Standing Committee on Transport and Communications to launch a study of Canadian news media in March 2003. (This topic had been examined twice in the past, by the Davey Commission (1970) and the Kent Commission (1981), both of which produced recommendations that were never implemented in any meaningful way.)

The Senate Committee's final report, released in June 2006, expressed concern about the effects of the current levels of news media ownership in Canada. Specifically, the Committee discussed their concerns regarding the following trends: the potential of media ownership concentration to limit news diversity and reduce news quality; the Canadian Radio-television and Telecommunications Commission]] (CRTC) and Competition Bureau's ineffectiveness at stopping media ownership concentration; the lack of federal funding for the CBC and the broadcaster's uncertain mandate and role; diminishing employment standards for journalists (including less job security, less journalistic freedom, and new contractual threats to intellectual property); a lack of Canadian training and research institutes; and difficulties with the federal government's support for print media and the absence of funding for the internet-based news media.

The report provided 40 recommendations and 10 suggestions (for areas outside of federal government jurisdiction), including legislation amendments that would trigger automatic reviews of a proposed media merger if certain thresholds are reached, and CRTC regulation revisions to ensure that access to the broadcasting system is encouraged and that a diversity of news and information programming is available through these services.

Media democracy advocates argue in favour of such legislative policies that encourage a stronger commitment to serving the public interest and a commercial framework that facilitates independent media ownership.

Public Broadcasting

Public broadcasting serves as an important counterweight to commercial media, and as such, it is a key element of media democracy. Since public television and radio broadcasters are usually funded by government and/or individual donations, they are not subject to the same commercial pressures as private broadcasters and are therefore an important source of a more diverse and in-depth media content. However, in many countries, public broadcasters are subject to funding instability, which jeopardizes their ability to fulfill their public service role consistently.

Alternative and Citizen Media

As a response to the shortcomings of the mainstream media, proponents of media democracy often advocate supporting and engaging in independent and alternative media, in both print and electronic forms. Through citizen journalism and citizen media, individuals can produce and disseminate information and opinions that are marginalized by the mainstream media. In the book We the Media: Grassroots Journalism by the People, for the People, Dan Gillmor urges individuals who are concerned about media ownership concentration and the decreasing amount of public-interest broadcasting to use technology like the internet to create and distribute information they believe is not properly reported in the mainstream news media. This book details strategies that individuals and groups can use to democratize the media.

Media Democracy Activism

There is a growing grassroots media democracy movement in western industrialized countries. As well as encouraging people to create and disseminate their own news, this movement encourages individuals to critically examine their media content and demand appropriate reforms. The principles of most Media Democracy organizations can be found in the Bill of Media Rights.

The organizations themselves have been active in lobbying for media reform and fighting further deregulation and consolidation of big media. While they have had limited success in the area of media reform, they have been able to put roadblocks in further consolidation of large media companies. When in June 2003 the Federal Communications Commission removed restrictions that limited ownership of the media within a local area, media advocacy organizations such as the Prometheus Radio Project and Media Alliance were able to successfully challenge the changes in court. The FCC is currently revising its June 2003 decision.

Wikipedia and Wikinews as Tools of Media Democracy

Wikipedia has become a powerful media democracy tool. Anyone-regardless of educational background, experience, or in-depth knowledge-can edit, expand, or remove content. Individuals do not have to get the approval of an editorial board to post content. While there are administrators on Wikipedia, they have roughly the same powers as ordinary users. Wikipedia also lacks corporate control: Wikipedia operates as a not-for-profit, and accepts no advertising or corporate investment which can influence or silence particular ideas. Operating costs are paid by typically small individual donations.

However, there are criticisms. While internet access is pervasive throughout North America, there is far less access in many other parts of the world. Those without access obviously cannot benefit from, or add information to, Wikipedia. There is also a concern that Wikipedia's content is biased towards a particular group, since a small number of relatively similar individuals contribute much of Wikipedia's content. To address this concern, a group of Wikipedia users have established Wikipedia:WikiProject Countering systemic bias to create articles and further develop existing articles in neglected subject areas on Wikipedia.

In 2004, Wikimedia established a site called Wikinews dedicated solely to providing news coverage using wiki technology and the open collaborative philosophy. The site's mission statement commits it to, "present up-to-date, relevant, newsworthy and entertaining content without bias" in the spirit of participatory journalism. Wikinews contains synthesis articles, where a number of news sources are condensed into a single article, and original reporting, where individuals write news stories to fill the gaps of the traditional news media due to various systemic constraints, blind spots, and biases of traditional news media sources do not allow.

Unfortunately, Wikinews has not received the same public interest as Wikipedia. Consequently, there is a relatively small number of contributors, and some stories are very short. However, the number of contributor accounts and new articles is increasing.

REPORT ON THE MEDIA FREEDOM DAY

Media Freedom day celebrations for Journalsim students were held on the 4th of May at the the University of the South Pacific Journalism newsroom.

The President of the Journalsim Students Association Losana Mcgowan and her committee members had set out a day of educational activities for the young journalist and other students to participate in and enjoy the World wide celebrated United Nations event as part of World Press Freedom Day.

"I found the panel discussion really good because I got to learn more of the media in Tonga, Tuvalu and samoa," said a second year student

Michelle Reddy a Bachelor of Education Third year student said that she found some revelation by one of the guest speakers, Ken Clark Director of Fiji TV shocking, when he said that the people from the Presidents office requested Fiji TV to guarantee them three things during the Fiji coup last year.

Firstly that they should not fly above parliament grounds, Secondaly stay one kilometre away from parliament complex when covering stories and lastly not to give coverage to George Speight and his supporters.

Fiji TV told the Presidents office that they would follow their request only if the other international media organisations and local media were told to do the same thing.

The president's office agreed to this and an agreement was reached, however Ms Reddy found it appalling that the presidents office did not keep their part of the agreement.

Fiji TV had folowed what they requested for a few days but then resumed normal shooting disregarding the agreement with the Presidents office,when Fiji TV found out that the other media organisations were not told of the arrangement requested by the Presidents office.

Also new to her was that just the previous weekend before the event the military had just moved away from Fiji TV, months after the staging of the coup. "However I loved the day because being a non Journalism student attending one of the workshop I got to learn more of how the media operates and especially the role of Good governance in guiding the media, especially the employers of the journalist," said Ms Reddy

Journalism students attended work shops that set out for the day which included speakers to the likes of Aziz Chaudry from APEC Monitoring group based in New Zealand who talked on globallization and the Media access and Chris Hodges from the Embassy of the United States of America who spoke on The Role of the Media in Good Governance.

The celebrations had run for three days, a pre workshop event on Thursday and Friday and a community broadcasters Hands-on Workshop practicum on Saturday the 5th of May.

The days event was funded by the Canada Fund.

On a lighter note Latu Matoto a third year Journalism student said that he really enjoyed the day." I liked the days celebrations because there was alot of food, we had morning tea, lunch and afternoon tea.

One thing is for sure Pacific islanders jump to the opportunity when free food is involved. This was seen when asking those participating on the day how they liked the celebrations.The main response was " Oh man! the food was great and so much food, whew!!

Political Issues Ahead of Pakistan Elections

As the country marches towards the February 18 elections, many ensuing issues so glaringly remain unresolved and the masses are absolutely clueless about them. These issues pertain to host of different areas and dimensions.

A browse through of Pakistan's history suggests that other than the polls of 1970, elections in Pakistan have been increasingly fought on the basis of race, ethnicity and faith. Real issues of the people have been compromised every time as soon as a political party or military dictator comes to power.

"Popular politics in Pakistan started from the days of Zulfiqar Ali Bhutto. Our national political structure is charismatic," explains local journalist Humair Ishtiaq. When asked that why in his opinion, elections in Pakistan are not being contested on the basis of ideas, issues and policies, as is the case with the world's major democracies, he claims "our circumstances and dimensions are different. Our prevailing social notions are based on our illiteracy."

Because of massive illiteracy, the masses become easy prey for the forces of ideological deception. Foreign intervention in Pakistani politics has become all the more clear in recent times. The machinations of the military establishment to fix election results in the past and arm twisting of the political parties has been well documented and reported in the English press in the past.

Keeping in mind this fact, renowned economist Shahid Siddiqi opines, "parties also do believe that the will of the voters does not count in the end."

This point further proves the idea that amidst massive illiteracy, collapse of law and order and rising levels of civic insecurities, free and fair elections cannot be held and democracy cannot flourish. Explaining this point further, Miss Natasha Khan, a teacher at Szabist, says "we do not have the basic amenities for conducting free and fair elections. We have made a fun of ourselves."

Presenting a slightly different opinion, Mr Abid Azad, who is a local journalist working at the Election cell of a private TV channel, AAJ TV, says that "elections are being fought in Pakistan on the basis of survival. He who has the wealth and power, wins." He further adds on that "Pakistanis are living like slaves. The people just give votes on the basis of personality only."

"Elections in Pakistan would not be free and fair, as things are being determined and announced before hand," suggests Mr Ishtiaq, who works for the Dawn newspaper. He further went on to acknowledge that members of the former ruling party were going on the record to say that the next parliament would indemnify the state of emergency that General Musharraf imposed in his capacity as the then Army Chief, on November 3 last year.

Such allegations and statements, according to Mr Ishtiaq go very much against the spirit of democracy and free and fair elections. "Elections in Pakistan would not be free and fair as things are being determined and announced before hand," was his concluding statement on this topic.

Identifying acts of rigging, corruption and other wrong doings, has been amongst the major professional duties of media correspondents during this election season, according to many local journalists and observers contacted by this correspondent. There is no certified way of picking out acts of rigging as these are committed in different forms and manifestations, far away from the outreach of the media and international observers.

Vote counting and the associated fairness and transparencies can still however be ensured by investigative media reporting. "The media should take all official results from the polling stations. These would add up to form the results of constituencies," says journalist Ishtiaq. This is how according to him any discrepancies with regards vote counts and other statistical details, along with locations of rigging can be clearly picked out.

Adding to this, a correspondent for a local television channel, Azmat Abbas says that "media correspondents can get election result copies from the candidates." These copies, he added, were to be distributed to them by the Chief Returning Officers of all constituencies.

Because of the ban on live coverage, Mr Abbas emphasised on the role of digital technologies in unravelling acts of rigging, once the official results were out. He further went on to say that at the moment, restrictions on media coverage were great. "According to new media laws, announcing unofficial results is not allowed," says Assadullah Khan, who heads the election cell at Dawn News, Pakistan's first English language channel.

This new ban, he claims would erect an information gap and stifle the initiative of investigative reporting as media organisations would now have to wait for the official announcement of the results.

Talking about the 1970 elections, Mr Ishtiaq argued that they were free and fair because PTV was announcing results on the basis of each polling station. He and Mr Azad believe that a similar mechanism or news media reporting and analysis can be taken up this time around as well.

"We would give progressive results on our channel," confides Mr Azad. "We would try to identify areas and stations where rigging has taken place," he adds. Mr Azad and Mr Ishtiaq however concluded that the ban on live television coverage is an obstacle that prevents television journalists to do incisive investigative reporting.

Talking further, Mr Azad explains the outstanding issues that the media has been facing in this country, in recent times. According to him, during the initial days of the emergency and the PCO, "it was very tough to do balanced reporting with editorial independence." According to him, the electronic media in the country was also exposed to threats and some restraints even before the emergency. "The channel that I work for, had been advised by the government and the agencies before as well," he added.

The reinstatement of the judiciary that stands deposed since the 3rd of November, has becoming an issue assuming great political importance in the country at the moment. "The issue of the judiciary is a tough and controversial one," according to barrister Shabnam Noorali However under the prevailing circumstances, "deposed judiciary would not come back," suggests Natasha Khan, a teacher at the SZABIST University.

The Benazir factor would surely have a major impact on the upcoming elections. "The assassination was a major ditch in the democratic process," argues Mr Azad.

Analysts and professionals who were asked for comments, refused to accept the findings of the Scotland Yard on the murder of PPP chairwoman Benazir Bhutto. "The investigations were done on the basis of second hand data," comments barrister Shabnam. While further adding on, she explains that "the Scotland Yard's team did not have access to primary sources of information, that is, the real crime scene and the dead body." On the basis of these ideas, she questions the authenticity of the report. While rejecting the report, TV journalist Abid Azad reaffirms that "inherent controversies suggest that the government wants to hide the facts and damage the information delivery mechanism."

Regarding the future set up, Mr Ishtiaq suggests, "the PPP would be able to reconcile with General Musharraf." However, according to barrister Shabnam "the upcoming set up would depend on the transparency of the elections." When asked that whether the future parliament would question the proclamation of emergency of November 3, Professor Mahmood Ghaznavi of the Karachi University said, "The parliament would not be able to question Musharraf as politicians are part of the same military establishment."

What is easily evident this time during the elections is that public interests have largely waned out. Voter turn out is expected to be low as usual, which according to Professor Ghaznavi, means that large-scale rigging might take place. However, what is pertinent here is that how do people react to the political wheeling-dealing that takes place after the vote is cast, according to lawyer Sahabnam. If these elections are not free and fair, irrespective of the turn out, public reaction would "boil up in the times to come," according to her.

6

PRESENT SCENARIO

A basic issue in the discussion of the role of the mass media in today's society is whether they do reflect social reality in a broad sense, or whether, instead, the elites which control them filter out the view of reality which they see fit to be made public. To my mind, the answer to this question is that the media do both, depending on the way we define reality.

To take, first, political reality, mass media, in one sense, do not provide a faked view of it. Taking into account what is considered as politics today, i.e. the activity of professional politicians 'representing' the people, one may argue that it is politics itself, which is faked, and mass media simply reproduce this reality. In this sense, the issue is not whether the mass media manipulate democracy, since it is democracy itself, which is faked, and not its mass media picture, which simply reflects the reality of present 'democracy'. But, at the same time, if we give a different definition to political reality, mass media do provide, in general, a distorted picture of it. In other words, if we define as real politics the political activity of people themselves (for instance, the collective struggles of various sectors of the population around political, economic or social issues) rather than that of professional politicians, then, the mass media do distort the picture they present about political reality. They do so, by minimising the significance of this type of activity, by distorting its meaning, by marginalising it, or by simply ignoring it completely.

Furthermore, mass media do provide a distorted picture of political reality when they come to report the causes of crises, or of the conflicts involving various sections of the elites. In such cases they faithfully reflect the picture that the sections of the elites controlling them wish to reproduce. The latest example of this was the way in which the Anglo-American media, in particular, distorted the real meaning of the criminal bombardment of the Iraqi people at the end of 1998. Thus, exactly, as in their reporting during the war in the Gulf, the real cause of the conflict, (i.e. who controls the world's oil, irrespective of where the oil stocks are located -- the elites of the North versus those in the South), was distorted as a conflict between the peace loving regimes in the North versus the rogue regimes in the South, or, in more sophisticated versions supported by socialdemocrat intellectuals, as a conflict between the 'democracies' in the North versus the 'despotic regimes' in the South over the control of oil.

Under these circumstances, it is obvious that the mass media usually offer a true glimpse of reality only when the elites are divided with respect to their conception of a particular aspect of political reality. From this point of view, concentration in the mass media industry is significant and whether the media are owned by 100 or 10 owners does indeed matter in the struggle for social change. It is for instance such divisions among the European elites over the issue of joining the European Monetary Union which have allowed a relatively wide media discussion on the true meaning of European integration, particularly in countries like Britain where the elites were split. It was also similar divisions between the Anglo-American and the European elites over the latest war crime in the Gulf which made a bit clearer the directly criminal role of the former (support for the bombardments), as well as the indirectly criminal role of the latter (support for the embargo). It is not accidental that in the USA and UK, where the media played a particularly despicable role in distorting the truth and misinforming the public, the polls showed consistently vast majorities in favour of the criminal activities of their elites. Of course, this does not mean that decentralisation of power in the mass media industry (or anywhere else) represents by itself, even potentially, a radical social change leading to an authentic democracy. Still, the significance of decentralisation in the media industry with respect to raising consciousness should not be ignored.

As regards economic reality, mass media, in one sense again, do provide a relatively accurate picture of what counts as economic reality today. This is when the media, taking for granted the system of the market economy, end up with a partial picture of economic reality where what matters is not whether the basic needs of the population are covered adequately but whether prices (in commodity and stock markets), interest rates, exchange rates and consequently profit rates are going up or down. Still, in another sense, the very fact that mass media take for granted the system of the market economy means that they cannot 'see' the 'systemic' nature of most of the real economic problems (unemployment, poverty and so on) and therefore inevitably end up with a faked image of economic reality. This way of seeing economic reality is not imposed on the media by their owners, important as their influence may otherwise be, or by their internal hierarchical structure etc. The media simply reflect the views of orthodox economists, bankers, businessmen and professional politicians, i.e. of all those who express the dominant social paradigm.

But if the picture of political and economic reality offered by the media is mixed this is not the case with respect to ecological reality. As no meaningful reporting of the ecological crisis is possible unless it refers to the systemic causes of it, which by definition are excluded by the discourse in the mainstream media, the result is a complete misinformation, or just straightforward description of the symptoms of the crisis. The mass media are flooded by the 'realist' Greens who fill the various ecological parties and who blame technology, consumerist values, legislation etc-- anything but the real cause of the crisis, i.e. the very system of the market economy. Similarly, the reporting of the present social crisis never links the explosion of crime and drug abuse, for instance, with their root cause, i.e. the increasing concentration of political, economic and social power in the hands of various elites. Instead, the symptoms of the social crisis are distortedly reported as its causes and the media blame, following the advice of the establishment 'experts', the breaking of the traditional family, or of the school, as the causes of crime. Similarly, various 'progressive' intellectuals (like the lamentable ex 'revolutionary' and now well promoted by the mainstream media Euro-parliamentarian Con Bendit) blame the prohibitive legislation on drugs for the massive explosion of drug abuse!

However, there is another approach being promoted recently by system theorists, according to which mass media do not just either reflect or distort reality but also manufacture it. This is not said in the usual sense of manufacturing consent described by Chomsky and Herman or, alternatively, by Bourdieu, which is basically a one-way process whereby the elites controlling the mass media filter out the information, through various control mechanisms, in order to create consent around their agenda. Instead, system theorists talk about a two-way process whereby social reality and mass media are seen as two interdependent levels, the one intruding into the other. This is based on the valid hypothesis that reality is not just something external to the way it is conceived. TV watching is a constituent moment of reality since our information about reality consists of conceptions that constitute reality itself. At the same time, the conception of reality is conditioned by the media functioning, which is differentiated in relation to the other social systems (political, economic etc).

In the systems analysis problematique, it is not the economic, or the political systems, which control the media functioning. What determines their functioning, as well as their communicative capability, is their ability to generate irritation- a fact that could go a long way to explain the high ratings of exciting or irritating TV programs. The diversified functioning of mass media creates, in turn, the conditions for a social dynamic which, in a self-reflective and communicative way, reproduces, as well as institutes, society. Thus, whereas the early modern society is instituted through a transcendental subjectivity and a material mode of production, the present post-modern society's reproduction depends on the processes of communicative rationality. The mass media are an integral and functional part of the communicative processes of post-modern society.

However, one may point out here that although it is true that social reality and mass media are interacting, i.e. that our conception of TV news is a constituent element of reality and at the same time our conception of reality is conditioned by TV functioning, this does not imply that the diversified functioning of mass media creates the conditions for a social dynamic which acts for the institution of society, although it does play this role as far as its reproduction is concerned. The meaning we assign to TV reporting is not determined exogenously but by our world view, our own paradigm, which in turn, as we have seen above, is the result of a process of socialisation that is conditioned by the dominant social paradigm. Furthermore, TV functioning plays a crucial role in the reproduction of the dominant social paradigm and the socialisation process generally. So, the diversified functioning of TV does indeed create the conditions for a social dynamic leading to the reproduction of the status quo, but in no way could be considered as doing the same for instituting society.

CONTROL MECHANISMS

The goals of the mass media are determined by those owning and controlling them, who, usually, are members of the economic elites that control the market economy itself. Given the crucial role that the media could play in the internalisation of the dominant social paradigm and therefore the reproduction of the institutional framework which secures the concentration of power in the hands of the elites, it is obvious that those owning and controlling the mass media have broader ideological goals than the usual goals pursued by those owning and controlling other economic institutions, i.e. profit maximising. Therefore, an analysis that would attempt to draw conclusions on the nature and significance of media institutions on the basis of the profit dimension alone, (i.e. that they share a common goal and consequently a similar internal hierarchical structure with all other economic institutions and that they just sell a product, the only difference with other economic institutions being that the product is the audience,) is bound to be one-dimensional. Profit maximising is only one parameter, often not even the crucial one, which conditions the role of mass media in a market economy. In fact, one could mention several instances where capitalist owners chose even to incur significant losses (which they usually cover from other profitable activities) in order to maintain the social influence (and prestige), which ownership of an influential daily offers to them (Murdoch and The Times of London is an obvious recent example).

Given the ultimate ideological goal of mass media, the main ways in which they try to achieve it are:

- first, by assisting in the internalisation of the dominant social paradigm and,
- second, by marginalising, if not excluding altogether, conceptions of reality which do not conform with the dominant social paradigm.

But, what are the mechanisms through which the media can achieve their goals? To give an answer to this question we have to examine a series of mechanisms, most of them 'automatic' built-in mechanisms, which ensure effective achievement of these goals. It will be useful here to distinguish between 'internal' and 'external' control mechanisms, which function respectively as internal and external constraints on the freedom of media workers to reproduce reality. Both internal and external mechanisms work mainly through competition which secures homogenisation with respect to the media's main goals. Competition is of course the fundamental organisational principle of a market economy; but, it plays a special role with respect to the media. As Bourdieu points out, competition 'rather than automatically generating originality and diversity tends to favour uniformity'. Still, competition is not the only force securing homogenisation. In a similar way as with the market economy itself, competition provides only the dynamic mechanism of homogenisation. It is the fact that owners of mass media, as well as managers and the highest paid journalists, share the same interest in the reproduction of the existing institutional framework which constitutes the 'base', on which this competition is developed. But, let us consider briefly the significance of the various control mechanisms. The main 'internal control' mechanisms are ownership and the internal hierarchical structure, which are, both, crucial in the creation of the conditions for internal competition among journalists, whereas the 'ratings' mechanism plays a similar role in the creation of the conditions for external competition among media.

Starting with ownership, it matters little, as regards the media's overall goals defined above, whether they are owned and controlled by the state and/or the state-controlled institutions or whether, instead, they are owned and controlled by private capital. However, there are certain secondary differences arising from the different ownership structures which may be mentioned. These secondary differences have significant implications, particularly with respect to the structure of the elites controlling the media, their own organisational structure and their 'image' with respect to their supposedly 'objective' role in the presentation of information. As regards the elite structure, whereas under a system of state ownership and control the mass media are under the direct control of the political elite and the indirect control of the economic elites, under a system of private ownership and control, the media are just under the direct control of the economic elites.

This fact, in turn, has some implications on whether filtering out of information takes place directly through state control, or indirectly through various economic mechanisms (e.g. ratings).As regards the media organisational structure, whereas state-owned media are characterised by bureaucratic rigidity and inefficiency, privately owned media are usually characterised by more flexibility and economic efficiency. Finally, the 'objective' image of mass media suffers less in case of private ownership compared to the case of state ownership. This is because in the latter case control of information is more direct and therefore more obvious than in the former.

Another important internal control mechanism is the hierarchical structure which characterises all media institutions (as it does all economic institutions in a market economy) and which implies that all-important decisions are taken by a small managerial group within them, who are usually directly responsible to the owners. The hierarchical structure creates a constant internal competition among journalists as to who will be more agreeable to the managerial group (on which their career and salary prospects depend). Similarly, people in the managerial group are in constant competition as to who will be more agreeable to the owners (on which their highly paid position depends). So, everybody in this hierarchical structure knows well (or soon learns) what is agreeable and what is not and acts accordingly. Therefore, the filtering of information works through self-censorship rather than through any kind of 'orders from above'. The effect of the internal hierarchical structure is to impose, through the internal competition that it creates, a kind of homogenisation in the journalists' performance. But, does this exclude the possibility that some media workers may have incentives other those determined by career ambitions? Of course, not. But, such people, as Chomsky points out, will never find a place in the corridors of media power and, one way or another, will be marginalised:

> They (journalists) say, quite correctly, "nobody ever tells me what to write. I write anything I like. All this business about pressures and constraints is nonsense because I'm never under any pressure." Which is completely true, but the point is that they wouldn't be there unless they had already demonstrated that nobody has to tell them what to write because they are going to say the right thing... it is not purposeful censorship.
>
> It is just that you don't make it to those positions. That includes the left (what is called the left), as well as the right. Unless you have been adequately socialised and trained so that there are some thoughts you just don't have, because if you did have them, you wouldn't be there.

But, how is it determined what is agreeable? Here it is where the 'external' control mechanisms come into play. It is competition among the various media organisations, which homogenises journalists' behaviour. This competition takes the form of a struggle to improve ratings (as regards TV channels) or circulation (as regards newspapers, magazines etc). Ratings or circulation are important not per se but because the advertising income of privately owned mass media (which is the extra income determining their survival or death) depends on them. The result is, as Pierre Bourdieu points out that:

Ratings have become the journalist's Last Judgement... Wherever you look, people are thinking in terms of market success. Only thirty years ago, and since the middle of the nineteenth century---since Baudelaire and Flaubert and others in avant-garde milieux of writers' writers, writers acknowledged by other writers or even artists acknowledged by other artists--- immediate market success was suspect. It was taken as a sign of compromise with the times, with money... Today, on the contrary, the market is accepted more and more as a legitimate means of Iegitimation.

The pressures created by the ratings mechanism, as Bourdieu points out, have nothing to do with the democratic expression of enlightened collective opinion or public rationality, despite what media ideologues assert. In fact, as the same author points out, the ratings mechanism is the sanction of the market and the economy, that is, of an external and purely market law. I would only add to this that given how 'public opinion' is formed within the process of socialisation and internalisation of the dominant social paradigm, it is indeed preposterous to characterise the ratings mechanism as somehow expressing the democratic will of the people. Ratings, as well as polls generally, is the 'democracy of the uninformed'. They simply reflect the ignorance, the half-truths, or the straightforward distortions of the truth which have been assimilated by an uninformed public and which, through the ratings mechanism, reinforce the role of the mass media in the reproduction of the dominant social paradigm.

One may therefore conclude that the role of the media today is not to make the system more democratic. In fact, one basic function of the media is, as Chomsky stresses, to help in keeping the general population out of the public arena because 'if they get involved they will just make trouble. Their job is to be "spectators," not "participants". Furthermore, the media can play a crucial role in offsetting the democratic rights and freedoms won after long struggles. This has almost always been the case when there was a clash between the elites and trade unions, or popular movements generally. Walter Lippmann, the revered American journalist was explicit about it, as Chomsky points out.

For Lippmann, there is a new art in the method of democracy, called "manufacture of consent." By manufacturing consent, you can overcome the fact that formally a lot of people have the right to vote. We can make it irrelevant because we can manufacture consent and make sure that their choices and attitudes will be structured in such a way that they will always do what we tell them, even if they have a formal way to participate. So we'll have a real democracy. It will work properly. That's applying the lessons of the propaganda agency.

Within this analytical framework we may explore fruitfully the particular ways through which the filtering of information is achieved, as, for instance, is described by Chomsky and Herman in their 'propaganda model'.

Similarly Bourdieu shows in a graphic way how the filtering of information takes place in television, through the structuring of TV debates, the time limits, the methods of hiding by showing etc. Particularly important is the way in which the media, particularly television, control not just the information flow, but also the production of culture, by controlling the access of academics as well as of cultural producers, who in turn, as a result of being recognised a public figures, gain recognition in their own fields. Thus, at the end, the journalistic field, which is structurally very strongly subordinated to market pressures and as such is a very heteronomous field, applies pressure, in turn, to all other fields.

An illustrative application of the above analytical framework is the crucial contribution of the mass media in the creation of the subjective conditions for the neoliberal consensus. Thus, the mass media have played a double ideological role with respect to the neoliberal consensus. On the one hand, they have promoted directly the neoliberal agenda:

- by degrading the economic role of the state,

- by attacking the 'dependence' on the state which the welfare state supposedly creates,
- by identifying freedom with the freedom of choice, which is supposedly achieved through the liberation of markets etc. (talk radio and similar TV shows play a particularly significant role in this respect).

On the other hand, the media have also attempted to divert attention from the consequences of the neoliberal consensus (in terms of growing inequality and poverty, the explosion of crime and drug abuse and so on):

- by promoting irrational beliefs of all sorts (religion, mystical beliefs, astrology etc). The film and video explosion on the themes of exorcism, supernatural powers etc (induced mainly by Hollywood) has played a significant role in diverting attention from the evils of neoliberalism.
- by manufacturing irrelevant and/or insignificant 'news stories' (e.g. Monica Lewinsky affair), which are then taken over by opposition politicians who are eager to find fictitious ways (because of the lack of real political differences within the neoliberal consensus) to differentiate themselves from those in power.
- by creating a pseudo 'general interest' (for instance around a nationalist or chauvinist cause) in order to unite the population around a 'cause' and make it forget the utterly dividing aspects of neoliberalism.

At the same time, the creation of the neoliberal conditions at the institutional level had generated the objective conditions for the mass media to play the aforementioned role. This was because the deregulation and liberalisation of markets and the privatisation of state TV in many European countries had created the conditions for homogenisation through the internal and external competition, which I mentioned above. It is not accidental anyway that major media tycoons like Murdoch in the Anglo-Saxon world, Kirsch in Germany, or Berlusconi in Italy have also been among the main exponents of the neoliberal consensus agenda.

CULTURE AND A DEMOCRATIC CONCEPTION OF CITIZENSHIP

I am not going to repeat here the discussion on the fundamental components of an inclusive democracy and the necessary conditions, which have to be met for the setting up of it. Instead, I will try to focus on the implications of the democratic institutional arrangements on culture and the role of media. The starting point is that the conditions for democracy imply a new conception of citizenship: economic, political, social and cultural.

Thus, political citizenship involves new political structures and the return to the classical conception of politics (direct democracy). Economic citizenship involves new economic structures of community ownership and control of economic resources (economic democracy). Social citizenship involves self-management structures at the workplace, democracy in the household and new welfare structures where all basic needs (to be democratically determined) are covered by community resources, whether they are to be satisfied in the household or at the community level. Finally, cultural citizenship involves new democratic structures of dissemination and control of information and culture (mass media, art, etc.), which allow every member of the community to take part in the process and at the same time develop his/her intellectual and cultural potential.

It is obvious that the above new conception of citizenship has very little in common with the liberal and socialist definitions of citizenship, which are linked to the liberal and socialist conceptions of human rights respectively. Thus, for the liberals, the citizen is simply the individual bearer of certain freedoms and political rights recognised by law which, supposedly, secure equal distribution of political power. Similarly, for the socialists, the citizen is the bearer not only of political rights and freedoms but, also, of some social and economic rights, whereas for Marxists the citizenship is realised with the collective ownership of the means of production.

Furthermore, the conception of citizenship adopted here is not related to the current social-democratic discourse on the subject, which, in effect, focuses on the institutional conditions for the creation of an internationalised market economy 'with a human face'.

The proposal for instance for a redefinition of citizenship within the framework of a "stakeholder capitalism" belongs to this category. This proposal involves an 'active' citizenship, where citizens have 'stakes' in companies, the market economy and society in general and managers have to take into account these stakes in the running of the businesses and social institutions they are in charge of.

The conception of citizenship adopted here, which could be called a democratic conception, is based on our definition of inclusive democracy and presupposes a 'participatory' conception of active citizenship, like the one implied by the work of Hannah Arendt. In this conception, "political activity is not a means to an end, but an end in itself; one does not engage in political action simply to promote one's welfare but to realise the principles intrinsic to political life, such as freedom, equality, justice, solidarity, courage and excellence". It is therefore obvious that this conception of citizenship is qualitatively different from the liberal and social-democratic conceptions, which adopt an 'instrumentalist' view of citizenship, i.e. a view which implies that citizenship entitles citizens with certain rights that they can exercise as means to the end of individual welfare.

Although the above conception of citizenship implies a geographical sense of community which is the fundamental unit of political, economic and social life, still, it is assumed that it interlocks with various other communities (cultural, professional, ideological, etc.).

Therefore, the community and citizenship arrangements do not rule out cultural differences based on language, customs etc, or other differences based on gender, age, ethnicity and so on; they simply provide the public space where such differences can be expressed.

Furthermore, these arrangements institutionalise various safety valves that aim to rule out the marginalisation of such differences by the majority. What therefore unites people in a political community, or a confederation of communities, is not a set of common cultural values, imposed by a nationalist ideology, a religious dogma, a mystical belief, or an 'objective' interpretation of natural or social 'evolution', but the democratic institutions and practices, which have been set up by citizens themselves.

However, as I attempted to show elsewhere this cultural pluralism does not mean a kind of cultural relativism where 'everything goes'.

In other words, it is possible to derive an ethical system and correspondingly a set of cultural values which is neither 'objective', (in the sense that it is derived from a supposedly objective interpretation of social evolution-Marx, or natural evolution---Bookchin), nor just a matter of individual choice. There can be a set of common or general moral criteria by which individual actions could be judged, i.e. a code of democratic ethics, which would be based on the fundamental principle of organising a democratic society around a confederal inclusive Democracy, (i.e. a democracy based on a confederation of demoi, or democratic communities).

DEMOCRATIC ETHIC CODE

This code of democratic ethics may be derived out of the two fundamental principles of organisation of a confederal inclusive Democracy, i.e. the principle of autonomy and the principle of community. Thus, out of the fundamental principle of autonomy one may derive a set of cultural values about equality and respect for the personality of every citizen, irrespective of gender, race, ethnic identity etc. Out of the same fundamental principle one could derive the principle of protecting the quality of life of each individual citizen -- something that would imply a relationship of harmony with nature. Similarly, out of the fundamental principle of community life one may derive a set of values involving solidarity and mutual aid, caring and sharing. These values should constitute an integral part of the dominant social paradigm so that democracy can reproduce itself. This of course does not exclude the possibility, or rather the probability, of the existence of alternative cultural values, or perhaps even of a conflict between personal and collective values ---particularly with respect to those citizens who cannot reconcile themselves with the tragic truth that it is we who determine our own truth and might still adhere to moral codes derived from irrational belief systems (religions, mystical beliefs etc). However, as long as these people are in a minority, (hopefully, a dwindling one, through the Paedeia of a democratic society), the conflict in their personal values with the collectively defined values should not be a problem for the community as a whole.

DEMOCRATIC MEDIA

The sufficient condition which has to be met so that democracy will not degenerate into some kind of "demagocracy", where the demos is manipulated by a new breed of 'professional' politicians, is crucially conditioned by the citizens' level of democratic consciousness. This, in turn, is conditioned by Paedeia. It is therefore obvious that the cultural institutions, particularly the media, play a crucial role in a democracy, given their role in the formation of Paedeia.

So, let us now consider the nature and role of the mass media, as cultural institutions, in a democratic society. First, there is no reason why the mass media in a democratic society will distort rather than reflect reality. As political and economic power would be equally distributed among citizens and therefore the existence of institutionalised elites would be excluded, the media would face none of the present dilemmas whether to reflect the reality of the elite, or particular sections of it, versus the reality of the rest of the population. Still, even in an inclusive democracy there is still the problem of the possible emergence of informal elites, which may attempt to exercise some sort of control over the information flows.

It is also clear that no democracy is possible unless its citizens are fully informed on anything affecting their life. Therefore, a way has to be found to organise the decision-taking process in the media so that, on the one hand, citizens are always fully informed and, on the other, the media are under the real control of the community.

It is obvious that it is citizens as citizens, through their assemblies, who should determine the overall operation of mass media and supervise them. This function could not just be assigned to the councils of media workers because in that case the democratic society will run the double risk of media not expressing the general interest, as well as of the possible emergence of new media elites within, at least, some of them.

This does not, obviously, mean that the assemblies will determine every day what the content of TV news bulletins will be, or what the papers would say next day. What it does mean is that the community assemblies would set strict rules on how full diversity and accountability could be achieved and then supervise the application of these principles in media practice.

Diversity implies that all sorts of views should be given full access to the media, provided that that they have been approved by the community and media workers' assemblies. Assuming that these assemblies have internalised the dominant democratic social paradigm, one could expect that they would not give easy access to views which contradict the democratic values (e.g. views promoting racial, sexist, religious values etc). However, the decision will always rest with the assemblies and if they see no contradiction involved in giving full access to such views this will simply herald the degradation and eventual collapse of the democratic society itself. Accountability implies that the media workers would be accountable for their decisions to the media workers' assemblies in the first instance and, next, to the community assemblies. Such a structure of accountability would be compatible with the lack of hierarchical structures in the media and the fact that it will be the communities themselves that would 'own' the media institutions.

So, this dual system of decision-taking, whereby overall decision-taking and supervision rests with the community assemblies, whereas the determination of detailed operational functioning of the media is left to the media workers' assemblies, to my mind, guarantees that not only the general interest is adequately taken into account but also that the day-to-day decisions are taken democratically by the media workers themselves.

WAYS TO BRING ABOUT SYSTEMIC SOCIAL CHANGE

As I tried to show above the culture of a democratic society will be characterised by very different values than those of a market economy. The values of heteronomy, competition, individualism and consumerism which are dominant today have to be replaced in a democratic society by the values of individual and collective autonomy, co-operation, mutual aid, solidarity and sharing. Furthermore, as far as the mass media is concerned, the role, organisation and nature of media in a democratic society will also drastically differ from the corresponding role, nature and organisation today. The media will not have the role to reflect reality, basically, as seen from the elites' point of view, but, as seen from the people's viewpoint; their organisation will not be based on hierarchical structures, but, on democratic structures; finally, the media will cease to be profit-making enterprises owned and controlled by elites and will become, instead, democratically owned and controlled institutions of communicating information.

The obvious issue, which arises here, is how we move from 'here' to 'there'. This basic question involves a series of other issues concerning social change, which have been discussed extensively, particularly during the century which is now expiring. Can there be a drastic change of values, like the one discussed above, without a parallel change of institutions? Do we need a systemic change to bring about the required change in values and institutions? Should the social struggle have as explicit aim the systemic change as part of a comprehensive political program for it? To attempt to give an answer to all these questions we will have to discuss briefly the main approaches to social change.

But, first, we have to be clear about the meaning of social change. As it is obvious from the above analysis, social change here means systemic change, i.e. a change in the entire socio-economic system of the market economy, representative democracy and hierarchical structures. As I attempted to show elsewhere the fundamental cause of the multi-dimensional crisis we face today (economic, ecological, social, political) is the concentration of power at the hands of various elites (economic, political etc) and therefore the only way out of this crisis is the abolition of power structures and relations, i.e. the creation of conditions of equal distribution of power among citizens. One way that could bring about this sort of society is the Inclusive Democracy proposal which involves the creation of political, economic and social structures that secure direct democracy, economic democracy, ecological democracy and democracy in the social realm. It also involves the creation of a new social paradigm (based on the values I mentioned above) which, for the reproduction of inclusive democracy to be secured, it has to become dominant.

So, assuming that the aim is to bring about systemic social change involving the creation of conditions for the equal distribution of power among citizens, there are, schematically, four main approaches which claim that they may bring about this result: reforms (from 'above' or from 'below'), revolution (from 'above' or from 'below'), 'life-style strategies' and the Inclusive Democracy approach.

THE REFORMIST APPROACH

The reformist approach claims that it can bring about systemic change through either the conquest of state power (reforms 'from above') or through the creation of autonomous from the state power bases which would press the state for reforms (reforms 'from below'). The main example of the former strategy is the social democratic approach, whereas the main example of the latter is the civil societarian approach. The social democratic approach reached its peak during the period of statism and particularly in the first thirty years after WWII, when the social democratic consensus was dominant all over the Western world. However, the internationalisation of the market economy since the mid '70s brought about the end of this consensus and the rise of the neoliberal consensus-which, in my view, is irreversible as long as the market economy is internationalised, in other words, as long as the market economy reproduces itself.

The recent deletion from the program of the British Labour Party (which was the last socialdemocratic party still committed to full socialisation of the means of production) of 'clause four', which committed it to full socialisation, marked the formal end of socialdemocratic claims towards real systemic change.

In fact, the neoliberal agenda for 'flexible' labour markets, minimisation of social controls on markets, replacement of the welfare state by a safety net etc has now become the agenda of every major socialdemocratic party in power or in opposition.

The parallel degradation of social democracy and the reversal of most of its conquests (comprehensive welfare state, state commitment to full employment, significant improvement in the distribution of income) has clearly shown that supporters of the revolutionary approach were always right on the impossibility of bringing about a systemic change through reforms.

As regards the civil societarian approach, the strategy here is to enhance 'civil society', that is, to strengthen the various networks which are autonomous from state control (unions, churches, civic movements, co-operatives, neighbourhoods, schools of thought etc.) in order to impose such limits (i.e. social controls) on markets and the state, so that a kind of systemic change is brought about. However, this approach is based on a number of unrealistic assumptions.

Thus, first, it implicitly assumes a high degree of statism where the state can still play the economic role it used to play during the socialdemocratic consensus. Second, it assumes, in effect, an almost closed market economy where the state can ignore the instant movement of capital in case a government attempts to meet demands of civil societarians which threaten capital's interets. No wonder that civil societarians usually deny (or try to minimise) the importance of the present internationalisation of the market economy. It is also indicative that when civil societarians attempt to internationalise their approach the only limits on the internationalised market economy that they view as feasible are various 'regulatory controls'. But, such controls have very little in common with the sweeping social controls that they have in mind when they discuss, abstracting from the present internationalised market economy, the limits that civil society networks should impose on markets (drastic reduction of inequalities, massive creation of jobs etc).

So, the civil societarian approach is both a-historical and utopian. It is a-historical, since it ignores the structural changes, which have led to the present neoliberal consensus and the internationalised market economy. And it is utopian because it is in tension both with the present internationalised market economy and the state. So, given that civil societarians do not see the outcome of this inevitable tension in terms of the replacement of the market economy and the state by the civil society, it is not difficult to predict that any enhancement of the civil society will have to be compatible with the process of further internationalisation of the market economy and the implied role of the state. In other words, the 'enhancement' of civil society, under today's conditions, would simply mean that the ruling political and economic elites will be left undisturbed to continue dominating society, while, from time to time, they will have to try to address the demands of the civil societarians-provided, of course that these demands are not in direct conflict to their own interests and the demands of oligopolistic production.

In conclusion, enhancing the civil society institutions has no chance whatsoever of either putting an end to the concentration of power, or of transcending the present multidimensional crisis. This conclusion may be derived from the fact that the implicit, although not always explicit, aim of civil societarians is to improve the functioning of existing institutions (state, parties, market), in order to make them more responsive to pressures from below when, in fact, the crisis is founded on the institutions themselves and not on their malfunctioning! But, in the present internationalised market, the need to minimise the socio-economic role of the state is no longer a matter of choice for those controlling production.

It is a necessary condition for survival. This is particularly so for European capital that has to compete with capital blocks, which operate from bases where the social-democratic tradition of statism was never strong (the United States, the Far East). But, even at the planetary level, one could seriously doubt whether it is still possible to enhance the institutions of civil society within the context of the market economy. Granted that the fundamental aims of production in a market economy are individual gain, economic efficiency and growth, any attempt to reconcile these aims with an effective `social control' by the civil society is bound to fail since, as historic experience with the statist phase has shown, social control and market efficiency are irreconcilable objectives. By the same token, one could reasonably argue that the central contradiction of the market economy today is the one arising from the fact that any effective control of the ecological implications of growth is incompatible with the requirements of competitiveness, which the present phase of the marketization process imposes.

THE LIFE-STYLE APPROACH

The second type of approach which claims capable to bring about systemic social change is the presently fashionable, particularly among Anglo-Saxon anarchists, life-style strategy. There are several versions of this strategy. Sometimes this approach involves no intervention at all in the political arena and usually not even in the general social arena --other than in struggles on specific 'Green' issues, like animal rights campaigns etcetera. Alternatively, this approach may involve a process which, starting from the individual, and working through affinity groups, aims at setting an example of sound and preferable life-styles at the individual and social level: alternative media, Community Economic Development projects, 'free zones' and alternative institutions (free schools, self-managed factories, housing associations, Local Employment and Trading Systems (LETS), communes, self-managed farms and so on).

However, this approach, in any of the above versions, is, by itself, utterly ineffective in bringing about a systemic social change. Although helpful in creating an alternative culture among small sections of the population and, at the same time, morale-boosting for activists who wish to see an immediate change in their lives, this approach does not have any chance of success--in the context of today's huge concentration of power-

-in building the democratic majority needed for systemic social change. The projects suggested by this strategy may too easily be marginalised, or absorbed into the existing power structure (as has happened many times in the past) whereas their effect on the socialisation process is minimal--if not nil.

Furthermore, life-style strategies, by usually concentrating on single issues which are not part of a comprehensive political program for social transformation, provide a golden opportunity to the ruling elites to use their traditional divide and rule tactics (the British elites, for instance, frequently use security guards recruited from the underclass to fight Green activists rather than 'exposing' the police on this role!)

Furthermore, systemic social change can never be achieved outside the main political and social arena. The elimination of the present power structures and relations can neither be achieved "by setting an example", nor through education and persuasion. A power base is needed to destroy power. But, the only way that an approach aiming at a power base would be consistent with the aims of the democratic project is, to my mind, through the development of a comprehensive program for the radical transformation of local political and economic structures.

A variation of the life-style strategy which however has, also, elements of the civil societarian approach is, to my mind, the strategy proposed by Noam Chomsky, Michael Albert and the group around Z magazine. Thus, Albert sees the setting up of alternative media institutions just 'as part of a project to establish new ways of organising media and social activity', without even mentioning the need to incorporate them into a comprehensive political program for systemic change. In fact, what differentiates the alternative from the mainstream media in his argument is, basically, their internal structure:

Being alternative can't just mean that the institution's editorial focus is on this or that topical area. And being alternative as an institution certainly isn't just being left or right or different in editorial content. Being alternative as an institution must have to do with how the institution is organised and works... An alternative media institution sees itself as part of a project to establish new ways of organising media and social activity and it is committed to furthering these as a whole, and not just its own preservation.

Similarly, Chomsky does not raise either the issue of incorporating alternative institutions into a comprehensive political program for systemic change. Thus, to the question whether we should just continue supporting efforts to set up alternative media institutions etc, or whether, instead, we should direct our striving towards integrating such attempts in a struggle to build a new political and social movement that will fight for alternative systems of social organisation, his reply is that these two possibilities 'should not be regarded as alternatives... these are not conflicting goals; rather, mutually supportive efforts, all of which should proceed'.

It is therefore obvious that for Chomsky and Albert the establishment of alternative media is seen as a kind of life-style strategy, rather than as part of a political strategy and a comprehensive program for systemic change. Similarly, Chomsky's argument above that, even within the existing institutional framework, we could reverse the present concentration of power involves elements of the civil societarian approach. It is illustrative how Chomsky justifies his argument on the matter:

These are not the operations of any mysterious economic laws; they are human decisions that are subject to challenge, revision and reversal. They are also decisions made within institutions, state and private. These have to face the test of legitimacy, as always; and if they do not meet that test they can be replaced by others that are more free and more just, exactly as has happened throughout history.

However, although it is true that there are no historical or natural laws determining social evolution this does not mean that 'anything goes' within the existing institutional framework, as Chomsky seems to assume. The institutional framework does set the parameters within which social action takes place. This means that both the nature and the scope of radical social action cannot transcend these parameters -unless social action explicitly aims at the institutional framework itself. The neoliberal consensus was not just a policy change, as social democrats assume, but a structural change imposed by the needs of internationalisation of the market economy.

This implies that the basic elements of the neoliberal consensus and particularly flexible markets and minimisation of social controls on markets will not go away, as long as the present internationalised market economy exists. But, today, the market economy can only be internationalised, since the growth (and therefore profitability) of the multinationals, which control the world market economy, depends on enlarging their markets worldwide. And as long as the market economy has to be internationalised, markets have to be as open and as flexible as possible. All this means that, as long as the system of the market economy and representative democracy reproduces itself, all that reforms ('from above', or 'from below') can bring about today is temporary victories and reversible social conquests like, for instance, those made during the period of the social democratic consensus which are now being systematically dismantled by the neoliberal consensus.

THE REVOLUTIONARY APPROACH

Coming now to the revolutionary strategy, by 'revolution from above' I mean the strategy, which aims at systemic change through the conquest of state power. The Marxist- Leninist tradition is a classical example of this type of strategy. This approach, implied that the change in the social paradigm even among a minority of the population, the vanguard of the proletariat, (organised in the communist party and equipped with the 'science' of socialism, i.e. Marxism), could function as a catalyst to bring about a socialist revolution. The socialist revolution would then lead to the conquest of state power by the proletariat (effectively by its vanguard, i.e. the communist party) which would bring about a change in the institutional framework as well as a change in the dominant social paradigm. The socialist society would give way to a communist society only when the rapid development of productive forces, through the socialisation of production relations, would lead to the abolition of scarcity and division of labour and the withering away of the state. History however has shown that this strategy could only lead to new hierarchical structures, as the vanguard of the working class becomes at the end the new ruling elite. This was the main lesson of the collapse of 'actually existing socialism' which has clearly shown that, if the revolution is organised, and then its program carried out, through a minority, it is bound to end up with new hierarchical structures rather than with a society where concentration of power has been abolished.

By 'revolution from below', I mean the strategy which aims at systemic change through the abolition of state power and the creation of federations of communes, or of workers' associations. The various trends within the anarchist movement (community-oriented versus worker-oriented) aim at revolution, in order to abolish state power and transform society 'from below', rather than in order to conquest state power and transform society 'from above'.

But, attempts for revolutions from below in History have usually ended up either as insurrections, which failed to lead to a systemic change (the major recent example being the May '68 insurrection in France) or to civil wars, where the superior means, organisation and efficiency of their enemies (either the state army and/or statist socialists) led to the suppression of revolutionaries (the major recent example being the Spanish civil war in 1936).

To my mind, the major problem of any revolutionary strategy, either from above or from below, is the uneven development of consciousness among the population, in other words, the fact that a revolution, which assumes a rupture with the past both at the subjective level of consciousness and at the institutional level, takes place in an environment where only a minority of the population has broken with the dominant social paradigm.

Then, if it is a revolution from above, it has a good chance to achieve its first aim, to abolish state power and establish its own power. But, exactly because it is a revolution from above with its own hierarchical structures etc, it has no chance to change the dominant social paradigm but only formally, i.e. at the level of the official ideology. On the other hand, although the revolution from below is the correct approach to convert people democratically to the new social paradigm, it suffers from the fact that the uneven development of consciousness among the population may not allow revolutionaries to achieve even their very first aim of abolishing state power.

Therefore, the still unresolved problem with systemic change is how it could be brought about, from below, but by a majority of the population, so that a democratic abolition of power structures could become feasible.

INCLUSIVE DEMOCRACY APPROACH

The Inclusive Democracy (ID) project does offer a strategy, which aims at resolving this problem. It starts first with the assumption that radical systemic change would never come about through reforms, or life-style strategies. This is because systemic change requires a rupture with the past, which extends to both the institutional and the subjective level. Such a rupture is only possible through the development of a new political organisation and a new comprehensive political program for systemic change.

This means that the various activities to set up communes, co-ops, alternative media institutions etc are just irrelevant to a process of systemic change --- unless they are an explicitly integral part of such a comprehensive political program. It is in this sense that one may argue that the two strategies are not complementary as Chomsky argues, but mutually exclusive.

The ID political strategy comprises the gradual involvement of increasing numbers of people in a new kind of politics and the parallel shifting of economic resources (labour, capital, land) away from the market economy. The aim of such a transitional strategy should be to create changes in the institutional framework, as well as to value systems, which, after a period of tension between the new institutions and the state, would, at some stage, replace the market economy, statist democracy, and the social paradigm "justifying" them, with an inclusive democracy and a new democratic paradigm respectively.

The immediate objective should be the creation, from below, of 'popular bases of political and economic power', that is, the establishment of local public realms of direct and economic democracy which will confederate in order to create the conditions for the establishment of a new society.

Contesting local elections (the only form of elections which is not incompatible with the aims of the ID project) could provide the chance to put into effect such a program on a massive social scale, although other forms of establishing new types of social organisation should not be neglected, as long as they are part of a program which explicitly aims at systemic change. Once the institutions of inclusive democracy begin to be installed, and people, for the first time in their lives, start obtaining real power to determine their own fate, then the gradual erosion of the dominant social paradigm and of the present institutional framework will be set in motion. A new popular power base will be created.

Town by town, city by city, region by region will be taken away from the effective control of the market economy and the nation-state, their political and economic structures being replaced by the confederations of democratically run communities. A dual power in tension with the state will be created, an alternative social paradigm will become hegemonic and the break in the socialisation process--the precondition for a change in the institution of society--will have occurred. The legitimacy of today's 'democracy' will have been lost.

The implementation of a strategy like the one outlined above requires a new type of political organisation, which will mirror the desired structure of society. This would not be the usual political party, but a form of 'democracy in action', which would undertake various collective forms of intervention at:

- the political level (creation of 'shadow' political institutions based on direct democracy, neighbourhood assemblies, etc.),
- the economic level (establishment of community units at the level of production and distribution which are collectively owned and controlled),

- the social level (democracy in the workplace, the university etc.), and
- the cultural level (creation of community-controlled art and media activities).

However, all these forms of intervention should be part of a comprehensive program for social transformation aiming at the eventual change of each municipality won in the local elections into an inclusive democracy. The alternative media established as part of this program would play a crucial role in developing an alternative consciousness to the present one, as regards the methods of solving the economic and ecological problems in a democratic way. They should connect today's economic and ecological crisis to the present socio-economic system and make proposals on how to start building the new society. For example: by setting up a democratic economic sector, (i.e. a sector owned by the demos); by creating a democratic mechanism to make economic decisions affecting the demotic sector of the community; by 'localising' decisions affecting the life of the community as a whole (local production, local spending, local taxes, etc.).

Without underestimating the difficulties involved in the context of today's all-powerful methods of brain control and economic violence, which, in fact, might prove more effective methods than pure state violence in suppressing a movement for the inclusive democracy, I think that the proposed strategy is a realistic strategy on the way to a new society.

MASS MEDIA AND COMMUNICATION

At the beginning of the third millennium, it hardly needs any emphasis that journalism and mass media or simply the "press" plays a central role in modern society. Even in the early 18th century, the press was recognised as a powerful entity. Thomas Carlyle (1795-1881) wrote that the British statesman Edmund Burke (1729-97) called the reporters' gallery in the British Parliament "a Fourth Estate more important by far" than the other three estates of Parliament-the peers, bishops, and commons. A Similar statement, however, is attributed to the English historian, Thomas Babington Macaulay (1800-1859) who in his Essay On Hallam's Constitutional History Published in Edinburgh Review (September 1828), observed with reference to the press gallery of the House of Commons, "The gallery in which the reporters sit has become a fourth estate of the realm".

And over time, newspapers, news magazines, radio, television, cable video, video Cassettes and movies have been demanding more and more of our attention and leisure time. The mass media now markedly affect our politics, our recreation, our education in general and profoundly our culture, our perception and our understanding of the world around us. However, Prof. (Herbert) Marshall Mcluhan (1911-1980), whose theories on mass communication caused widespread debate, argued that each major period of history is characterised, not by the mass media per se, but by the nature of the medium of communication (print or electronic) used most widely at the time. In this Chapter will be discussed educational opportunities in four interrelated areas of studies, viz., Journalism and Mass Communication, Communication Studies, Public Relations, and Advertising. However, it would be in order to present first an overview of the media world, the role of the government, and to explain several terminologies.

First, a few words about the various terms used in this field because many such terms occur in admission advertisements. The term "journalism" often referred to as "news business" involves the gathering, processing, and delivery of important information relating to current affairs by the print media (news papers and new magazines), and electronic media (radio and TV). This integrated entity is also simply called "media". News and entertainment are communicated in a number of different ways using different media. The world "media" is often used to refer to the communication of news, and in this context means the same as news media. Media and mass media are often used when discussing the power of modern communication.

If there is a term that has appeared in more diverse publications than any other over the last few years, it is "multimedia". The number of definitions for it is as numerous as the number of companies that are involved in multimedia business. In essence, multimedia is the use or presentation of information in two or more forms. The combination of audio and video in film and television was probably the first multimedia application. It is the advent of the PC, with its ability to manipulate data from different sources and offer this directly to the consumers or subscribers that has sparked the current interest. In the context of mass media and communication, multimedia is an effective tool for the profession. Still journalism, which has long history beginning almost with the invention of printing, continues to be the core concept of the entire process of communication. The newer communication technologies, in fact, have been strengthening the cause of journalism and newspapers, the latest to appear on the scene being the Internet. However, education in multimedia is mainly offered by private IT institutes (e.g., Arena Multimedia).

THE MEDIA WORLD

The media world consists of a wide variety of agencies and organisations which are involved in media related activities. At its core are the mass media organisations per se and the users of mass media. The first category consists of (i) the print media (newspapers and magazines), (ii) the electronic media (radio and television channels), and (iii) the news agencies. The electronic media now includes the World Wide Web (WWW) which hosts Internet versions of most of the well-known newspapers and news magazines and is also emerging as a potential advertisement medium. In the second category are (i) the advertisers and advertising agencies, and (ii) the public relations agencies. Advertising provide the financial sustenance to the mass media and their survival depends upon advertisements. Public relation agencies interact with the mass media to put across their messages.

They also have their own mechanisms to reach their target audience groups. Besides, there are other institutions and organisations associated with media related activities. They include (1) audit agencies which vouch for the circulation figures of the print media; (2) agencies conducting readership surveys;

(3) schools of journalism and mass communication; (4) statutory and non-statutory organisations dealing with regulatory and ethical issues; and (5) organisations representing various interest groups in the media world. Last but not the least, there are facilitators, such as the chain of distributors of the print media and the TV cable operators, who provide the vital link between the products of media organisations and their consumers.

However, apart from functional relationships among mass media, advertising, and public relations, from academic point of view what is necessary to appreciate is that at the heart of these three activities is the art and science of communication. The practitioners is these areas strive to communicate with their respective target audience groups, adopting the most effective communication strategies.

The term communication, however, has a much wider connotation encompassing many fields of studies, the major areas being sociology and psychology, linguistics, cybernetics and information theory, and the study of non-verbal communication. Sociology and psychology produced the first academic studies in mass communication during the 1930s. Thereafter, many scholars studied the effects of mass communication on individuals and society. The theory and process of communication indeed has profoundly influenced the study of journalism and mass communication.

MASS MEDIA AND GOVERNMENT

Governments and press are widely perceived as mutual adversaries. Freedom of the Press-the right of the press to report and to criticise the wrong doings of the powerful without retaliation or threat of retaliation-is the cornerstone of democracy. Freedom of the Press in the United States is more than a legal concept-almost a religious tenet. The First Amendment to the US Constitution states clearly and unequivocally that the "Congress Shall Make No Law. Abridging Freedom of Speech or of the Press".

The Indian Constitution does not have similar provision, but Art 19 (1) (a) protects the right to freedom of speech and expression subject to reasonable restrictions as mentioned in Art 19 (2) Though many governments vouch for protecting the freedom of the press, there are instances galore of throttling the press. There are several agencies in various countries which fight for the cause of press freedom. Be that as it may, governments themselves are also major users of mass media for putting across their messages.

The Ministry of Information and Broadcasting which was set up during the Second World War to mobilise support for war efforts, is now a very large mass media organisation of the Government of India.

It performs its tasks through a number of specialised media units and other organisation. One of its most important units, the Directorate of Advertising and Visual Publicity (DAVP), is the primary multimedia advertising agency of the Central Government which uses about 6,240 newspapers for press advertisement.

The Ministry, besides its own mass media activities performs several statutory functions, the most important of which is the registration of newspapers and periodicals. The Office of the Registrar of Newspapers in India (RNI), commonly known as Press Registrar, was created in 1956 in accordance with the Section 19A of the Press and Registration of regulation of titles of newspapers and periodicals, followed by their registration and allocation of registration numbers.

It is also responsible for the verification of circulation claims, receiving Annual Statements of registered newspapers and periodicals, and compiling and publishing the annual report titled `Press in India' containing detailed information about the print media, a valuable media reference tool.

Another important statutory quasi-judicial authority, under the umbrella of the Ministry, is the Press Council of India (PCI). The objectives of the PCI established under the Indian Press Council Act 1978, are to preserve the freedom of the press and to maintain and improvement of standards of newspapers and news agencies. The Ministry of Labour, on the other hand, is responsible for the operation of the provisions of two Acts relating to the employees of newspaper establishments: (1) The Working Journalists and Other Newspaper Employees (Conditions of Service) and Miscellaneous Provisions Act, 1955, and (2) The Working Journalists (Fixation of Rates of Wages) Act, 1958. The first Act provides for the constitution of two separate Wage Boards for fixing or revising rates of wages of working journalists (including those working in news agencies) and non-journalist newspaper employees.

So far five Wage Boards had been set up (1956, 1963, 1975, 1985, and 1994). The fifth one (Manisana Wage Board) set up in 1994, has submitted its tentative proposals on December 12, 1999. Besides, there are a number of Acts which directly or indirectly affect the mass media. In December, 1999, the Government has introduced in the Parliament the Freedom of Information Bill. When enacted, it is likely to have a far reaching favourable effect on mass media. So far five States viz., Goa, Karnataka, Maharashtra, Rajasthan, and Tamil Nadu also have enacted similar laws.

JOURNALISM AND MASS COMMUNICATION

Journalism education in the narrow sense prepares students for careers in newspapers, news magazines, broadcast news, and news services. Now it encompasses a much wider area under the broad label "mass communication ". By what ever name it may be called, journalism and mass communication study is not a discipline in the sense that sociology, economics, political science or history is, but a rather loose interdisciplinary field covering a wide range of issues somehow related to public concerns. As such, the field reflects in general, the growth of mass communication itself.

A brief account of the development of journalism education in the USA will be helpful in understanding the current trend in journalism and mass communication education in India. Journalism education which has a beginning in English Departments in America universities focussed more on techniques, such as, reporting, news writing, editing, design, photography. Often they were taught by former journalists. Willard G Bleyer, a professor of English in the University of

Wisconsin may be called the father of journalism education. He was instrumental in introducing the first journalism course in the University in 1905 and his scholarly interests later greatly influenced the field.

However, the country's first school of Journalism came into existence in 1908 at the University of Missouri. This was followed by the establishment of the Graduate School of Journalism in 1911 at the Columbia University backed with a $2 million gift from Joseph Pulitzer (1846-1911), publisher of the New York World, Pulitzer is also remembered for the Pulitzer Prizes, also funded by him, and annually awarded for excellence in journalism, letters and music.

The School, still rated as one of the best journalism schools in the USA, is the publisher of the scholarly journal Columbia Journalism Review published since 1961. Now there are 427 colleges and universities which offer programmes in journalism and mass communication.

The focus on newspapers continued to dominate journalism education throughout the 1940s at leading Schools of Journalism in the USA. With the emergence of radio and television as major news and entertainment media, the journalism schools incorporated such topics as radio news, television news and broadcasting production techniques in their programmes. Even the Speech Departments, offshoots of English Departments, became involved in the preparation of students for careers in broadcasting. In some universities, the speech of communication arts department were merged with the journalism programmes.

Around the same time, more and more journalism schools started offering courses in advertising and public relations, giving rise to the term "mass communication" to describe this amalgam of courses on newspapers, radio, television, news magazines, and an increasing involvement with the study of communication itself. Communication study as an academic discipline has long been a part of social sciences in the American higher education. It involves the study of mass media and other social institutions devoted, among other, to persuasion, communication processes and their effects, audience studies, contents analysis, and interpersonal communication.

Wilbur Schramm, a leading scholar of communication studies, who taught at University of Iowa, Illinois and Stanford, is credited with popularising communication studies in journalism departments. Increasingly, graduate programmes became more concerned with communication theory while undergraduate courses stressed pre-professional training for careers in news media, advertising, and public relations. However, such emphasis on communication has its share of criticism too. It has been argued that communication and media studies hardly have anything to do with the practice of journalism.

The increased emphasis on communication theory at the expense of basic reporting and writing skill has also led to the scrapping of exclusive journalism courses in some universities. The shifting of focus from conventional journalism to communication is reflected in the rechristening the Schools and Departments of Journalism as School of Journalism and Mass Communication, Department of Communication, or Schools of Communication. Some of the well-known schools, however, did not change their names. At Missouri and at Columbia they continue to be the School of Journalism and Graduate Department of Journalism, respectively.

JOURNALISM EDUCATION IN INDIA

In India, the very notion of journalism education in universities was looked at with askance. A write-up published in the Times of India (November 27, 1934) shares the most commonly held view of the time that "journalists are born and not made". It observed, "A faculty for criticism, a flair for essentials and a sense of news values can be developed by experience only if these qualities are innate from the beginning... The actual basis of journalism is its various departments can be only be acquired by direct contact and often bitter experience". Almost all the famous journalists of yesteryears learnt journalism on the job starting as "cub" reporters. Even many of the celebrated editors and columnists did not undergo any formal training in journalism. The credit for making journalism as a subject of study goes to Dr. Annie Besant, the distinguished theosophist and freedom fighter. The course in the National University (Adyar) introduced by her, however, did not survive.

There were several other abortive attempts also. The oldest surviving Department of Journalism in the Indian sub-continent was established at Punjab University in Lahore (now in Pakisthan) in 1914. After partition, the Department continued to function at the New Delhi campus of the Indian part of the divided Punjab University till July 1962. At present, it offers a two-year integrated Master of Mass Communication (MMC) programme. From 1947 to 1954, there were only five university departments of journalism: (1) University of Madras (1947), (2) University of Calcutta (1950), (3) University of Mysore (1951), (4) Nagpur University (1952) and (5) Osmania University (1954), Both the First (1952-54) and the Second (1980-82) Press Commissions emphasised the need for expanding the scope of journalism education. The Second Press Commission recommended the establishment of a National Council for Journalism and Communication Research. It also highlighted the need for inter-disciplinary approach in journalism education and recommended that admission should be based on the performance in aptitude tests.

It was in 1963, that the Ford Foundation Mass Communication Study Team headed by Wilbur Schramm, who, as stated earlier greatly influenced journalism education in the USA, recommended the expansion of the scope of journalism education by broadening the curriculum to include mass communication, advertising, public relations and Radio and TV journalism, to fall in line with the American system. The Ford Foundation report set the trend of journalism and mass communication education in India. It also led to the establishment in 1965, of the Indian Institute of Mass Communication at New Delhi, by the Ministry of Information and Broadcasting which over a period, has introduced separate courses in these areas. In 1981, the University Grants Commission published the Report on the Status of Journalism and Communication Education in India, which recommended various measures for the strengthening the University Departments of Journalism and improvement in the quality of education. In another document, English Plan Perspective on Journalism/Communication Education in India published in 1990-91, the UGC unveiled a proposal for strengthening of selected universities departments.

With the broadening of curriculum to include the various dimensions of mass communication, the Indian Universities followed the examples of their US counterparts and started incorporating the terms "communication" and "mass communication" in their names. Many new Departments do not even include the term "journalism" in their names. The nomenclature of both the degrees, Bachelor of Journalism (BJ), and Master of Journalism (MJ), accordingly were changed by some universities to incorporate the terms "communication", "mass communication", such as, Bachelor of Communication and Journalism (BCJ), Bachelor of Journalism and Mass Communication (BJMC), Master of Communication and Journalism (MCJ), and Master of Journalism and Mass Communication (MJMC).

In some other universities the nomenclature of the Master's degree courses in MA (Journalism), or MA (Communication and Journalism). Yet in some universities the term "Journalism" does not occur at all, for example, MA, MS or M.Sc (Communication, or Mass Communication), Master of Communication Studies (MCS), Master of Mass Communication (MMC), The choice of nomenclature often reflects the incorporation, in varying degrees, the components of the "journalism", "mass communication" and "communication" in the course curricula.

In the programmes with such labels as "Journalism" or "Journalism and Mass Communication", while topics such as communication theory and broadcast journalism (TV and Radio) are covered, the focus of graduate programmes is more on the basics of print journalism methods and techniques.

In the latter category, apart from the preponderance of communication theory and process along with such issued as development communication, rural communication, educational communication, media research, the trust of many programmes is shifting towards TV and video production, web reporting and publishing, and Internet journalism. However, course contents vary from university to university. Advertising and public relations are covered in almost all the courses. The application of Information Technology (IT) of late is demanding more attention in many programmes.

Educational Opportunities

There has been now a proliferation of university courses in journalism in packages of different combinations of topics. The number of universities offering journalism and related courses now exceeds 75. An exclusive journalism university, Makhanlal Chaturvedi Rashtriya Patrakarita Vishwavidyalaya, was established in Bhopal in 1990.

The objective of the university is to develop itself into a national centre for teaching, training and research of journalism and mass communication through the medium of Hindi. It however, received considerable flak for its greater involvement in franchising out its BCA course to all and sundry throughout the country, rather then striving to achieve excellence in Hindi journalism. At present it offers nine journalism related courses.

Several institutions outside the university system also offer these courses, which include, as stated, earlier, the Indian Institution of Mass Communication. Some of these institutions have been sponsored by newspaper establishments, such as, Eenadu School of Journalism, Times Journalism (Indian Express Group). Some members of the Indian Newspaper Society took the initiative to promote the Press Foundation of India to provide opportunities for training and retraining of journalists.

It may be mentioned that the Film and Television Institute of India (FTTI) (Pune) is the first institution to introduce courses in TV Production. Besides FTTI, its counterpart in Calcutta, Satyajit Ray Film & Television Institute, and several other institutions offer programmes in Television. This has been discussed in Chapter 45 (Performing Arts). The National Institute of Design (Ahmedabad) has courses in the area of Communication Design which include Print Media, Audiovisuals and Video Film. Levels of Education: Education in journalism and mass communication is offered at the first degree (three-year BA degree), postgraduate Bachelor's degree (BJ/BCJ/BJMC, etc.,) Master's degree (MJ/MCJ/MJMC, etc.,) and pre-doctoral and doctoral levels. Besides, some universities offer the subject as one of the combinations at the first degree levels. Three-year BA degree courses, open to candidates who have passed 10+2 examination, are available only in the affiliated colleges of University of Delhi and Bangalore University. There are also diploma and certificate courses in a number of universities. M.Phil and Doctoral programmes are also available in some universities. The Bachelor's degree course is of one year duration and open to degree holders in any discipline. Master's degree, also of one year duration, is open to Bachelor's degree holders in journalism.

The MA course in the subject, which is of two-year duration, is open to Bachelor's degree holders in any discipline. A number of universities have started introducing two year integrated programmes, instead of separate one year programmes leading successively to Bachelor and Master degrees. The diploma courses are of one-year duration and the entry requirement is mostly a degree in any discipline. The certificate courses are open to undergraduates.

DISTANCE LEARNING COURSES

About 18 universities offer journalism and mass communication courses at different levels through distance learning mode which include five open universities, viz., Indira Gandhi National Open University, Kota Open University, Karnataka State Open University, Nalanda Open University, and Yashwantrao Chavan Maharashtra Open University.

SPECIALISED COURSES

There are stray instances of journalism courses in specific areas e.g.,

1. PG Diploma (one year) in Agriculture Journalism (Chaudhary Charan Singh Agricultural University),
2. Certificate (trimester) in Fashion Communication and a short term programme in Fashion Journalism (National Institute of Fashion Technology),

3. MA in Development Communication (Madurai Kamaraj University),
4. M.Sc in Agricultural Communication and Extension (GB Pant university of Agriculture & Technology),
5. PG Diploma in Electronic Journalism & Mass Communication (MJP Rohilkhand University),
6. Diploma in TV/AIR (Guru Nanak Dev University),
7. MA/M.Phil/Ph.D in Educational Communication, Distance Education, Subject Communication, M.Com (Subject Communication), and M.Sc (Subject Communication) (Yashwantrao Chavan Maharashtra Open University, Nashik-422005),
8. PG Diploma in Radio and Television Journalism (Indian Institute of Mass Communication).

Two other institutions, Asian College of Journalism and Indian Institute of Journalism and Mass Media focus on Radio, TV and Web journalism. The focus of the MJ course in Punjab Agricultural University is on agricultural journalism. In fact, the M.Sc and Ph.D courses in agricultural extension in agricultural universities include specialisation in mass communication for diffusion of agricultural information to farmers.

LANGUAGE JOURNALISM

Although, both in terms of the number and circulation, Indian language newspapers far outnumber those in English, only a small number of universities offer courses in language journalism. As of now, there are courses only in Hindi, Urdu and Telugu journalism. Two universities offer courses in Hindi journalism:

(1) Avinashilingam Institute for Home Science of Higher Education for Women-MA in Hindi Journalism,

(2) Banaras Hindu University-MA (Functional Hindi) in Journalism, and PG Diploma in Hindi Journalism of two-year duration (after MA).

As stated earlier, the Makhanlal Chaturvedi Rashtriya Patrakarita Vishwavidyalaya was established to promote journalism and mass communication through the medium of Hindi. Indian Institute of Mass Communication has a postgraduate Diploma course in Hindi Journalism. Urdu journalism is taught only in Jawaharlal Nehru University. It offers an Advance Diploma in Mass Media course with Urdu as one of the subjects. Potti Sreeramulu Telugu University and Eenadu School of Journalism offer Journalism courses in Telugu. While the former offer BJ and MJ programmes, the latter has introduced a Diploma course. The Eenadu Journalism School established by Eenadu, the largest circulated Telugu daily, deserves special mention. Eenadu is the first newspaper in the country to establish a school of journalism. It offers a Diploma course in Journalism of six months duration.

Candidates who successfully complete the course with merit would undergo further TV channels. Candidates are paid a fellowship of Rs.2,000 per month during the course and Rs.3,400 per month while undergoing advanced training. After successful completion of the advances training, candidates will be put on probation. Eligibility requirements are:

(a) graduate degree,

(b) proficiency in English and Telugu,

(c) flair for writing in Telugu,

(d) age not more than 25 years.

Admissions are made on the basis of reporting and editing, and an orientation in political, economic, geographical, and legal aspects relevant to print and visual media.

PUBLIC RELATIONS

Public Relations (PR), one of the newest management disciplines, means different things to different people.

It is widely perceived as the profession of corporate image making, a "lobbying" mechanism or "fixing things", and also as a face-saving device employed by organisations who find themselves in deep trouble.

Yet others equated PR with publicity and propaganda. A PR professional once wryly described PR as "the art of making friends you don't need". Be that as it may, PR is a reality and is practised world over by organisations which have something to do with their publics. It has now attained the status of specialised profession of communication management.

However, the definitions of PR are legion. There are as many definitions as there are PR "gurus".

Dr R F Harlow, a PR practitioner, culled out 472 definitions from various sources. Analysing them, he put forward a sort of working definition thus: "Public relations is a distinctive management function which helps establish and maintain mutual lines of communication.

Understanding, acceptance and cooperation between an organisation and its publics; involves the management of problems or issues; help management to keep informed on and responsive to public opinion; defines and emphasizes the responsibility of management to serve the public interest; helps management keep abreast of effectively utilising change, serving as an early warning system to help anticipate trends; and uses research and sound and ethical communication as its principle tools".

The concept of PR as a distinct branch of communication is comparatively a recent one, though it is an ancient practice. Perhaps, it was the American Telephone and Telegraph Company (now AT & T) which coined the term "public relations" and used it in its annual report for 1908. It is the Second World War that brought about new opportunities to the PR work. The International Public Relations Association was formed in 1955 and simultaneously many countries including India established national professional for a. In India it was the Tatas which first set up a PR Department in 1942.

In a sense, in India the first PR exercise on a very large scale was undertaken by the Government of India with the creation of a new Ministry of Information and Broadcasting in the 1940s. Its main function was to mobilise public opinion in favour of the war efforts in a situation where the Indian National Congress and national sentiment generally were against the war efforts.

The professionalism in PR may be said to have emerged with the establishment in 1958 of the Public Relations Society of India (PRSI). It was not until 1968 when the first national level conference of PRSI which adopted Code of Ethics and defined the parameters of the PR profession that it earned a sort of professional respectability.

With 28 regional chapters, the PRSI is now a national organisation involved in promoting PR along ethical lines and develop human resources through seminars, conferences and training programmes. It also publishes a professional journal `Public Relations'.

As stated earlier PR has a symbiotic relationship with mass media and advertising. Though public relations, and advertising are different professions yet they are interdependent. Often, the two have similar goals, a shared audience and the same media vehicles. As such, PR practitioners need the same level of communication skills and the knowledge of communications techniques as that of journalism and advertising professionals.

Public Relations Departments, often known as Corporate Communication Departments, exist in major business and industrial organisations.

All the government agencies at different levels, both at the Centre and the States, have PR Departments. The international organisations of the Un family and even large non-governmental organisations (NGOs) fell the need for PR units. Besides, there are a large number of PR organisations, often set up by the advertising agencies, which provide PR service to a large number organisations although some of them have their own PR outfits. There are also a large number of individual PR consultants.

Among the PR tools are press releases, press conferences, seminars, annual reports of the organisations, house magazines and newsletters, films, charitable donations, sponsorship of events (such as, sports and games, music recitals), community relations and last but not the least PR advertising, as distinct aimed at building a positive corporate image of an organisation in the context of its community on subjects of welfare or seeking to educate or inform the community on subjects of public interest, such as, road safety, immunisation; AIDS, family welfare.

Educational Opportunities

It has been mentioned earlier that PR is one of the essential components of almost all the courses in journalism and mass communication. The number of stand-alone courses in PR, however, is limited. Often the courses cover both PR and advertising. Most of the courses are at the diploma level offered by both universities and non-universities institutions. The courses generally cover such subjects as communication tools media of PR, media planning, editing and proof reading, advertising writing press releases, media production techniques.

Advertising

Way back in 1759, Samuel Johnson (1709-84) the English poet, critic and lexicographer observed "Promise, large promise, is the soul of an advertisement" (The Idler No.40, 20 January 1759). Stephen Leacock (1869-1944), a Canadian humourist described advertising "as the science of arresting human intelligence long enough to get money from it" (Garden of Folly (1924)-"The Perfect Salesman"). Leacock's dig at advertising perhaps signifies its enormous power.

Though many TV watchers curse advertisers and their advertising agencies for the number of commercial breaks to show advertisements in between TV programmes, consciously and often willingly or unwillingly, they listen to their message and more often than not succumb to the allurements. In fact, we now live in an "advertisement-laden" society. Advertisements stare at us from the pages of newspapers and glossy magazines, TV screen and the huge outdoor billboards, often illuminated ones in the night. We cannot escape online advertisements while surfing the Internet. And now advertising via wireless devices carrying messages to the cell phone is in the offing!

Advertisements, a Marketing Management function, has been defined by the American Marketing Association as "any paid form of non-personal presentation and promotion of ideas, goals or services by an identified sponsor". In other words, advertisements involve purchasing time or space in such mass media as television, radio newspapers or magazines to explain, or to urge or to persuade the use or adoption of a product, service or an idea. The field of advertisement management is made up of a system of interacting organisations and institutions, all of which play a role in the advertising process.

At the core of the system are advertisers, the organisations that provide financial resources that support advertising. Advertisers are private and public sector organisations, that use mass media to achieve their respective organisational objectives. Increasingly, political parties are using advertising as a major tool for election campaign.

The two other components of the system are: (i) advertising agencies, and (ii) the media that carry the advertisements. Another important adjunct of the advertising industry is the advertising models. Many celebrated women models went on to win laurels in beauty contests, both national and international, and made their marks in films. The expenditure incurred by advertisers provides the basis for estimates of the size of the burgeoning advertising industry.

According to the Eleventh A&M Agency Report prepared by the prestigious A&M magazines (15 September 2000), the total advertisement expenditure of 200 top spenders in 1998-99 was Rs.3,914.7 crore representing 2.3% of their sales.

The top 200 spenders account for 90% of the total expenditure. However, the report is based on the data provided by advertising agencies and thus excludes expenditures incurred by small and private organisations which buy media space or time directly, the Central Governments and State Governments which release advertisements through the Directorate of Audio-Visual Publicity (DAVP), and Departments of Information and Public Relations, respectively.

Though the advertisers provide the nutrients, it is advertising agencies which are the backbone of the advertising industry and make things happen. The importance of advertising agencies has increased because the era of brand loyalty is almost a thing of the past. It is the agencies which now create brand images for new products and resurrect those of the fading ones. The agencies vary in size, organisation structure and services they offer. Large agencies have networks of branch offices in major cities.

According to the A&M Agency Report referred to above, during 1999-2000, of the top 89 agencies, the first 15 garnered more than 65% of the gross income. Advertisement agencies do the planning for their clients, create advertisements, and select the appropriate media for placing them. Advertisement planning involves market research.

Most of the big agencies, therefore, have in-house market research facilities, e.g., Indian Market Research Bureau, (IMRB), a Division of the Hindustan Thompson Associate. Besides, there are also independent agencies, such as, MARG Marketing and Research Group, and Operations Research Group (ORG). The Advertisers' Handbook (1999-2000), listed more than 690 accredited agencies.

Two of the oldest agencies are Hindustan Thompson Associates (1929) and Ogilvy & Mather (1928). Incidentally, David M Ogilvy (1911-1999), the most revered, albeit controversial, advertisement "guru" is the founder of Ogilvy & Mather. Besides, about 660 non-accredited agencies are also listed in it. As stated elsewhere, the Indian Newspaper Society (INS) operates the system of accreditation of advertising agencies.

One of the conditions for accreditation is that the agency should be completely independent without control or ownership of the media or clients.

The INS also has framed conditions for accepting advertisements from accredited advertising agencies by INS member publications. The income of advertising agencies comes mostly from commissions received not from the clients but from the advertising media.

As stated earlier, the Directorate of Advertisement and Visual Publicity (DAVP) is the advertising agency of the Government of India. The Advertisement policy of the Government of India says that in "pursuance of broad social objectives of the Government and in order to achieve parity of rate between various categories of newspapers, appropriate weightage/consideration may be given to:

(1) small and medium newspapers and journals,

(2) specialised scientific and technical journals,

(3) language newspapers and journals, and

(4) newspapers and journals published especially in backward, remote, and border areas."

Many big advertisers and the print an electronic media have their own advertising departments which generally liaise with advertising agencies.

Advertising agencies have three different associations, to look after the business interest, viz., the Advertising Agencies Association of India (1948) (Mumbai), the National Council of Advertising Agencies (1967) (New Delhi), and the Indian Society of Advertisers (Mumbai).

Besides, the Advertising Standards Council of India (1985) (Mumbai) comprising advertisers, advertising agencies, newspapers, magazines and others involved in advertising has prepared a Code for Self-Regulation in Advertising to create a sense of responsibility for its observance amongst advertisers, advertising agencies and others connected with the creation of advertising, and the media.

Educational Opportunities

Educational opportunities in advertising are very limited, although advertising along with relations are included in the journalism and mass communication courses. Advertisement Management is also component of marketing management in management programmes.

The programmes offered by the Mudra Institute of Communications (MICA) set up by Mudra Communications, the third largest advertisement agency, deserves mention.

It offers three programmes:

(1) Postgraduate Programme in Communication,

(2) Programme in Creating Advertising, and

(3) Faculty Induction Programme.

The postgraduate programme open to graduates, offers specialisation in Brand Stewardship and Account Management, Marketing Research, Direct Marketing, Corporate Communication, and Media Planning and Marketing. Admission is based on the CAT score. The second programme of three-month duration is offered in collaboration with the National Institute of Design. The specialisation offered copywriting and Art Direction.

Eligibility requirement is a Bachelor's degree for the Art direction course. Computer literacy is an essential requirement. The third programme of two-year duration is aimed at developing teachers to be absorbed in MICA itself, Eligibility requirement is a Master's degree with experience in research, teaching, marketing, journalism, media and advertising. The selected candidates are given a stipend of Rs.10,000 per month during the first year and Rs.12,000 per month in the second year.

Indian Newspaper Society (INS): INS brings out a comprehensive annual reference publication titled the INS Press Handbook (both print and CD version) which contains detailed particulars of member newspapers and magazines, accredited advertising agencies, important newspapers and media organisations, accredited press correspondents, etc.

Course on Online Journalism and Internet: Career Launcher, a Delhi-based preparatory education outfit had set up a journalism school called School of Contemporary Media to offer a programme on online journalism and web writing.

Career Opportunities

Journalism and Mass Communication: Career opportunities in journalism and mass communication exist in newspapers, news magazines, news agencies, TV Channels as well as in advertising and PR agencies. However, the bulk of journalists are employed in newspapers, news magazines and news agencies.

Newspapers differ in language, size, circulation and as such the number and the category of staff vary widely. As stated earlier, the wage structure of journalists (rather working journalists) is governed by the recommendations of the Wage Boards for Working Journalists set up by the Ministry of Labour from time to time.

The wage structure of various categories of working journalists is in turn determined by the size of the gross revenue of newspapers.

The Bachawar Wage Board (1984) classified the newspaper establishments into ten classes. At the top is Class IA with a gross revenue of Rs.100 crore followed by Class I (Rs.50 crore and above, but less than Rs.100 crore) and at the lowest level is the Class IX (less than Rs.25 lakh).

The Manisana Wage Board (1994) reportedly has introduced a new classification with ten classes, introducing a new class IB at the top and merging Class IX with VIII. The Bachawat Wage Board grouped the working journalists into eight categories for newspaper establishments belonging to Class IA to VII. However, the designations may vary. A perusal of such news magazines, as India Today, The Week, Outlook will give an idea about the positions obtaining in the increasing crop of news magazines.

Generally, fresh entrants to the profession being as sub-editors or junior reporters, often as trainees. Merely passing out of journalism school does not make one a good journalist. Four most important qualities of a prospective journalist are:

(i) possession of what is called a "nose for news",

(ii) general acquaintance with socio-economic, and political environment;

(iii) knowledge of authoritative sources of background information about issues handled;

(iv) skills for gathering sifting and analysing information and present it as lucidly as possible.

The last one needs command over the language of the newspaper and a flair for writing. In addition, computer literacy is a must in modern day journalism. All these skills can be developed only through hard painstaking work.

This is now the age of specialisation. More and more specialised features and supplements relating to science, technology, education, environment, women, fashion are now being added to newspapers.

The number of news magazines in the areas of business and industry, finance, economics are also growing. A formal educational qualification in these subjects would go a long way for making a mark in specialised areas of the profession.

Whether electronic newspapers will be economically viable enough to replace the print media is still a matter of conjecture. However, the stunning possibility of Internet for journalism and the news business are somewhat obvious.

The Internet multimedia information retrieval system on the WWW is on the verge of becoming a mass medium itself. The journalists of today and tomorrow must take note of the ongoing information revolution and prepare themselves for the future.

The schools of Journalism in the country, therefore, should catch up with the revolutionary developments that are taking place in the field of information technology. Students should be taught how to navigate the www to get most out of the cast information resources now available online. Besides, they need to be exposed to some of the techniques involved in the creation of web pages, reporting and writing for electronic newspapers, cyber laws and ethics.

Public Relations

As has been states earlier, hardly there are any institution and organisations, which do not need PR professionals. However, job profiles differ from organisation to organisation. For new entrants. PR is a job that literally keeps them on their toes where only sheer hard work leads to a successful career. At this stage, they are often little more than errand boys doing different kinds of work. This is particularly true in the PR units of an organisation. As they go up the career ladder they enter into specialised functional areas. It is in the large PR agencies that the job prospects are bright.

Advertising

Though the advertisers and advertising departments of mass media organisations offer opportunities in advertising, it is the advertising agencies which provides really challenging professionals responsibilities. The types of tasks in advertising agencies vary from department to department and as such each task needs different type of training requirement and skills.

A mid-size agency has typically four core departments, viz., client servicing, creative, media, and art production departments, besides other support services, such as, finance and accounts. The client servicing department provided the link between the agency and the client on the one hand, and with other departments in the agency, on the other. It is basically, a management function. Larger agencies, therefore, prefer persons with a management degree or advertising qualification.

The Creative Department, which actually creates the advertisement, is perceived as the most glamorous one in an advertising agency. It engages two types of people-visualisers and copywriters. Visualisers are artists who are responsible for the layout and visual aspects of the advertisement. Copywriters, on the other hand, prepare the copy, i.e., the written part of the advertisement or scripts for TV commercials. A visualiser should have a formal qualification in art or design. With increasing use of computers in designing work, familiarity with its use is a desirable requirement.

A short-term course in multimedia designing would help in the profession. Though for copywriters, no specific formal qualification is necessary, they should have a good command over the language used for the copy, and have the ability to get across the message most effectively.

By and large, the copy is written in English and thereafter translated into the language of the medium. Proficiency in

English and a regional language (mother tongue) is the desirable requirement.

The media Department is responsible for media planning and buying space or time. Media planning largely involves market research about, among others, media habit and preferences of consumers.

A formal management qualification majoring in marketing is a desirable entry qualification. And finally, the Art Production Department is responsible for giving physical shape to the concept created by the Creative Department in the form of final product to be passed on to the client for publication. The staff of the Department includes commercial artists.

7

Antisocial Effects on Reporting

The antisocial effect of viewing television and motion pictures is one of the most heavily researched areas in all mass media studies. Comstock, Chaffee, and Katzman (1978) reported that empirical studies focusing on this topic outnumbered work in all other problem areas by four to one, and this emphasis is still apparent more than a decade later. Paik and Comstock (1994) reviewed the results of 217 such studies conducted between 1959 and 1990.

The impact of prosocial content is a newer area and grew out of the recognition that the same principles underlying the learning of antisocial activities ought to apply to more positive behavior. Applied and academic researchers share an interest in this area: All the major networks have sponsored such research, and the effects of antisocial and prosocial content have been popular topics on college and university campuses for the past 30 years. It is not surprising that there has been a certain amount of friction between academic researchers and industry executives.

HISTORY

Concern over the social impact of the mass media was evident as far back as the 1920s, when many critics charged that motion pictures had a negative influence on children. In 1928, the Motion Picture Research Council, with support from the Payne Fund, a private philanthropic organization, sponsored a series of 13 studies on movies' influence on children. After examination of film content, information gain, attitude change, and influence on behavior, it was concluded that the movies were potent sources of information, attitudes, and behavior for children. Furthermore, many of the things that children learned had antisocial overtones. In the early 1950s, another medium, the comic book, was chastised for its alleged harmful effects (Wertham, 1954).

In 1960, Joseph Klapper summarized what was then known about the social impact of mass communication. In contrast to many researchers, Klapper downplayed the potential harmful effects of the media. He concluded that the media most often reinforced an individual's existing attitudes and predispositions. Klapper's viewpoint, which became known as the *minimal effects position,* was influential in the development of a theory of media effects.

In the late 1950s and early 1960s, concern over the antisocial impact of the media shifted to television. Experiments on college campuses by Bandura and Berkowitz (summarized in Comstock & Paik, 1991) showed that aggressive behavior could be learned by viewing violent media content and that a stimulation effect was more probable than a cathartic (or cleansing) effect. Senate subcommittees examined possible links between viewing violence on television and juvenile delinquency, and in 1965, one subcommittee concluded that televised crime and violence were related to antisocial behaviors among juvenile viewers.The civil unrest and assassinations in the middle and late 1960s prompted the formation of the National Commission on the Causes and Prevention of Violence, chaired by Milton Eisenhower. The staff report of the Eisenhower Commission, which concluded that television violence taught the viewer how to engage in violence, included a series of recommendations about reducing the impact of television violence.

The early 1970s saw extensive research on the social effects of the mass media. Just three years after the publication of the Eisenhower Commission report came the release of a multi-volume report sponsored by the Surgeon General's Scientific Advisory Committee on Television and Social Behavior (1972, p. 10). In *Television and Growing Up,* the committee cautiously summarized its research evidence:

There is a convergence of fairly substantial evidence on short-run causation of aggression among children by viewing violence . . . and the much less certain evidence from field studies that . . . violence viewing precedes some long-run manifestation of aggressive behavior. This convergence . . . constitutes some preliminary evidence of a causal relationship.

The committee tempered this conclusion by noting that in accordance with the reinforcement notion, "any sequence by which viewing television violence causes aggressive behavior is most likely applicable only to some children who are predisposed in that direction" (p. 10).

At about the same time, the three television networks were sponsoring research in this area. CBS commissioned two studies: a field experiment that found no link between television viewing and subsequent imitation of antisocial behavior (Milgram & Shotland, 1973), and a longitudinal study in Great Britain that found an association between viewing violence on television and committing antisocial acts such as damaging property and hurting others (Belson, 1978). ABC sponsored a series of studies by two mental health consultants who concluded that television stimulated aggression to only a tiny extent in children (Heller & Polsky, 1976). NBC began a large-scale panel study, but results were not released until 1983. In addition to television violence, the potential antisocial impact of pornography was under scrutiny. The Commission on Obscenity and Pornography (1970), however, reported that such material was not a factor in determining antisocial behavior. The commission's conclusions were somewhat controversial in political circles, but in general they supported the findings of other researchers in human sexuality (Tan, 1986). Subsequent efforts in this area were directed primarily toward examining links between pornography and aggression.

Along with violence and pornography, the contrasting prosocial effect of television was investigated as well. One stimulus for this research was the success of the television series *Sesame Street*. A substantial research effort went into the preparation and evaluation of these children's programs. It was found that the series was helpful in preparing young children for school but not very successful in narrowing the information gap between advantaged and disadvantaged children (Minton, 1975). Other studies by both academic researchers and industry researchers demonstrated the prosocial impact of other programs. For example, the series *Fat Albert and the Cosby Kids* was found to be helpful in teaching prosocial lessons to children (CBS Broadcast Group, 1974).

Studies of these topics continued between 1975 and 1985, although there were far fewer than in the early 1970s. An update to the 1972 Surgeon General's Report, issued in 1982, reflected a broader research focus than the original document; it incorporated investigations of socialization, mental health, and perceptions of social reality. Nonetheless, its conclusions were even stronger than those of its predecessor: "The consensus among most of the research community is that violence on television does lead to aggressive behavior" (National Institute of Mental Health, 1982, p. 8). Other researchers, notably Wurtzel and Lometti (1984) and Bear (1984), argued that the report did not support the conclusion of a causal relationship, whereas Chaffee (1984) and Murray (1984), among others, contended that the conclusions were valid.

Not long after the Surgeon General's report was updated, the results of the NBC panel study begun in the early 1970s were published (Milavsky, Kessler, Stipp, & Rubens, 1983). This panel study, which used state-of-the-art statistical analyses, found a nonsignificant relationship between viewing television violence during the early phases of the study and subsequent aggression. The NBC data have been reexamined by others, and at least one article suggests that the data from this survey do show a slight relationship between violence viewing and aggression among at least one demographic subgroup—middle-class girls (Cook, Kendzierski, & Thomas, 1983).

From 1985 to 2001, the controversy subsided, but this topic remained popular among academic researchers. Williams (1986) conducted an elaborate field experiment in three Canadian communities. One town was about to receive television for the first time, another received Canadian TV, and the third received both Canadian and U.S. programs. Two years later,

Williams and her colleagues found that when compared to children in the other two communities, children in the town that had just received TV scored higher on measures of physical and verbal aggression. Additional evidence on the topic of television and violence comes from a series of panel studies conducted by an international team of researchers (Huesmann & Eron, 1986). Data were gathered from young people in the United States, Finland, Australia, Israel, and Poland. Findings from the U.S. and Polish studies reached a similar conclusion: Early TV viewing was related to later aggression. The Finnish study found this relationship for boys but not for girls. The Israeli study found that TV viewing seemed to be related to aggression for children living in urban areas but not for those in rural areas. The Australian study failed to find a relationship. In all countries where a relationship between TV viewing and violence was found, the relationship was relatively weak. Rosenthal (1986), who concluded that even a weak relationship could have substantial social consequences, examined the practical implications of this weak relationship.

More recently, Congress passed the Telecommunications Act of 1996. Part of the act specified that newly manufactured TV sets had to contain a V-chip, a computer chip that allows parents to block out violent and other objectionable programming from their TV sets. The chip would work in concert with a ratings system developed by the industry. (Recent research suggests that consumers have largely ignored the V-chip. One study found that 53% of consumers who had recently purchased a new TV set were not even aware they had a V-chip. A Kaiser Family Foundation study discovered that only 17% of families were using the V-chip to screen programs.)

Another recent research area examined mediating effects on the viewing of TV violence.

Nathanson (1999), for example, confirmed that parental mediation of TV viewing helped curtail the antisocial inclinations of their children. The same researcher (Nathanson, 2001) also examined the influence of peer mediation on antisocial TV viewing. She found that peer influence was more frequent and more potent than parental mediation and that it tended to promote a positive attitude toward antisocial TV. The violence at Columbine High School in Littleton, Colorado, and in other high schools at the end of the century, sparked renewed interest in media violence among parents and policy makers. Media leaders were called before a congressional committee investigating this topic. In 2001, the Surgeon General issued a report entitled *Youth Violence,* a document that included a study of the factors that contributed most to antisocial behavior among young people. The report concluded that media violence was less of a risk factor than family influences, peer group attitudes, socioeconomic status, and substance abuse (U.S. Department of Health and Human Services, 2001).

The increasing popularity of video games during the early years of this decade opened up another avenue of inquiry for researchers. Since more than 90% of young people report that they sometimes play these games, and since some of the more popular games feature graphic and explicit violence, social concern over their impact was widespread.

Results of some of the early studies in this area (for example, Silvern & Williamson, 1987) suggest that playing video games can lead to increased aggression levels in young children and is related to their self-concepts (Funk & Buchman, 1996). More-recent research has reinforced this conclusion. Anderson and Dill (2000) measured aggressive personality traits, recent delinquent behaviors, and video-game playing habits of 227 college students.

Those who reported playing more violent video games in the past engaged in more aggressive behavior and had lower academic grades in college. Sherry (2001) conducted a meta-analysis on 20 studies that examined a possible link between video-game playing and antisocial attitudes and behaviors. He concluded that, like the research results on exposure to TV violence and antisocial behavior, there was a weak but statistically significant link between playing violent video games and aggression.

Research about the antisocial effects of pornography increased in the late 1980s but has recently declined. One controversial research area examined if prolonged exposure to nonviolent pornography had any antisocial effects (Donnerstein, Linz, & Penrod, 1987; Zillmann & Bryant, 1989; Allen, D'Alessio, & Brezgel, 1995). The most recent studies have focused on exposure to pornographic Internet sites (for example, Lo & Weir, 2002).

Research interest in the prosocial effects of media exposure decreased in the 1980s and mid-1990s. Sprafkin and Rubinstein (1979) reported on a correlational study in which the viewing of prosocial television programs accounted for only 1% of the variance in an index of prosocial behavior exhibited in school.

The apparent lack of a strong relationship between these two variables, coupled with the absence of general agreement on a definition of *prosocial content,* might have discouraged researchers from selecting this area. In any case, few studies of the media impact on prosocial behavior have appeared in the scholarly literature in the last five years. The meta-analysis of Anderson and Bushman (2001) found only a handful of prosocial studies to analyze but concluded that playing violent video games is linked to a decline in prosocial behavior.

METHODS

Researchers who study the effects of mass media have used most of the techniques discussed in this book: content analysis, laboratory experiments, surveys, field experiments, observations, and panels. In addition, they have used some advanced techniques, such as meta-analysis, that have not been discussed. Given the variety of methods used, it is not possible to describe a typical approach. Instead, this section focuses on five different methods as illustrations of some research strategies.

The Experimental Method. A common design used to study the antisocial impact of the media is to show one group of subjects violent media content while a control group sees nonviolent content. This was the approach used by Berkowitz and Bandura in their early work. The dependent variable, aggression, is measured immediately after exposure—either by a pencil-and-paper test or by a mechanical device like the one described next. For example, Liebert and Baron (1972) divided children into two groups. The first group saw a 3.5-minute segment from a television show depicting a chase, two fistfights, two shootings, and a knifing. Children in the control group saw a segment of similar length in which athletes competed in track and field events. After viewing, the children were taken one at a time into another room that contained an apparatus with two buttons, one labeled "Help" and the other labeled "Hurt." An experimenter explained to the children that wires from the device were connected tc a game in an adjacent room. The subjects were told that in the adjacent room, another child was starting to play a game. (There was, in fact, no other child.) At various times, by pressing the appropriate buttons, each child was given a chance either to help the unseen child win the game or to hurt the child. The results showed that children who had seen the violent segment were significantly more likely than the control group to press the "Hurt" button. Of course, there are many variations on this basic design. For example, the type of violent content shown to the subjects can be manipulated (cartoon versus live violence, entertainment versus newscast violence, justified versus unjustified violence). Also, some subjects may be frustrated before exposure. The degree of association between the media violence and the subsequent testing situation may be high or low. Subjects can watch alone or with others who praise or condemn the media violence. Media exposure can be a one-time event or it can be manipulated over time. For a thorough summary of this research, see Comstock and Paik (1991) and Liebert and Sprafkin (1992).

Experimental studies to examine the impact of media exposure on prosocial behavior have used essentially the same approach. Subjects see a televised segment that is either prosocial or neutral, and the dependent variable is then assessed. For example, Forge and Phemister (1987) randomly assigned preschoolers to one of four conditions: prosocial animated program (*The Get-along Gang*), neutral animated (*Alvin and the Chipmunks*), prosocial nonanimated (*Mr. Rogers' Neighborhood*), and neutral nonanimated (*Animal Express*). The children watched the program and were then placed in a free-play situation where their prosocial behaviors were observed and recorded. The results demonstrated an effect for the program variable (prosocial programs prompted more prosocial behaviors than did neutral programs) but no effect for the animated versus nonanimated variable.

The operational definitions of *prosocial behavior* have varied widely: Studies have examined cooperative behaviors, sharing, kindness, altruism, friendliness, creativity, and absence of stereotyping. Almost any behavior with a positive social value seems to be a candidate for study, as exemplified by the experiment by Baran, Chase, and Courtright (1979): Third-graders were assigned to one of three treatment conditions. One group saw a condensed version of a segment of *The Waltons* demonstrating cooperative behavior; the second group saw a program portraying noncooperative behavior; and the third group saw no program. After answering a few written questions dealing with the program, each subject left the viewing room only to encounter a confederate of the experimenter who passed the doorway and dropped an armload of books. There were two dependent measures: whether the subject attempted to retrieve the books and how much time elapsed until the subject began to help. The group that saw the cooperative content was more likely to help, and their responses were quicker than those of the control group. It is interesting that there was no difference in helping behavior or in time elapsed between the group that saw *The Waltons* and the group that saw the noncooperative content.

The Survey Approach. Most survey studies have used questionnaires that incorporate measures of media exposure (such as viewing television violence or exposure to pornography) and a pencil-and-paper measure of antisocial behavior or attitudes. In addition, many recent studies have included measures of demographic and sociographic variables that mediate the exposure–antisocial behavior relationship. Results are usually expressed as a series of correlations.

A survey by McLeod, Atkin, and Chaffee (1972) illustrates this approach. Their questionnaire contained measures of violence viewing, aggression, and family environment. They tabulated viewing by giving respondents a list of 65 prime-time television programs with a scale measuring how often each was viewed. An index of overall violence viewing was obtained by using an independent rating of the violence level of each show and multiplying it by the frequency of viewing. Aggression was measured by seven scales. One measured respondents' approval of manifest physical aggression (sample item: "Whoever insults me or my family is looking for a fight"). Another examined approval of aggression ("It's all right to hurt an enemy if you are mad at him"). Respondents indicated their degree of agreement with each of the items on the separate scales. Family environment was measured by asking about parental control over television, parental emphasis on nonaggressive punishment (such as withdrawal of privileges), and other variables. The researchers found a moderate positive relationship between the respondents' level of violence viewing and their self-reports of aggression. Family environment showed no consistent association with either of the two variables.

Sprafkin and Rubinstein (1979) used the survey method to examine the relationship between television viewing and prosocial behavior. They used basically the same approach as McLeod, Atkin, and Chaffee (1972), except their viewing measure was designed to assess exposure to television programs established as prosocial by prior content analysis. Their measure of prosocial behaviors was based on peer nominations of people who reflected 12 prosocial behaviors, including helping, sharing, following rules, staying out of fights, and being nice. The researchers found that when the influence of the child's gender, the parents' educational level, and the child's academic level were statistically controlled, exposure to prosocial television explained only 1% of the variance in prosocial behaviors.

Field Experiments. Parke, Berkowitz, and Leyens (1977) conducted a field experiment in a minimum-security penal institution for juveniles. The researchers exposed groups to unedited feature-length films that were either aggressive or nonaggressive. On the day after the last film was shown, in the context of a bogus learning experiment, the boys were told they had a chance to hurt a confederate of the experimenters who had insulted one group of boys and had been neutral to the other.

The results on an electric shock measure similar to the one used in the Liebert and Baron (1972) study, described previously, revealed that the most aggressive of all the experimental groups were the boys who had seen the aggressive films and had been insulted. In addition to this laboratory measure, the investigators collected observational data on the boys' aggressive interpersonal behavior in their everyday environment. These data showed that boys who saw the violent movies were more interpersonally aggressive. However, there was no apparent cumulative effect of movies on aggression. The boys who watched the diet of aggressive films were just as aggressive after the first film as after the last.

The dependent variable of aggression was measured in three ways: observations of behavior on school playgrounds, peer ratings, and teacher ratings. On the observational measure, the aggressive acts of children in the town labeled A (the town that just received TV) increased from an average of 0.43 per minute in Phase 1 to 1.1 per minute in Phase 2. Children in the other towns showed only a slight and statistically insignificant increase in the same period. Peer and teacher ratings tended to support the behavioral data. As yet, there have been no large-scale field experiments examining prosocial behavior.

Panel Studies. Primarily because of the time and expense involved in panel studies, this method is seldom used to examine the antisocial effects of the media. Five studies relevant to this topic are briefly reviewed here. Lefkowitz, Eron, Waldner, and Huesmann (1972), using a catch-up panel design, reinterviewed 427 of 875 youthful subjects 10 years after they had participated in a study of mental health. Measures of television viewing and aggression had been administered to these subjects when they were in the third grade, and data on the two variables were gathered again a decade later.

Slightly different methods were used to measure television viewing on the two occasions. Viewing in the third grade was established based on mothers' reports of their children's three favorite television shows. Ten years later, respondents rated their own frequency of viewing. The data were subjected to cross-lagged correlations and path analysis. The results supported the hypothesis that aggression in later life was caused in part by television viewing during early years. However, the panel study by Milavsky and colleagues (1983), sponsored by NBC, found no evidence of a relationship.

The difference between the results of these studies might be due to several factors. The Milavsky study did not vary its measure of "violent television viewing" throughout its duration. In addition, the NBC researchers used LISREL (linear structural equations), a more powerful statistical technique, which was not available at the time of the Lefkowitz study. Finally, the Lefkowitz measures were taken 10 years apart; the maximum time lag in the NBC study was 3 years.

Another panel study of the media and possible antisocial effects was conducted by Huesmann and Eron (1986). The investigators followed 758 children who were in the first and third grades in 1977 and reinterviewed them in 1978 and 1979. Aggression was measured by both peer nominations and self-ratings. Multiple regression analyses disclosed that, for both boys and girls, watching TV violence was a significant predictor of the aggression they would later demonstrate. Other significant variables were the degree to which children identified with violent TV characters, the perceived reality of the violence, and the amount of a child's aggressive fantasizing.

More recently, two longitudinal panel studies have found long-term effects of viewing TV violence. Huesmann, Moise-Titus, Podolski and Eron (2003) did a 15-year follow-up study with more than 300 respondents from surveys originally conducted in the 1970s. They found that respondents who watched violent shows at age 8 were more likely to be more aggressive in their 20s. The results remained significant even when such factors as IQ, social class, and parenting differences were statistically controlled. A second study (Johnson, Cohen, Smailes, Kasen, & Brook, 2002) found a significant association between the amount of time spent watching TV during their respondents' teenage years and aggressive behavior as young adults. The results of this study, however, were criticized because the researchers measured general TV viewing rather than viewing of violent programs.

Meta-analysis. A complete description of the techniques of meta-analysis is beyond the scope of this book. For our purposes, meta-analysis is defined as the quantitative aggregation of many research findings and their interpretations. It allows researchers to draw general conclusions from an analysis of many studies that have been conducted concerning a definable research topic. Its goal is to provide a synthesis of an existing body of research. Given the large number of research studies that have been conducted concerning antisocial and prosocial behavior, it is not surprising that the mid- to late-1990s saw the growth in popularity of meta-analytic research in this area. Five examples of meta-analysis are discussed here.

Paik and Comstock (1994) performed a meta-analysis on 217 studies from 1959 to 1990 that tested 1,142 hypotheses. They concluded that the magnitude of the impact of exposure to media violence varied with the method used to study it.

Experiments produced the strongest effects, and time-series studies the weakest. Nonetheless, there was overall a highly significant positive association between exposure to portrayals of violence and antisocial behavior. In addition, they found that males were affected by exposure to media violence only slightly more than females and that violent cartoons and fantasy programs produced the greatest magnitude of effects. The latter finding is at odds with the conventional argument that cartoon violence does not affect viewers because it is unrealistic.

A second meta-analysis on the impact of exposure to pornography and subsequent aggressive behavior was done by Allen, D'Alessio, and Brezgel (1995). They analyzed the results of 30 studies and found that there was indeed a connection between exposure to pornography and subsequent antisocial behavior. More specifically, they noted that exposure to nudity actually decreased aggressive behavior. In contrast, consumption of material depicting nonviolent sexual activity increased aggressive behavior, while exposure to violent sexual activity generated the highest levels of aggression. These findings are in accord with those discussed by Paik and Comstock (1994). A meta-analysis of studies examining exposure to pornography and acceptance of rape myths (Allen, Emmers, Gebhardt, & Geiry, 1995) revealed that experimental studies showed a positive relationship between pornography and rape myth acceptance but nonexperimental studies displayed no such effects.

Friedlander (1993) reported the results of a meta-analysis that compared the magnitude of effects reported by studies that looked at antisocial behavior with those that examined prosocial behavior. He found that, with few exceptions, the effects found for prosocial media messages were larger than the effect found for antisocial messages. Finally, Hogben (1998) looked at the results of 56 analyses from 30 studies and concluded that viewing televised violence was associated with a small increase in viewer aggression. In addition, there was a correlation between the year a study was done and the effect size; the later the study, the greater the effect size, suggesting that prolonged exposure has a greater effect on viewers. Last, justified violence and violence that did not accurately portray the consequence of violence generated greater effect sizes.

Experiments and surveys have been the most popular research strategies used to study the impact of media on antisocial and prosocial behavior. The more elaborate techniques of field experiments and panel studies have been used infrequently. Laboratory experiments have shown a stronger positive relationship between viewing media violence and aggression than have the other techniques. Meta-analyses have offered general conclusions about the scope and magnitude of these effects.

THEORETICAL DEVELOPMENTS

One of the earliest theoretical considerations in the debate on the impact of media violence was the controversy of catharsis versus stimulation. The catharsis approach suggests that viewing fantasy expressions of hostility reduces aggression because a person who watches filmed or televised violence is purged of his or her aggressive urges. This theory has some obvious attraction for industry executives because it implies that presenting violent television shows is a prosocial action. The stimulation theory argues the opposite: Viewing violence prompts more aggression on the part of the viewer. Research findings in this area have indicated little support for the catharsis position. A few studies did find a lessening of aggressive behavior after viewing violent content, but these results apparently were an artifact of the research design. The overwhelming majority of studies found evidence of a stimulation effect.

Since these early studies, many experiments and surveys have used social learning as their conceptual basis. As spelled out by Bandura (1977), the theory explains how people learn from direct experience or from observation (or modeling). Some key elements in this theory are attention, retention, motor reproduction, and motivations. According to Bandura, *attention* to an event is influenced by characteristics of the event and by characteristics of the observer. For example, repeated observation of an event by a person who has been paying close attention should increase learning. *Retention* refers to how well an individual remembers behaviors that have been observed. *Motor reproduction* is the actual behavioral enactment of the observed event. For example, some people can accurately imitate a behavior after merely observing it, but others need to experiment. The *motivational* component of the theory depends on the reinforcement or punishment that accompanies performance of the observed behavior.

Applied to the effects area, social learning theory predicts that people can learn antisocial or prosocial acts by watching films or television. The model further suggests that viewing repeated antisocial acts makes people more likely to perform these acts in real life. Another suggestion is that desensitization accounts for people who are heavily exposed to violence and antisocial acts becoming less anxious about the consequences.

Bandura (1977) summarized much of the research on social learning theory. In brief, some key findings in laboratory and field experiments suggest that children can easily perform new acts of aggression after a single exposure to them on television or in films. The similarity between the circumstances of the observed antisocial acts and the post-observation circumstances is important in determining whether the act is performed.

If a model is positively reinforced for performing antisocial acts, the observed acts are performed more frequently in real life. Likewise, when children are promised rewards for performing antisocial acts, they exhibit more antisocial behavior. Other factors that facilitate the performance of antisocial acts include the degree to which the media behavior is perceived to be real, the emotional arousal of the subjects, and the presence of cues in the post-observation environment that elicit antisocial behavior. Finally, as predicted by the theory, desensitization to violence can occur through repeated exposure to violent acts.

Other research has continued to refine and reformulate some of the elements in social learning theory. For example, the *arousal hypothesis* (Tannenbaum & Zillmann, 1975) suggests that, for a portrayal to have a demonstrable effect, increased arousal may be necessary. According to this model, if an angered person is exposed to an arousing stimulus, such as a pornographic film, and is placed in a situation to which aggression is a possible response, the person will become more aggressive. (*Excitation transfer* is the term used by the researchers.)

Zillmann, Hoyt, and Day (1979) offer some support for this model. It appears that subjects in a high state of arousal after seeing a violent film will perform more prosocial acts than nonaroused subjects. Like aggressive behavior, prosocial behavior seems to be facilitated by media-induced arousal (Mueller, Donnerstein, & Hallam, 1983). Other research has shown that social learning theory can be applied to the study of the effects of viewing pornography.

Zillmann and Bryant (1982) showed that heavy exposure to pornographic films apparently desensitized subjects to the seriousness of rape and led to decreased compassion for women as rape victims. A similar finding was obtained by Linz, Donnerstein, and Penrod (1984). Men who viewed five movies depicting erotic situations involving violence toward women perceived the films as less violent and less degrading to women than did a control group not exposed to the films. In sum, social learning theory is a promising framework for integrating many findings in this area.

Another promising theory, outlined by Berkowitz and Rogers (1986), is based on priming effects analysis. Drawing upon the concepts of cognitive neo-associationism, *priming effects analysis* posits that elements of thought, feeling, or memories are parts of a network connected by associative pathways. When a thought element is activated, the activation spreads along the pathways to other parts of the network. Thus, for some time after a concept is activated, there is an increased probability that it and other associated parts of the network will come to mind again, thus creating the priming effect.

As a result, aggressive ideas prompted by viewing media violence trigger other semantically related thoughts, thereby increasing the probability that associated aggressive thoughts will come to mind. Berkowitz and Rogers note that priming analysis can explain why much exposure to media violence results in short-term, transient effects. They point out that the priming effect attenuates over time to lower the probability of subsequent violent effects.

Van Evra (1990) suggests that "script theory" might also be useful in explaining the impact of viewing TV violence. Since most viewers, particularly younger ones, have little real-life experience with violence but see a lot of it on TV, their behavior patterns or scripts might be influenced by the TV exposure. Those who watch a large amount of violent TV might store these scripts in their memory and display violence when an appropriate stimulus triggers the acting out of their scripts. Moreover, Huesmann and Eron (1986) argue that if a young child learns early in his or her developmental cycle that aggression is a potent problem-solving technique, that behavior will be hard to change because the script has been well rehearsed by the child.

Drawing upon the this information, Comstock and Paik (1991) proposed a three-factor explanation of the influence of media violence on antisocial and aggressive behavior:

1. Violent portrayals that are unique, compelling, and unusual are likely to prompt viewer aggression because of their high attention and arousal.
2. Social cognition theory suggests that repetitive and redundant portrayals of violence prompt viewers to develop expectations and perceptions of violence.
3. Violent media content encourages the early acquisition of stable and enduring traits. Children who are only 3 or 4 years old may learn some violent scripts.

More recently, Sander (1997) proposed a new theoretical approach, the dynamic transaction model, to explain how viewers perceive violence. The model posits that a person's reaction to media violence is a function of the precise form of the media stimulus and the interpretive ability of the receiver. A quasi-experimental study of viewers revealed that audience members and researchers perceive violence differently and that specific content variables (physical vs. psychological violence, serious vs. comic violence, real vs. fantasy violence, and so on) have the greatest influence on perceptions, followed by the emotional state of the receiver while watching violence. Krcmar's (1998) study suggested that family communication patterns are also important in determining how children perceive violence. These last two studies support the idea that perceptions of violence may be a key concept in formulating theories about the impact of this kind of material.

USES AND GRATIFICATIONS

The uses and gratifications perspective takes the view of the media consumer. It examines how people use the media and the gratifications they seek and receive from their media behaviors. Uses and gratifications researchers assume that audience members are aware of and can articulate their reasons for consuming various media content. The uses and gratifications approach has its roots in the 1940s, when researchers became interested in why people engaged in various forms of media behavior, such as radio listening or newspaper reading.

These early studies were primarily descriptive, seeking to classify the responses of audience members into meaningful categories. For example, Herzog (1944) identified three types of gratification associated with listening to radio soap operas: emotional release, wishful thinking, and obtaining advice. Berelson (1949) took advantage of a New York newspaper strike to ask people why they read the paper.

The responses fell into five major categories: reading for information, reading for social prestige, reading for escape, reading as a tool for daily living, and reading for a social context. These early studies had little theoretical coherence; in fact, many were inspired by the practical needs of newspaper publishers and radio broadcasters to know the motivations of their audience in order to serve them more efficiently.

The next step in the development of this research began during the late 1950s and continued into the 1960s. In this phase, the emphasis was on identifying and operationalizing the many social and psychological variables that were presumed to be the antecedents of different patterns of consumption and gratification. For example, Schramm, Lyle, and Parker (1961), in their extensive study, found that children's use of television was influenced by individual mental ability and relationships with parents and peers, among other things. Gerson (1966) concluded that race was important in predicting how adolescents used the media. These studies and many more conducted during this period reflected a shift from the traditional effects model of mass media research to the functional perspective.

According to Windahl (1981), a primary difference between the traditional effects approach and the uses and gratifications approach is that a media effects researcher usually examines mass communication from the perspective of the communicator, whereas the uses and gratifications researcher uses the audience member as a point of departure. Windahl argues for a synthesis of the two approaches, believing that it is more beneficial to emphasize their similarities than to stress their differences. He has coined the term *conseffects* of media content and use to categorize observations that are partly results of content use in itself (a viewpoint commonly adopted by effects researchers) and partly results of content mediated by use (a viewpoint adopted by many uses and gratifications researchers).

Windahl's perspective links the earlier uses and gratifications approach to the third phase in its development. Recently, uses and gratifications research has become more conceptual and theoretical as investigators have offered data to explain the connections between audience motives, media gratifications, and outcomes. As Rubin (1985, p. 210) notes: "Several typologies of mass media motives and functions have been formulated to conceptualize the seeking of gratifications as variables that intervene before media effects." For example, Rubin (1979) found a significant positive correlation between the viewing of television to learn something and the perceived reality of television content: Those who used television as a learning device thought television content was more true to life. DeBock (1980) notes that people who experienced the most frustration at being deprived of a newspaper during a strike were those who used the newspaper for information and those who viewed newspaper reading as a ritual. These and many other recent studies have revealed that a variety of audience gratifications are related to a wide range of media effects. These "uses and effects" studies (Rubin, 1985) have bridged the gap between the traditional effects approach and the uses and gratifications perspective.

In the last several years, the uses and gratifications approach has been used to explore the impact of new technologies on the audience. For example, Lin (1993) posited that audience activity (planning viewing, discussing content, remembering the program) would be an important intervening variable in the gratification-seeking process because of the viewing options opened up by cable, VCRs, and remote controls. Her results supported her hypothesis. Viewers who were most active had a greater expectation of gratification and also reported obtaining greater satisfaction.

Albarran and Dimmick (1993) combined the uses and gratifications approach with niche theory in their study of the utility of the video entertainment industries. They found that broadcast TV was the most diverse in serving the cognitive gratifications of the audience, whereas cable TV and the VCR were the most effective in meeting needs related to feeling and emotional states. The advent of the Internet has spurred a renaissance in uses and gratifications research as investigators describe Internet motivations and compare and contrast their results with the uses and gratifications from traditional media.

To illustrate, Valkenburg and Soeters (2001) found that Internet use among their sample of 8- to 13-year-olds was most related to an enjoyment of using computers and finding information.

Ferguson and Perse (2000) examined the World Wide Web as a functional alternative to TV and discovered that many of the motivations for using the web were similar to those for viewing television. Finally, Papacharissi and Rubin (2000) came up with a set of five motivations for using the Internet: utility, passing time, seeking information, convenience, and entertainment.

Methods

Uses and gratifications researchers have relied heavily on the survey method to collect their data. As a first step, researchers have conducted focus groups or have asked respondents to write essays about their reasons for media consumption.

Closed-ended Likert-type scales are then constructed based on what was said in the focus group or written in the essays. The closed-ended measures are typically subjected to multivariate statistical techniques such as factor analysis, which identifies various dimensions of gratifications. For example, in their study of the uses and gratifications of VCRs, Rubin and Bantz (1989) first asked selected groups of respondents to list 10 ways in which they used their VCRs and to provide reasons for those uses. This procedure resulted in a list of categories and statements describing VCR usage.

A questionnaire was then developed from this master list and administered to respondents, who were asked to indicate how frequently they used their VCRs for these purposes and to rate how much importance they placed on the statements detailing the reasons for usage. After revisions, a final questionnaire was developed; it contained 95 motivational statements. This questionnaire was administered to a sample of 424 VCR owners.

Through factor analysis, the 95 statements were then reduced to eight main motivational categories. These are some examples of the factors and statements that went with them: "I want to keep a permanent copy of the program" (library storage); "I use music video for parties" (music videos); "I don't have to join an exercise class" (exercise tapes).

Rubin and Bantz then correlated these factors with demographic and media exposure variables. Note that this technique assumes that the audience is aware of its reasons and can report them when asked.

The method also assumes that the pencil-and-paper test is a valid and reliable measurement scale. Other assumptions include an active audience with goal-directed media behavior; expectations for media use that are produced from individual predispositions, social interaction, and environmental factors; and media selection initiated by the individual. The experimental method has not been used widely in uses and gratifications research. When it has been chosen, investigators typically manipulated the subjects' motivations and measured differences in their media consumption.

To illustrate, Bryant and Zillmann (1984) placed their subjects in either a state of boredom or a state of stress and then gave them a choice of watching a relaxing or a stimulating television program.

Stressed subjects watched more tranquil programs, and bored subjects opted for the exciting fare. McLeod and Becker (1981) had their subjects sit in a lounge that contained public affairs magazines.

One group of subjects was told that they would soon be tested about the current situation in Pakistan; a second group was told they would be required to write an essay on U.S. military aid to Pakistan; while a control group was given no specific instructions. As expected, subjects in the test and essay conditions made greater use of the magazines than did the control group. The two test groups also differed in the type of information they remembered from the periodicals. Experiments such as these two indicate that different cognitive or affective states facilitate the use of media for various reasons, as predicted by the uses and gratifications rationale.

MEDIA EFFECTS RESEARCH: WHETHER THE WEATHER MAKES A DIFFERENCE

Uses and gratifications research has shed a good deal of light on viewer motivations for watching TV, but the approach has not been particularly successful in predicting the actual amount of television use. Roe and Vandebosch (1996) suggest that one reason for the inability to predict is that researchers sometimes overlook the obvious—such as the weather.

Seasonal variations in TV viewing are well documented: People watch more in the winter and less in the summer. Roe and Vandebosch, however, suggest that specific weather effects occur with each season.

The researchers gathered detailed meteorological data in Belgium for a year, including temperature, precipitation amount, wind speed, cloud cover, barometric pressure, and hours of sunlight. They also collected television-viewing statistics encompassing the percentage viewing and the daily average amount of time spent watching.

Their results showed strong correlations between all their weather-related measures, except for barometric pressure, and viewing with some correlations reaching as high as .75. Furthermore, there was consistency within each individual season. People watched more TV when there were fewer hours of daylight, when the temperature was low, when wind speed was high, and when there was some precipitation.

The implication in this finding for broadcasters was clear. The single most important determiner of TV audience size was wholly beyond their control.

Theoretical Developments

As mentioned earlier, researchers in the academic sector are interested in developing theory concerning the topics they investigate. This tendency is well illustrated in the history of uses and gratifications research. Whereas early studies tended to be descriptive, later scholars have attempted to integrate research findings into a more theoretical context.

In an early explanation of the uses and gratifications process, Rosengren (1974) suggested that certain basic needs interact with personal characteristics and the social environment of the individual to produce perceived problems and perceived solutions.

The problems and solutions constitute different motives for gratification behavior that can come from using the media or from other activities.

Together the media use or other behaviors produce gratification (or nongratification) that has an impact on the individual or society, thereby starting the process anew. After reviewing the results of approximately 100 uses and gratifications studies, Palmgreen (1984) stated that "a rather complex theoretical structure . . . has begun to emerge." He proposed an integrative gratifications model that suggested a multivariate approach.

The gratifications sought by the audience form the central concept in the model. There are, however, many antecedent variables such as media structure, media technology, social circumstances, psychological variables, needs, values, and beliefs that all relate to the particular gratification pattern used by the audience.

Additionally, the consequences of the gratifications relate directly to media and nonmedia consumption behaviors and the perceived gratifications that are obtained. As Palmgreen admits, this model suffers from lack of parsimony and needs strengthening in several areas, but it does represent an increase in our understanding of the mass media process.

Further refinements in the model will come from surveys and experiments designed to test specific hypotheses derived from well-articulated theoretical rationales and from carefully designed descriptive studies. For example, Levy and Windahl (1984) examined the assumption of an active audience in the uses and gratifications approach. They derived a typology of audience activity and prepared a model that linked activity to various uses and gratifications, thus further clarifying one important postulate in the uses and gratifications process. Swanson (1987) called for more research to encourage the theoretical grounding of the uses and gratifications approach.

Specifically, Swanson urged that research focus on (1) the role of gratification seeking in exposure to mass media, (2) the relationship between gratification and the interpretive frames through which audiences understand media content, and (3) the link between gratifications and media content.

Van Evra (1990) presents an integrated theoretical model of television's impact in which the use of the medium is considered along with the amount of viewing, presence of information alternatives, and perceived reality of the medium. Her description highlights the complex interactions that need to be examined in order to understand the viewing process.

Additionally, uses and gratifications researchers have incorporated a theory from social psychology, expectancy-value theory, into their formulations (Babrow, 1989). This theory suggests that audience attitude toward media behavior is an important factor in media use.

Rubin (1994) summarized the growth of theory in the area and concludes that single-variable explanations of media effects are inadequate.

He suggests that more attention be given to antecedent, mediating, and consequent exposure conditions. Finn (1997) investigated a five-factor personality model as a correlate of mass media use. He found that people who scored high on the extroversion and agreeableness dimensions of a personality measure were more likely to choose nonmedia activities (such as conversation) to meet their communication needs.

In a comprehensive review of the theoretical developments relevant to uses and gratifications theory, Ruggiero (2000) argues that researchers must expand the uses and gratifications model to accommodate the unique features of the Internet such as interactivity and demassification. He also contends that the growing popularity of the Internet will make the uses and gratifications approach even more valuable in the future.

The uses and gratifications approach also illustrates the difference in emphasis between academic and applied research objectives. Newspaper publishers and broadcasting executives, who want guidance in attracting readers, viewers, and listeners, seem to be particularly interested in determining what specific content is best suited to meeting the needs of the audience.

College and university researchers are interested not only in understanding content characteristics but also in developing theories that explain and predict the public's media consumption based on sociological, psychological, and structural variables.

8

Basic Media Tools

The notion of agenda setting by the media can be traced back to Walter Lippmann (1922), who suggested that the media were responsible for the "pictures in our heads." Forty years later, Cohen (1963) further articulated the idea when he argued that the media may not always be successful in telling people what to think, but they are usually successful in telling them what to think about. Lang and Lang (1966, p. 468) reinforced this notion by observing, "The mass media force attention to certain issues. . . . They are constantly presenting objects, suggesting what individuals in the mass should think about, know about, have feelings about."

The first empirical test of agenda setting came in 1972 when McCombs and Shaw (1972) reported the results of a study done during the 1968 presidential election. They found strong support for the agenda-setting hypothesis. There were strong relationships between the emphasis placed on different campaign issues by the media and the judgments of voters regarding the importance of various campaign topics. This study inspired a host of others, many of them concerned with agenda setting as it occurred during political campaigns. For example, Tipton, Haney, and Baseheart (1975) used cross-lagged correlation to analyze the impact of the media on agenda setting during statewide elections.

Patterson and McClure (1976) studied the impact of television news and television commercials on agenda setting in the 1972 election. They concluded that television news had minimal impact on public awareness of issues but that television campaign advertising accounted for increased audience awareness of candidates' positions on issues.

Agenda setting continued to be a popular research topic through the 1980s and 1990s. Its focus has expanded from looking at political campaigns to examining other topics. The agenda-setting technique is now being used in a variety of areas: history, advertising, foreign news, and medical news. McCombs (1994) and Wanta (1997) present useful summaries of this topic.

In recent years the most popular subjects in agenda-setting research are (1) how the media agenda is set (this research is also called *agenda building*), and (2) how the media choose to portray the issues they cover (called framing analysis). With regard to agenda building, Wanta, Stephenson, Turk, and McCombs (1989) noted some correlation between issues raised in the president's State of the Union address and the media coverage of those issues. Similarly, Wanta (1991) discovered that the president can have an impact on the media agenda, particularly when presidential approval ratings are high. Boyle (2001) found that major party candidate political ads can have an influence on media coverage of a campaign. Reese (1990) presents a review of the agenda-building research.

Framing analysis recognizes that media can impart a certain perspective, or "spin," to the events they cover and that this, in turn, might influence public attitudes on an issue. Framing analysis has been called the second level of agenda setting. As Ghanem (1997, p. 3) put it:

> Agenda setting is now detailing a second level of effects that examines how media coverage affects both what the public thinks about and how the public thinks about it. This second level of agenda setting deals with the specific attributes of a topic and how this agenda of attributes also influences public opinion.

For example, Iyengar and Simon (1993) found a framing effect in their study of news coverage of the Gulf War. Respondents who relied the most on television news, where military developments were emphasized, expressed greater support for a military rather than a diplomatic solution to the crisis. In their study of the way media framed breast cancer coverage in the 1990s, Andsager and Powers (1999) discovered that women's magazines offered more personal stories and more comprehensive information, while news magazines focused more on the economic angle, stressing research funding and insurance. Finally, Andsager (2000) analyzed the attempts by interest groups to frame the abortion debate of the late 1990s and the impact their efforts had with news media. She found that the pro-life group was more successful in getting their interpretation into press coverage.

METHODS

The typical agenda-setting study involves several of the approaches discussed in earlier chapters. Content analysis is used to define the media agenda, and surveys are used to collect data on the audience agenda. In addition, since determining the media agenda and surveying the audience are not done simultaneously, a longitudinal dimension is present. More recently, some studies have used the experimental approach.

Measuring the Media Agenda. Several techniques have been used to establish the media agenda. The most common method involves grouping coverage topics into broad categories and measuring the amount of time or space devoted to each category. The operational definitions of these categories are important because the more broadly a topic area is defined, the easier it is to demonstrate an agenda-setting effect. Ideally, the content analysis should include all media: television, radio, newspaper, and magazines. Unfortunately, this is too large a task for most researchers to handle comfortably, and most studies have been confined to one or two media, usually television and the daily newspaper. For example, Williams and Semlak (1978) tabulated the total air time for each topic mentioned in the three television network newscasts over a 19-day period. The topics were rank-ordered according to their total time. At the same time, the newspaper agenda was constructed by measuring the total column inches devoted to each topic on the front and editorial pages of the local newspaper. McLeod, Becker, and Byrnes (1974) content-analyzed local newspapers for a 6-week period, totaling the number of inches devoted to each topic, including headlines and pertinent pictures on the front and editorial pages. Among other things, they found that the front and editorial pages adequately represented the entire newspaper in their topical areas.

The development of new technologies has created problems for researchers when it comes to measuring the media agenda. Cable TV, fax machines, email, online computer services, and the Internet have greatly expanded the information outlets available to the public. The role of these new channels of communication in agenda setting is still unclear.

Measuring Public Agendas. The public agenda has been measured in at least four ways. First, respondents are asked an open-ended question such as "What do you feel is the most important political issue to you personally?" or "What is the most important political issue in your community?" The phrasing of this question can elicit either the respondent's intrapersonal agenda (as in the first example) or interpersonal agenda (the second example).

A second method asks respondents to rate in importance the issues in a list compiled by the researcher. The third technique is a variation of this approach. Respondents are given a list of topics selected by the researcher and asked to rank-order them according to perceived importance. The fourth technique uses the paired-comparisons method. Each issue on a preselected list is paired with every other issue, and the respondent is asked to consider each pair and to identify the more important issue. When all the responses have been tabulated, the issues are ordered from the most important to the least important.

As with all measurement, each technique has its own advantages and disadvantages. The open-ended method gives respondents great freedom in nominating issues, but it favors those people who are better able to verbalize their thoughts. The closed-ended ranking and rating techniques make sure that all respondents have a common vocabulary, but they assume that each respondent is aware of all the public issues listed and restrict the respondent from expressing a personal point of view. The paired-comparisons method provides interval data, which allows for more sophisticated statistical techniques, but it takes longer to complete than the other methods, and this might be a problem in some forms of survey research.

Three important periods used in collecting the data for agenda-setting research are (1) the duration of the media agenda measurement period, (2) the time lag between measuring the media agenda and measuring the personal agenda, and (3) the duration of the audience agenda measurement. Unfortunately, there is little in the way of research or theory to guide the investigator in this area. To illustrate, Mullins (1977) studied media content for a week to determine the media agenda, but Gormley (1975) gathered media data for 4.5 months. Similarly, the time lag between media agenda measurement and audience agenda measurement has varied from no time at all (McLeod et al., 1974) to a lag of 5 months (Gormley, 1975). Wanta and Hu (1994a) discovered that different media have different optimum time lags. Television, for example, has a more immediate impact, whereas newspapers are more effective in the long term.

It is not surprising that the duration of the measurement period for audience agendas has also varied widely. Hilker (1976) collected a public agenda measure in a single day, whereas McLeod and colleagues (1974) took 4 weeks. Eyal, Winter, and DeGeorge (1981) suggested that methodological studies should be carried out to determine the optimal effect span or peak association period between the media emphasis and public emphasis. Winter and Eyal (1981), in an example of one of these methodological studies, found an optimal effect span of 6 weeks for agenda setting on the civil rights issue. Similarly, Salwen (1988) found that it took from 5 to 7 weeks of news media coverage of environmental issues before they became salient on the public's agenda.

In a large-scale agenda-setting study of German television, Brosius and Kepplinger (1990) found that the nature of the issue had an impact on the time lag necessary to demonstrate an effect. For general issues such as environmental protection, a lag of a year or two might be appropriate. For issues raised in political campaigns, 4 to 6 weeks might be the appropriate lag. For a breaking event within an issue, such as the Chernobyl disaster, a lag of a week might be sufficient.

Agenda-setting researchers are now incorporating more complicated longitudinal analysis measures into their designs. Gonzenbach and McGavin (1997) for example, present descriptions of time series analysis and time series modeling and a discussion of nonlinear analysis techniques.

Several researchers have used the experimental technique to study the causal direction in agenda setting. For example, Heeter, Brown, Soffin, Stanley, & Salwen (1989) examined the agenda-setting effect of teletext. One group of subjects was instructed to abstain from all traditional news media for five consecutive days and instead spend 30 minutes each day with a teletext news service. The results indicated that a week's worth of exposure did little to alter subjects' agendas. The experimental method has also been employed to measure the impact of different message frames. Valentino, Buhr, and Beckmann (2001) manipulated the frame of a news story about a politician by creating one version in which an elected official's policy decision was represented as a sincere choice to benefit constituents and another version in which the same decision was represented as a selfish effort to win votes in the next election. The frame that emphasized the vote-getting effort produced more negative reactions than did the sincere choice interpretation.

THEORETICAL DEVELOPMENTS

The theory of agenda setting is still at a formative level. In spite of the problems in method and time span mentioned earlier, the findings in agenda setting are consistent enough to permit some first steps toward theory building. To begin, longitudinal studies of agenda setting have permitted some tentative causal statements. Most of this research has supported the interpretation that the media's agenda causes the public agenda; the rival causal hypothesis—that the public agenda establishes the media agenda—has not received much support (Behr & Iyengar, 1985; Roberts & Bachen, 1981). Thus, much of the recent research has attempted to specify the audience-related and media-related events that condition the agenda-setting effect.

It is apparent that constructing an agenda-setting theory will be a complicated task. Williams (1986), for example, posited eight antecedent variables that should have an impact on audience agendas during a political campaign. Four of these variables (voter interest, voter activity, political involvement, and civic activity) have been linked to agenda setting (Williams & Semlak, 1978). In addition, several studies have suggested that a person's "need for orientation" should be a predictor of agenda holding. (Note that such an approach incorporates uses and gratifications thinking.) For example, Weaver (1977) found a positive correlation between the need for orientation and a greater acceptance of media agendas.

These antecedent variables define the media-scanning behavior of the individual (McCombs, 1981). Important variables at this stage of the process are the use of media and the use of interpersonal communication (Winter, 1981). Other influences on the individual's agenda-setting behavior are the duration and obtrusiveness of the issues themselves and the specifics of media coverage (Winter, 1981). Three other audience attributes that are influential are the credibility given to the news media, the degree to which the audience member relies on the media for information, and the level of exposure to the media (Wanta & Hu, 1994b).

Despite the tentative nature of the theory, many researchers continue to develop models of the agenda-setting process. Manheim (1987), for example, developed a model of agenda setting that distinguished between content and salience of issues.

Brosius and Kepplinger (1990) used time series analysis in their study of German news programs to test both a linear model and a nonlinear model of agenda setting. The linear model assumes a direct correlation between coverage and issue importance; an increase or decrease in coverage results in a corresponding change in issue salience. Four nonlinear models were also examined:

(1) the threshold model—some minimum level of coverage is required before the agenda-setting effect is seen;

(2) the acceleration model—issue salience increases or decreases to a greater degree than coverage;

(3) the inertia model—issue importance increases or decreases to a lesser degree than coverage; and

(4) the echo model—extremely heavy media coverage prompts the agenda-setting effect long after coverage recedes.

Their data showed that the nature of the issue under study was related to the model that best described the results. The acceleration model worked better for issues that were considered subjectively important by the audience (taxes) and for new issues. The linear model seemed to work better with enduring issues (the environment). Some support was also found for the threshold model. There was, however, little support for the inertia model, and not enough data were available for a convincing test of the echo model. In sum, these data suggest an agenda-setting process more complicated than that envisioned by the simple linear model.

CULTIVATION OF PERCEPTIONS OF SOCIAL REALITY

How do the media affect audience perceptions of the real world? The basic assumption underlying the cultivation, or enculturation, approach is that repeated exposures to consistent media portrayals and themes influence our perceptions of these items in the direction of the media portrayals. In effect, learning from the media environment is generalized, sometimes incorrectly, to the social environment.

As was the case with agenda-setting research, most of the enculturation research has been conducted by investigators in the academic sector. Industry researchers are aware of this work and sometimes question its accuracy or meaning (Wurtzel & Lometti, 1984), but they seldom conduct it or sponsor it themselves.

Some early research studies indicated that media portrayals of certain topics could have an impact on audience perceptions, particularly if the media were the main information sources. Siegel (1958) found that children's role expectations about a taxi driver could be influenced by hearing a radio program about the character. DeFleur and DeFleur (1967) found that television had a homogenizing effect on children's perceptions of occupations commonly shown on television.

The more recent research on viewer perceptions of social reality stems from the Cultural Indicators project of George Gerbner and his associates (1968). Since 1968, they have collected data on the content of television and have analyzed the impact of heavy exposure on the audience. Some of the many variables that have been content analyzed are the demographic portraits of perpetrators and victims of television violence, the prevalence of violent acts, the types of violence portrayed, and the contexts of violence. The basic hypothesis of cultivation analysis is that the more time one spends living in the world of television, the more likely one is to report conceptions of social reality that can be traced to television portrayals (Gross & Morgan, 1985).

To test this hypothesis, Gerbner and his associates have analyzed data from adults, adolescents, and children in cities across the United States. The first cultivation data were reported more than two decades ago (Gerbner & Gross, 1976). Using data collected by the National Opinion Research Center (NORC), Gerbner found that heavy television viewers scored higher on a "mean world" index than did light viewers. [Sample items from this index are "Do you think people try to take advantage of you?" and "You can't be too careful in dealing with people (agree/disagree)."] Data from both adult and child NORC samples showed that heavy viewers were more suspicious and distrustful. Subsequent studies reinforced these findings and found that heavy television viewers were more likely to overestimate the prevalence of violence in society and their own chances of being involved in violence (Gerbner, Gross, Jackson-Beeck, Jeffries-Fox, & Signorielli, 1978). In sum, their perceptions of reality were cultivated by television.

Not all researchers have accepted the cultivation hypothesis. In particular, Hughes (1980) and Hirsch (1980) reanalyzed the NORC data using simultaneous rather than individual controls for demographic variables, and they were unable to replicate Gerbner's findings. Gerbner responded by introducing resonance and mainstreaming, two new concepts to help explain inconsistencies in the results (Gerbner, Gross, Morgan, & Signorielli, 1986). When the media reinforce what is seen in real life, thus giving an audience member a "double dose," the resulting increase in the cultivation effect is attributed to resonance. Mainstreaming is a leveling effect.

Heavy viewing, resulting in a common viewpoint, washes out differences in perceptions of reality usually caused by demographic and social factors. These concepts refine and further elaborate the cultivation hypothesis, but they have not satisfied all the critics of this approach. Condry (1989) presents a comprehensive review of the cultivation analysis literature and of cultivation analysis and an insightful evaluation of the criticisms directed against it. Shanahan and Morgan (1999) also present a comprehensive review of cultivation research.

Additional research on the cultivation hypothesis indicates that the topic may be more complicated than first thought. There is evidence that cultivation may be less dependent on the total amount of TV viewing than on the specific types of programs viewed (O'Keefe & Reid-Nash, 1987).

Weaver and Wakshlag (1986) found that the cultivation effect was more pronounced among active TV viewers than among low-involvement viewers and that personal experience with crime was an important mediating variable that affected the impact of TV programs on cultivating an attitude of vulnerability toward crime. Additionally, Potter (1986) found that the perceived reality of the TV content had an impact on cultivation. Other research (Rubin, Perse, & Taylor, 1988) demonstrated that the wording of the attitude and the perceptual questions used to measure cultivation influenced the results.

Potter (1988) found that variables such as identification with TV characters, anomie, IQ, and informational needs of the viewer had differential effects on cultivation. In other words, different people react in different ways to TV content, and these different reactions determine the strength of the cultivation effect. More recently, there have been three key trends in cultivation research. The first is expanding the focus of cultivation into other countries and cultures. *Cultivation Analysis: New Directions in Media Effects Research* (Signorielli & Morgan, 1990) contains chapters on research done in Britain, Sweden, Asia, and Latin America.

The results regarding the cultivation effect were mixed. The second trend, discussed in more detail in the next section, is a closer examination of the measurements used in cultivation. Results suggest that the way TV viewing is quantified and the way the cultivation questions are framed all have an impact on the results. The final trend concerns the conceptual mechanisms that result in the occurrence of the cultivation effect and are discussed in the Theoretical Developments section, immediately following the Methods section.

AN INSIDE LOOK

Cultivating the Paranormal

Many television programs focus on the paranormal—*The X-Files, Unsolved Mysteries, Sightings,* and more. Could heavy viewing of these programs have a cultivation effect? This general question was examined by Sparks, Nelson, and Campbell (1997) in a survey of 120 residents of a Midwestern city. Respondents were asked to estimate the total amount of time they spent watching TV and how often they had seen specific programs that featured paranormal content.

The researchers next developed a 20-item scale to assess respondents' belief in paranormal activities, including UFOs, ESP, ghosts, palm reading, telekinesis, and astrology. This scale was factor- analyzed to yield two distinct elements: belief in supernatural beings and belief in psychic energy The researchers also asked respondents to report whether they had had any paranormal experiences. TV viewing was then correlated with the measures of belief in the paranormal.

The total number of hours of TV viewing was not related to either of the paranormal belief factors. Exposure to paranormal TV shows showed no correlation with belief in psychic energy. There was a significant relationship, however, between paranormal TV show viewing and belief in supernatural beings among those who had some prior experience with paranormal events. This relationship persisted even after controlling for several demographic variables. The authors suggest that this finding should have implications for journalists and program producers of content related to paranormal themes.

Methods

There are two discrete steps in performing a cultivation analysis. First, descriptions of the media world are obtained from periodic content analyses of large blocks of media content.

The result of this content analysis is the identification of the messages of the television world. These messages represent consistent patterns in the portrayal of specific issues, policies, and topics that are often at odds with their occurrence in real life. The identification of the consistent portrayals is followed by the construction of a set of questions designed to detect a cultivation effect. Each question poses two or more alternatives. One alternative is more consistent with the world as seen on television, while another is more in line with the real world. For example, according to the content analyses performed by Gerbner and colleagues (1977), strangers commit about 60% of television homicides. In real life, according to government statistics, only 16% of homicides occur between strangers. The question based on this discrepancy was, "Does fatal violence occur between strangers or between relatives and acquaintances?" The response "strangers" was considered the television answer. Another question was, "What percentage of all males who have jobs work in law enforcement and crime detection? Is it 1% or 5%?" According to census data, 1% of men in real life have such jobs, compared with 12% in television programs. Thus, 5% is the television answer.

Condry (1989) points out that the cultivation impact seems to depend upon whether respondents are making judgments about society or about themselves. Societal-level judgments, such as the examples just given, seem to be more influenced by the cultivation effect, but personal judgments (such as "What is the likelihood that you will be involved in a violent crime?") seem to be harder to influence. In a related study, Sparks and Ogles (1990) demonstrated a cultivation effect when respondents were asked about their fear of crime but not when they were asked to give their personal rating of their chances of being victimized. Measures of these two concepts were not related. Related findings were reported by Shanahan, Morgan, and Stenbjerre (1997), who found that TV viewing was associated with a general state of fear about the state of the environment but not related to viewers' perceptions of specific sources of environmental threats.

The second step involves surveying audiences about their television exposure, dividing the sample into heavy and light viewers (4 hours of viewing a day is usually the dividing line), and comparing their answers to the questions that differentiate the television world from the real world. In addition, data are often collected on possible control variables such as gender, age, and socioeconomic status. The basic statistical procedure consists of correlational analysis between the amount of television viewing and the scores on an index reflecting the number of television answers to the comparison questions. Also, partial correlation is used to remove the effects of the control variables. Alternatively, sometimes the *cultivation differential* (CD) is reported. The CD is the percentage of heavy viewers minus the percentage of light viewers who gave the television answers. For example, if 73% of the heavy viewers gave the television answer to the question about violence being committed between strangers or acquaintances compared to 62% of the light viewers, the CD would be 11%. Laboratory experiments use the same general approach, but they usually manipulate the subjects' experience with the television world by showing an experimental group one or more preselected programs.

Measurement decisions can have a significant impact on cultivation findings. Potter and Chang (1990) gauged TV viewing using five different techniques: (1) total exposure (the traditional way used in cultivation analysis); (2) exposure to different types of television programs; (3) exposure to program types while controlling for total exposure; (4) measure of the proportion of each program type viewed, obtained by dividing the time spent per type of program by the total time spent viewing; and (5) a weighted proportion calculated by multiplying hours viewed per week by the proportional measure mentioned in the fourth technique.

The results showed that total viewing time was not a strong predictor of cultivation scores. The proportional measure proved to be the best indicator of cultivation. This suggests that a person who watches 20 hours of TV per week, with all of the hours being crime shows, will score higher on cultivation measures of fear of crime than a person who watches 80 hours of TV a week with 20 of them consisting of crime shows. The data also showed that all of the alternative measures were better than a simple measure of total TV viewing.

Potter (1991a) demonstrated that deciding where to put the dividing point between heavy viewers and light viewers is a critical choice that can influence the results of a cultivation analysis. He showed that the cultivation effect may not be linear, as typically assumed. This finding may explain why cultivation effects in general are small in magnitude; simply dividing viewers into heavy and light categories cancels many differences among subgroups. Diefenbach and West (2001) offer another insight into possible ways of measuring the cultivation effect. In their study of the cultivation effect, they found no relationship between TV viewing and estimates of murder and burglary rates in society when using the traditional regression model. However, when they used a different form of regression analysis, one based on non-normally distributed dependent variables, they detected a cultivation effect.

Theoretical Developments

What does the research tell us about cultivation? After an extensive literature review in which they examined 48 studies, Hawkins and Pingree (1981) concluded that there was evidence for a link between viewing and beliefs regardless of the kind of social reality in question. Was this link real or spurious? The authors concluded that the answer did, in fact, depend on the type of belief under study. Relationships between viewing and demographic aspects of social reality held up under rigorous controls. As far as causality was concerned, the authors concluded that most of the evidence went in one direction—namely, that television causes social reality to be interpreted in certain ways. Twelve years later, Shrum and O'Guinn (1993) echoed the earlier conclusion by saying that cultivation research has demonstrated a modest but persistent effect of television viewing on what people believe the social world is like. More recently, Morgan and Shanahan (1997) performed a meta-analysis of 82 published cultivation studies and concluded that there is a small but reliable and pervasive cultivation effect that accounts for about 1% of the variance in people's perceptions of the world. The authors argue that although the effect is small, it is not socially insignificant.

How does this process take place? The most recent publications in this area have focused on conceptual models that explain the cognitive processes that cause cultivation. Potter (1993) presents an extensive critique of the original cultivation formulation and offers several suggestions for future research, including developing a typology of effects and providing a long-term analysis. Van Evra (1990) posits a multivariate model of cultivation, taking into account the use to which the viewing is put (information or diversion), the perceived reality of the content, the number of information alternatives available, and the amount of viewing. She suggests that maximum cultivation occurs among heavy viewers who watch for information, believe the content to be real, and have few alternative sources of information. Potter (1991b) proposes a psychological model of cultivation incorporating the concepts of learning, construction, and generalization. He suggests that cultivation theory needs to be extended and revamped in order to explain how the effect operates.

Tapper (1995) presents a possible conceptual model of the cultivation process that is divided into two phases. Phase one deals with content acquisition and takes into account such variables as motives for viewing, selective viewing, the type of genre viewed, and perceptions of the reality of the content. Phase two is the storage phase and elaborates those constructs that might affect long-term memory. Tapper's model allows for various cultivation effects to be examined according to a person's viewing and storage strategies. Shrum and O'Guinn (1993) present a psychological model of the cultivation process based on the notion of accessibility of information in a person's memory. They posit that human memory works much like a storage bin. When new information is acquired, a copy of that new information is placed on top of the appropriate bin. Later, when information is being retrieved for decision making, the contents of the bin are searched from the top down. Thus, information deposited most recently and most frequently stands a better chance of being recalled.

A person who watches many TV crime shows, for example, might store many exaggerated portrayals of crime and violence in the appropriate bin. When asked to make a judgment about the frequency of real-life crime, the TV images are the most accessible, and the person might base his or her judgment of social reality on them. Shrum and O'Guinn reported the results of an empirical test of this notion. They reasoned that the faster a person is able to make a response, the more accessible is the retrieved information. Consequently, when confronted with a social reality judgment, heavy TV viewers should be able to make judgments faster than light viewers, and their judgments should also demonstrate a cultivation effect. The results of Shrum and O'Guinn's experiment supported this reasoning. Shrum (1996) reported a study that replicated these findings. In this experiment, subjects who were heavier viewers of soap operas were more likely to show a cultivation effect and responded faster to the various cultivation questions that were asked of them.

The same author (Shrum, 2001) presents evidence that the cognitive information-processing strategy employed by the viewer has an impact on cultivation. Specifically, when subjects were asked to respond to questions about estimates of crime and occupations spontaneously, a cultivation effect was found. On the other hand, when subjects were asked to think systematically about their answers, the cultivation effect was not found. Shrum argues that those who thought systematically were more likely to discount TV as a source of their information and rely on other sources, thus negating a cultivation effect.

In sum, cultivation has proven to be an evocative and heuristic notion. It is likely that future research will concentrate on identifying key variables important to the process and on specifying the psychological processes that underlie the process.

Social Impact of the Internet

Mass media research follows a typical pattern when a new medium develops. Phase 1 concerns an interest in the medium itself: the technology used, functions, access, cost. Phase 2 deals with the users of the medium: who they are, why they use it, what other media it displaces. Phase 3 pertains to the social, psychological, and physical effects of the medium, particularly any harmful effects. Finally, Phase 4 involves research about how the medium can be improved. The Internet is such a recent development that this section departs from the organizational structure we used earlier. It is too early to write the history of Internet research or to talk about theoretical developments. The methods used to study the net are those discussed earlier in this book: surveys, content analysis, and the occasional experiment. Moreover, new research methods that use the unique resources of the Internet will continue to emerge. Consequently, this section divides the research into relevant topic categories.

Audience Characteristics

According to the 2000 Census, about 44 million U.S. households (about 42% of all households) had at least one member online. About 95 million people used the Internet in 2000, up from 57 million in 1998.

By the beginning of 2005, the demographic profile of the average Internet user was similar to that of the average American. According to *Nielsen//NetRatings* data, 52% of online users were women, a percentage that almost exactly mirrors that of the general population. In addition, the average household income of the online population was only slightly higher than that of the U.S. population. The Internet population was still generally younger, with 76% of the online users between 18 and 49, compared to 63% in the general population. Older Americans, however, were among the fastest-growing age category of Internet users. Education is related to Internet use. A Mediamark survey found that 80% of users had attended college, a proportion greater than the U.S. average. Research by the Pew Internet and American Life Project (2003) found that the demographic make-up of Internet users had not changed drastically from 2001 to 2003.

Longitudinal usage data suggest that the Internet deviates from the pattern followed by other new media. Lindstrom (1997) points out that initial use of a medium is abnormally high during the novelty phase and then declines over time as the medium becomes familiar. During the 1950s, for example, individuals who bought TV sets watched more TV during their first few months of ownership than they did during the rest of the year.

Lindstrom cites data from a Nielsen survey, however, showing that Internet use actually increased in the 12-month period following initial use. He hypothesizes that it requires both learning and practice to get the most utility out of the Internet, thus increasing use over time. A 2000 survey by the Stanford Institute for the Quantitative Study of Society lends support to this hypothesis (Nie & Erbring, 2000). Amount of Internet use was positively correlated with the number of years respondents had had Internet access.

Recent research on Internet usage suggests that time spent on the net displaces time spent on other media, particularly television. Television viewing suffers because a great deal of Internet usage is during the evening hours, when people traditionally watch TV (Weaver, 1998). The Stanford study found that 65% of their respondents who were online more than 10 hours per week reported they spent less time watching TV. Time spent on the Internet was also negatively related to time spent reading newspapers, but the effect was not as great as with TV (Nie & Erbring, 2000). Radio listening occurs mainly in cars and as a result does not seem to be affected by Internet use.

When it comes to news, however, using the Internet seems to have little impact. Stempel, Hargrove, and Bernt (2000) found that Internet users and nonusers were alike in their viewing of local and network newscasts, and, in a finding that is at odds with the Stanford results, they found that users actually were more regular readers of the daily newspaper. A more recent study (Stempel & Hargrove, 2003) also found that the Internet still lagged behind traditional media as a news source.

The audience still relies on and trusts traditional news sources for most of their information about the world. A Gallup survey of more than 1,000 Americans conducted in 1998 revealed that only a few people (about 11%) frequently used the Internet as a source of news. In addition, about 45% of the Gallup sample reported that they can't trust the accuracy of what's on the net. Only infomercials and talk shows were viewed with more distrust than the Internet (Newport & Saad, 1998). Johnson and Kaye (1998) found similar results. About 14% of their survey respondents rated online newspapers and online magazines as moderately or very credible sources. When compared to their traditional counterparts, however, online information sources fare relatively well. Flanagin and Metzger (2000) found that their respondents rated the credibility of Internet information sites as highly as they rated the credibility of information obtained from television, radio, and magazines. Only the traditional newspaper was rated higher in credibility.

Functions and Uses

Although a definitive list of uses and gratifications has yet to be designed, some preliminary results show a few general trends. At the risk of oversimplifying, the main functions seem to be (1) information, (2) communication, (3) entertainment, and (4) affiliation. The primary use seems to be information gathering. The Pew Center survey mentioned previously found that more than 80% of their sample had used the net to find information on some specific topic. A Nielsen survey found that about 75% used the net for informational needs, with most looking for information about products or services.

The communication function is best exemplified by the use of email. About 90% of the Pew Center survey respondents used the net to send email. The Stanford survey turned up a comparable result (Nie & Erbring, 2000).

Surfing the web and generally exploring websites illustrate the entertainment function of the Internet. The Stanford survey found that a little more than a third of their respondents surf the web and play games for fun. The Pew Center found an even greater percentage: 68% said they surf the web to be entertained.

The last function, affiliation, may be the most interesting. A Georgia Tech study found that 45% of respondents reported that after going on the net they felt more "connected" to people like themselves ("GVU Survey," 1998). About 35% of the Pew Center respondents reported participating in an online support group. Finally, the frequency of Internet uses seems to be related to age. Younger people use the net more for entertainment and socializing, whereas older people use it more for information (Cortese, 1997).

Social and Psychological Effects

Phase 3 research is still evolving, but existing studies provide some early guidance. One potential harmful effect has been labeled "Internet addiction" (Young, K., 1998). This condition is typified by a psychological dependence on the Internet that causes people to turn into "online-aholics" who ignore family, work, and friends as they devote most of their time to surfing the net. Young estimated that perhaps 5 million people may be addicted. Surveys have shown that middle-aged women, the unemployed, and newcomers to the net are most at risk (Hurley, 1997). Students are also susceptible. One study reported that one in three students knew someone whose grades had suffered because of heavy net use. Another found a positive correlation between high Internet use and dropout rate (Young, J., 1998). In New York an Internet addiction support group has started regular meetings to help addicts kick the habit. A 1998 study done at Carnegie Mellon University raised some interesting questions about the relationship between Internet use and feelings of depression and loneliness (Harmon, 1998). Somewhat unexpectedly, a 2-year panel study of 169 individuals found that Internet use appeared to cause a decline in psychological well-being. Even though most panel members were frequent visitors to chat rooms and used email heavily, their feelings of loneliness increased as they reported a decline in their amount of interaction with family members and friends. The researchers hypothesized that online communication does not provide the kind of support obtained from conventional face-to-face communication. These findings were reinforced by the results of the Stanford survey. Nie and Erbring (2000) reported that heavy Internet users spent less time talking to family and friends over the phone and spent less time with family and friends in person. On the other hand, the Pew survey found the opposite. Their results suggested that Internet use actually sustained and strengthened social and family ties. Subsequent studies have suggested a "rich get richer" effect. People who are outgoing and extroverted use the Internet to link up with friends and family and increase their social contacts. Those who are more introverted tended to shy away from online social contacts (Kraut, Kiesler, Bonera, Cummings, Hegelson, & Crawford, 2002).

Using the Internet

Some helpful websites for more information about media effects research include:

1. *www.pewinternet.org* The Pew Internet & American Life Project creates and funds original, academic-quality research that explores the impact of the Internet on children, families, communities, the workplace, schools, health care, and civic/political life. This is a good source for current data on Internet usage.
2. *http://www.aber.ac.uk/media/Documents/short/cultiv.html* contains a helpful overview of cultivation analysis and it s methods.

3. *www.surgeongeneral.gov/library/youthviolence/chapter4/sec1.html* will take you to the Surgeon General's Report on Youth Violence. Appendix 4B is entitled "Violence in the Media and Its Effect on Youth Violence," and it contains a readable and succinct summarization of the TV violence literature.
4. *http://zimmer.csufresno.edu/~johnca/spch100/7-4-uses.htm* This site contains an extended discussion of the uses and gratifications approach.

MASS MEDIA AS TOOL FOR TRANSFER OF INFORMATION

Mass media are tools for the transfer of information, concepts, and ideas to both general and specific audiences. They are important tools in advancing public health goals. Communicating about health through mass media is complex, however, and challenges professionals in diverse disciplines. In an article in the *Journal of Health Communication*, Liana Winett and Lawrence Wallack wrote that "using the mass media to improve public health can be like navigating a vast network of roads without any street signs—if you are not sure *where* you are going and *why*, chances are you will not reach your destination" (1996, p. 173).

Using mass media can be counterproductive if the channels used are not audience-appropriate, or if the message being delivered is too emotional, fear arousing, or controversial. Undesirable side effects usually can be avoided through proper formative research, knowledge of the audience, experience in linking media channels to audiences, and message testing.

Types and Functions of Mass Media

Sophisticated societies are dependent on mass media to deliver health information. Marshall McLuhan calls media "extensions of man." G. L. Kreps and B. C. Thornton believe media extend "people's ability to communicate, to speak to others far away, to hear messages, and to see images that would be unavailable without media" (1992, p. 144). It follows that employment of mass media to disseminate health news (or other matters) has, in effect, reduced the world's size. The value of health news is related to what gets reported and how it gets reported. According to Ray Moynihan and colleagues:

The news media are an important source of information about health and medical therapies, and there is widespread interest in the quality of reporting. Previous studies have identified inaccurate coverage of published scientific papers, overstatement of adverse effects or risks, and evidence of sensationalism. The media can also have a positive public health role, as they did in communicating simple warnings about the connection between Reye's syndrome and the use of aspirin in children (1999, p. 1645).

Despite the potential of news media to perform valuable health-education functions, Moynihan et al. conclude that media stories about medications continue to be incomplete in their coverage of benefits, risks, and costs of drugs, as well as in reporting financial ties between clinical trial investigators and pharmaceutical manufacturers.

The mass media are capable of facilitating short-term, intermediate-term, and long-term effects on audiences. Short-term objectives include exposing audiences to health concepts; creating awareness and knowledge; altering outdated or incorrect knowledge; and enhancing audience recall of particular advertisements or public service announcements (PSAs), promotions, or program names. Intermediate-term objectives include all of the above, as well as changes in attitudes, behaviors, and perceptions of social norms.

Finally, long-term objectives incorporate all of the aforementioned tasks, in addition to focused restructuring of perceived social norms, and maintenance of behavior change. Evidence of achieving these three tiers of objectives is useful in evaluating the effectiveness of mass media.

Mass media performs three key functions: educating, shaping public relations, and advocating for a particular policy or point of view. As education tools, media not only impart knowledge, but can be part of larger efforts (e.g., social marketing) to promote actions having social utility. As public relations tools, media assist organizations in achieving credibility and respect among public health opinion leaders, stakeholders, and other gatekeepers. Finally, as advocacy tools, mass media assist leaders in setting a policy agenda, shaping debates about controversial issues, and gaining support for particular viewpoints.

Television

Television is a powerful medium for appealing to mass audiences—it reaches people regardless of age, sex, income, or educational level. In addition, television offers sight and sound, and it makes dramatic and lifelike representations of people and products. Focused TV coverage of public health has been largely limited to crises. However, for audiences of the late 1950s, the 1960s, and the 1970s, television presented or reinforced certain health messages through product marketing. Some of these messages were related to toothpaste, hand soaps, multiple vitamins, fortified breakfast cereals, and other items.

Public health authorities have expressed concern about the indirect influence of television in promoting false norms about acts of violence, drinking, smoking, and sexual behavior. A hypothetical equation for viewers might be: drinking plus smoking equals sex and a good time. Safe sex practices are rarely portrayed on television. An additional public health concern is that TV viewing promotes sedentariness in a population already known for its multiple risk factors for cardiovascular disease and other chronic illnesses.

A more focused coverage of health matters occurred in the 1990s as a result of two events: (1) an expansion of "health segments" on news broadcasts, which included the hiring of "health" reporters, and (2) the expansion and wider distribution of cable television (CATV) and satellite systems. Television coverage of health issues reveals some of the medium's weaknesses as an educator, however. Health segments incorporated into news broadcasts are typically one to three minutes in length—the consumer receives only a brief report or "sound bite," while the broadcaster remains constrained by the fact that viewers expect the medium to be both visual and entertaining. Fortunately, with the advent and maturation of CATV, more selected audience targeting has become possible. The Health Network is dedicated entirely to health matters, while other cable networks (e.g., Discovery Channel) devote significant amounts of broadcast time to health. This narrowcasting allows the medium to reach particular market segments. However, the proliferation of cable channels decreases the volume of viewers for a given channel at any point in time. According to George and Michael Belch, even networks such as CNN, ESPN, and MTV draw only 1 to 2 percent of primetime viewers.

Although TV has the potential to deliver messages about HIV/AIDS (human immunodeficiency virus/acquired immunodeficiency syndrome), smoking, cardiovascular disease, cancer, and so on, televised messages have the characteristic of low audience involvement.

The main consumer effect of messages occurs through repetition and brand familiarity. Most health messages do not have the exposure level that brands of toothpaste, soap, or antiperspirant receive, for public health groups rarely can sustain the cost of television, thereby limiting their message's penetration.

For all its potential strengths, TV suffers many shortcomings. The cost of placing health messages on TV is high, not only because of the expense of purchasing airtime, but because of production time for PSA creation. Televised messages are fleeting—airing in most instances for only 15 to 30 seconds. Belch and Belch point out that for 13 to 17 minutes of every hour viewers are bombarded with messages, creating a clutter that makes retention difficult.

Radio

Radio also reaches mass and diverse audiences. The specialization of radio stations by listener age, taste, and even gender permits more selectivity in reaching audience segments. Since placement and production costs are less for radio than for TV, radio is able to convey public health messages in greater detail. Thus, radio is sometimes considered to be more efficient.

Radio requires somewhat greater audience involvement than television, creating the need for more mental imagery, or what Belch and Belch call "image transfer." Because of this, radio can reinforce complementary messages portrayed in parallel fashion on TV. However, the large number of radio stations may fragment the audience for health message delivery.

Radio health message campaigns have been effective in developing countries, especially when combined with posters and other mass media. Ronny Adhikarya showed that mass media message targeted at wheat farmers in Bangladesh increased the percentage of those who carried out rat control from 10 percent to 32 percent in 1983. Continuation of the campaign in subsequent years saw rat control efforts rise to 72 percent.

Internet

The advent of the World Wide Web and the massive increase in Internet users offers public health personnel enormous opportunities and challenges. The Internet places users in firmer autonomous control of which messages are accessed and when they are accessed. It is possible to put virtually anything on-line and disseminate it to any location having Internet access, but the user has little control over quality and accuracy. Internet search engines can direct users to tens of thousands of web sites after the user's introduction of one or more keywords. A critical task for public health educators will be to assist people in discriminating among Internet health-information sources. Efforts need to stop short of censorship, thus balancing accuracy, quality, and (in the U.S.) protection of free speech (First Amendment rights).

Unlike TV or radio, which are available in nearly all households, Internet access requires some technical skill, as well as the resources to purchase hardware and Internet subscription services. J. R. Finnegan and K. Viswanath explain that, as with its predecessor technologies, the Internet suffers from a certain "legacy of fear" about its impact on children, youth, and others. As with cinema since the 1940s and TV since the 1950s, the Internet has been accused of promoting mindlessness; exposing people to pornography, violence, and other examples of society's lowest common denominators; and enabling sedentary behavior. The Internet is said to facilitate activities of society's hate groups and to teach children and others how to construct bombs and obtain weapons. Unlike some other mass media, the Internet is presently not universally available across socioeconomic strata due to cost and other barriers. It is possible that this lack of universality has already contributed to existing information gaps between society's "haves" and "have-nots."

The Internet's utility for conveying health information can be illustrated by looking at three sample web sites. Considered by some to be the best source for public health data and information is the web site of the Centers for Disease Control and Prevention (http://www.cdc.gov).

From here persons can locate numerous government data sources, obtain facts on chronic and infectious diseases, and gain fingertip access to health updates, including the *Morbidity and Mortality Weekly Report (MMWR)*. Another valuable site is that of the Association for Toxic Substances and Disease Registry (http://www.atsdr.cdc.gov/HEC/primer.html), which includes a primer on health risk communication principles and practice. Through this site, persons learn how to communicate about health risks to a skeptical public, including factors that influence the public's risk perceptions.

Finally, Columbia University's health education web site (http://www.goaskalice.columbia.edu) makes it possible to access information on a voluminous array of health topics, with particular relevance to college students. This site also permits individuals to submit questions anonymously, receive responses, and be referred to other Internet links. These items are then archived for use by persons having similar queries.

Speculating about the Internet's future is not easy. However, the Internet offers all of the audio and visual strengths of other electronic media, plus interactivity and frequent updates. The challenge is to increase its availability and augment the skills of Internet users.

Newspapers

Belch and Belch estimate that newspapers are read daily in 70 percent of U.S. households, and in as many as 90 percent of high-income households. Newspapers permit a level of detail in health reporting not feasible with broadcast media. Whereas one can miss a television broadcast about breast cancer, and thus, lose its entire message, one can read the same (and more detailed) message in a newspaper at one's choice of time and venue. Although newspapers permit consumers flexibility concerning what is read, and when, they do have a brief shelf life.

In many households, newspapers seldom survive more than one or two days. Newspapers are available in daily and weekly formats, and local, regional, and national publications exist. In addition, there are numerous special audience newspapers (e.g., various ethnic groups, women and feminist related, gay and lesbian, geography-specific, neighborhood). Consequently, health messages contained in newspapers can reach many people and diverse groups. Newspapers often fall short of their dissemination potential, however. In addition to educating people about public health, deliberate efforts need to be directed at educating other media and politicians (McDermott 2000, p. 269).

Other authorities have illustrated the shortcomings of the newspapers in conveying health information. Few stories call for individual or community policy or action, and even fewer present a local angle.

Magazines

Belch and Belch divide magazines into three varieties: consumer (e.g., *Reader's Digest, Newsweek, People*), farm (e.g., *Farm Journal, National Hog Farmer, Beef*), and business (professional, industrial, trade, and general business publications). Magazines have several strengths, including audience selectivity, reproduction quality, prestige, and reader loyalty. Furthermore, magazines have a relatively long shelf life—they may be saved for weeks or months, and are frequently reread, and passed on to others. Magazine reading also tends to occur at a less hurried pace than newspaper reading. Health messages, therefore, can receive repeated exposure.

Other Print Media

Pamphlets, brochures, and posters constitute other print media used to disseminate health messages. These devices are readily found in most public health agencies, offices of private practitioners, health care institutions, and voluntary health organizations. They are common and familiar educational tools of the American Cancer Society, the American Heart Association, and the American Lung Association. Though widely used, their actual utility is infrequently evaluated (e.g., units distributed vs. changes in awareness, cost analysis). Until the 1990s, few of these print media were developed with the assistance of target audiences, and few contained varied messages, were culturally tailored, or employed readability and face validity techniques. The extent to which persons read, reread, and keep these devices—or circulate them to other readers—is not well evaluated. Thus, their permanence is unknown.

Outdoor Media

Outdoor media include billboards and signs, placards inside and outside of commercial transportation modes, flying billboards (e.g., signs in tow of airplanes), blimps, and skywriting. Commercial advertisers such as Goodyear, Fuji, Budweiser, Pizza Hut, and Blockbuster all make extensive use of their logo-bearing blimps around sports stadiums. In the United States, none of these outdoor modes are used extensively to convey health messages, although billboards and transit placards are the most likely forms to contain health information. For persons who regularly pass by billboards or use public transportation, these media may provide repeated exposure to messages. Pro-health messages displayed on urban public transportation may suffer, however, from the image problems that afflict urban buses and subways. In addition, the effectiveness of such postings wears out quickly as audiences grow tired of their sameness. Tobacco and alcohol manufacturers have made extensive use of billboards and other outdoor media. However, the 1998 Master Settlement Agreement between the states and the tobacco industries outlawed billboard advertising of cigarettes. In their 1994 Chicago-based study, Diana Hackbarth and her colleagues revealed how billboards promoting tobacco and alcohol were concentrated in poor neighborhoods. Similar themes were seen in other urban centers (Baltimore, Detroit, St. Louis, New Orleans, Washington, D.C., and San Francisco) where alcohol and tobacco billboards were much more concentrated in African-American neighborhoods than in white neighborhoods. The tobacco industry now pursues the same strategy in developing countries.

MEDIA EFFECTS

Decades of studies on the consequences of mass media exposure demonstrate that effects are varied and reciprocal—the media impact audiences and audiences also impact media by the intensity and frequency of their usage. The results of mass media for promoting social change, especially in developing countries, have become important for public health. J. R. Finnegan Jr. and K. Viswanath (1997) have identified three effects, or functions, of media: (1) the knowledge gap, (2) agenda setting, and (3) cultivation of shared public perceptions.

The Knowledge Gap

Health knowledge is differentially distributed in the population, resulting in knowledge gaps. Unfortunately, mass media are insufficient for distributing information in an egalitarian fashion—changes in social structure and institutions are also necessary for this to occur. Thus, the impact of mass media on audience knowledge gaps is influenced by such factors as the extent to which the content is appealing, the degree to which information channels are accessible and desirable, and the amount of social conflict and diversity there is in a community. Hence, public health media campaigns are more effective when structural factors that impede the distribution of knowledge are addressed.

Agenda Setting

The selective nature of what members of the media choose for public consumption influences how people think about health issues, and what they think about them. When Rudolph Giuliani, the mayor of New York City, publicly disclosed he had prostate cancer prior to the 2000 New York senatorial election, many news media reported the risks of prostate cancer, prompting greater public awareness about the incidence of the disease and the need for screening. A similar episode occurred in the mid-1970s when Betty Ford, wife of President Gerald R. Ford, and Happy Rockefeller, wife of Vice President Nelson Rockefeller, were both diagnosed with breast cancer.

A related theme is the extent to which the media set the public's perception of health risks. According to J. J. Davis, when risks are highlighted in the media, particularly in great detail, the extent of agenda setting is likely to be based on the degree to which a public sense of outrage and threat is provoked. Where mass media can be especially valuable is in the framing of issues. "Framing" means taking a leadership role in the organization of public discourse about an issue. Media, of course, are influenced by pressures to offer balance in coverage, and these pressures may come from persons and groups with particular political action and advocacy positions. According to Finnegan and Viswanath, "groups, institutions, and advocates compete to identify problems, to move them onto the public agenda, *and* to define the issues symbolically" (1997, p. 324). Thus, persons who desire to access mass media's agenda-setting potential must be aware of the competition.

Cultivation of Perceptions

Cultivation is the extent to which media exposure, over time, shapes audience perceptions. Television is a common experience, especially in the United States, and it serves as what S. W. Littlejohn calls a "homogenizing agent." However, the effect is often based on several conditions, particularly socioeconomic factors. Prolonged exposure to TV or movie violence may affect the extent to which people think community violence is a problem, though that belief is likely moderated by where they live. However, the actual determinants of people's impressions of violence are complex, and consensus in this area is lacking.

The Relationship of Mass Media to Other Forms of Communication

The interaction between media messages and interpersonal communication was first described by Elihu Katz and Paul Lazarsfeld in their two-step flow hypothesis. They argued that media effects were moderated principally by interpersonal encounters. Community opinion leaders scan the media for information, then communicate that information to others in interpersonal contexts. It is in this second step, interpersonal interaction, that opinion leaders wield enormous power, influencing others not only by what they choose to reveal but also the slant that they use in conveying the message. The two-step model has been expanded to include multistep models—most notably information diffusion models. Step models have been limited by their linear assumptions of one-way influence and causation. Media influence is undeniably linked to complex interpersonal dynamics. A shared influence likely results when people are exposed to health messages and then converge together in contexts that influence what they say to one another (and even how they say it), as well as what they selectively think.

George Gerbner describes a three-component framework. The first of these components is semiotics, the study of signs, symbols, and codes. Language comprises one such set of symbols and codes that can be further embellished by sights, sounds, and other visual and aural cues. The second aspect of the framework relates to behaviors and interactions associated with exposure to messages. Psychologists, marketers, and others attempt to predict behavior based on specially designed messages. The third element examines how communication is organized around social systems, and the extent to which history and human experience influence society's institutions.

Designers of health messages need to consider such models and frameworks. Modern views of health behavior change acknowledge eclectic approaches and consider multiple aspects of human experience, from the individual level to the community level. Individual channels of communication (e.g., face-to-face encounters) offer personal support and may invoke trust, but are labor intensive, have limited reach, and may require ancillary materials. Mass media channels transmit information rapidly and to general or specific audiences. Mass media can set agendas, but questions have been raised concerning their impartiality and integrity. Community channels (e.g., coalitions, community action groups, and the like), have less "reach" than mass media, but they reinforce, expand, and localize media messages and offer institutional and social support. Knowledge of the complementary strengths of various channels helps to optimize penetration and effectiveness of health messages.

Mass Media Public Health Campaigns—the Right "Mix"

Because of the inherent properties of various mass media, a U.S. Department of Health and Human Services publication advises that health-message designers consider a series of questions relative to choice of channels:

- Which channels are most appropriate for the health problem/issue and message?
- Which channels are most likely to be credible to and accessible by the target audience?
- Which channels fit the program purpose (e.g., inform, influence attitudes, change behavior)?
- Which and how many channels are feasible, considering your time and budget?

A 1999 article by A. G. Ramirez and colleagues describes a media mix that significantly increased adherence to recommended guidelines concerning cervical cancer screening among women in a predominantly Spanish-speaking Texas border city. The media mix included 82 television segments, 67 newspaper stories, and 48 radio programs, all featuring role models. In a 1998 study by Ramirez and other investigators, programs employing a similar strategy in New York, Florida, and California showed significant change in target behaviors among Hispanic populations.

In Project Northland, Cheryl Perry's team of researchers focused on moderating alcohol use by adolescents, but could not use radio and television spots due to their potential confounding properties (i.e., being heard or viewed by adolescents in a nonintervention comparison group) with respect to evaluation of this school-and community-based intervention. Print media, including posters, brochures, and newsletters, were used in the intervention communities to market health messages and advertise ancillary events, and adolescents and adults were trained in media advocacy to increase media coverage of underage use of alcohol.

The primary health communication tool used by the Centers for Disease Control and Prevention (CDC) is PRIZM, which was developed by Claritas, Inc. PRIZM divides the United States into sixty-two lifestyle clusters, or groups of people with similar "geodemographic characteristics, consumer behaviors, psychosocial beliefs, and media habits" (Parvanta and Freimuth 2000, p. 22). It provides data on 250 sociodemographic census variables and approximately 500 items concerning media preferences, purchasing behaviors, and lifestyle activities. Following a needs assessment that revealed an abnormally high birth-defect rate in a four-county area of Virginia, mass media were tapped to inform more than 22,000 women of child-bearing age about the health benefits of folic acid supplements and folate-rich foods. The campaign included television and radio PSAs, brochures, posters and display boards, as well as the cooperation of a local grocery store chain that provided other print media (food information cards and special food labels on folate-dense products). In a 1999 evaluation, CDC investigators reported a statistically significant increase in folic acid awareness between 1997 and 1999.

Mass media have been major sources of information about HIV/AIDS and other sexually transmitted infections. In a 2000 study, 96 percent of 1,290 men aged twenty-two to twenty-six reported hearing about these subjects through television advertisements, radio, or magazines. Some authorities have expressed skepticism about the mass media's future motivation to provide positive sex education messages, since portrayal of sex attracts viewers, which in turn, increases revenues.

Other evidence of the media's ability to improve reproductive health and promote population control exists, especially from developing countries. Mass media have made people aware of modern contraception and where to access it, as well as linking family planning to other reproductive health care and to broader roles for women. Communication about family planning and population control creates awareness, increases knowledge, builds approval, and encourages healthful behaviors. In Egypt, where nearly all households have television, population control objectives have been achieved through televised PSAs. Data also support the positive effects of mass media messages on contraception use in Zimbabwe, Ghana, Nigeria, and Kenya. In a 1999 Tanzania-based study, a team of researchers led by Everett M. Rogers showed how the popularity of a radio soap opera promoting family planning increased listeners' self-efficacy with respect to discussing contraception with spouses and peers.

Although mass media are important for disseminating health messages and encouraging an adoption of healthful lifestyles, they currently fall short of their potential. The realization of this potential in the future depends, in part, on increasing the media advocacy skills of public health authorities, improving understanding of competing antihealth media messages, and organizing channels for an optimal media mix.

The various agents of mass communication and entertainment: newspapers, magazines and other publications, television, radio, the cinema, and the Internet. They rely on widespread literacy, increased leisure, and ready access by the public to receiving equipment. Their entertainment function is usually predominant, attracting investment, providing revenue, and securing (and retaining) an audience.

Other functions, however, have greater political relevance, including the collection, organization, and transmission of news and information, the formation of opinion, and, in more or less open societies, some contribution to public debate. Nowhere have the media escaped regulation, control, and some censorship. Regulation usually relates to ownership, funding, and licensing arrangements, as well as providing for supervision of the length, content, and balance of programmes. With the rapid advance of technology there has been a growing concentration of media ownership, particularly in sectors where the audience is extensive and production costs are high.

Governments are finding it increasingly difficult to maintain close control and supervision, especially with the spread of satellite, cable, and Internet, the advent of global media networks, and increased cross-media ownership.

The emphasis has switched to deregulation, privatization, or a mix of public-private ownership. Meanwhile studies of media influence suggest that, outside elections and other big events, there is but a small audience for serious political debate and comment, and that even that restricted public is neither very receptive nor particularly retentive. Any effects are subtle and indirect. Nevertheless media access is indispensable to the main parties and groups and also allows minority candidates with unorthodox views to be heard.

> *Some have argued that the rapid advance of information technology has led to profound changes in political campaigning. Others retort that this is to confuse the medium with the message.* — Ian Campbell

US HISTORY ENCYCLOPEDIA

The term "mass media" refers to various audiovisual culture industries that send content from a particular source to a wide audience—for example, recorded music and television. The twentieth century in the United States was characterized by the transformation of artisanal, local hobbies and small businesses into highly centralized, rationalized industries working like production lines, and the entertainment and informational media were no different. In the process, pleasure was turned into profit. And when governments occasionally intervened to regulate, or alternative technologies destabilized established forms and interests, ways were found of accommodating threats or capitalizing on others' innovations, resulting in renewed corporate control over each medium. For instance, when newspapers were confronted with radio and then television, they bought into these sectors as quickly as possible, where cross-ownership laws permitted. Even the

Internet, initially celebrated as a source of freedom from centralized control, has gradually come under corporate domination. These tensions are played out in the history of radio and motion pictures. Radio began in the 1920s as a means of two-way communication, a source of agricultural stock-price and weather information, a boon to military technology, and a resource for ethnic cultural maintenance. Then radio became a broadcast medium of networked mass entertainment dominated by corporations in the 1930s that was confronted with wartime censorship and the advent of television as an alternative in the 1940s. It was transformed by popular music and the Top Forty in the 1950s; saw the emergence of college radio and frequency modulation as sites of innovation in the 1960s; and felt the impact of Spanish-language and right-wing talk stations in the increasingly deregulated environment of the 1980s and 1990s.

For its part, the motion picture industry began among textile merchants in New York City, who made films as segments of vaudeville shows. Around the time of World War I (1914–1918), the cinema shifted from depicting actual events and tricks to fictional narratives told in longer forms. This coincided with the rise of trade unions in New York, which, together with climatic considerations, encouraged the industry to shift to California. Filmmaking enterprises emerged and became fully integrated companies, called studios. Each studio owned the labor that made the films, the places where they were shot, the systems by which they were distributed, and the places where they were watched. The federal government intervened after World War II (1939–1945) because this vertical integration was seen to jeopardize competition, and the studios were required to sell off many of their assets.

Combined with the advent of television and the suburbanizing movement of population in the late 1940s away from the inner cities (where most theaters were located), this posed a threat to Hollywood. But it managed to reduce costs, sell its product to television, and survive, later becoming linked to other cultural sectors and diverse industries from banking to gin. Various debates about the mass media have recurred since the beginning of the twentieth century. Most of the U.S. population learned to read with the spread of public schooling. At that point, newspapers divided between those appealing to the middle and ruling classes (today's broadsheets) and the working class (today's tabloids). Ever since, there has been controversy about appeals to popular tastes versus educational ones (that the press will print, and people will prefer rap versus opera and sex crime versus foreign policy). This division is thought to exacerbate distinctions between people who have power and knowledge and other groups. There has also been a debate about concentration of media ownership, which has often generated conflicts of interest and minimized diverse points of view.

The most consistent disagreements have been about what are called hypodermic-needle effects on audiences. This concept assumes that what people read, hear, and see has an immediate and cumulative impact on their psyches. Beginning with 1930s panics about movies affecting young people, this perspective became especially powerful with the advent of television. There have been vast numbers of academic studies and public-policy debates on the topic of violence in the media ever since. Such debates reach the headlines whenever an individual embarks on a killing spree—but never when the U.S. military invades another country or engages in covert action and the media accept images and stories provided by the government itself, as per conflicts in Panama and Afghanistan.

Another recurring debate, which began in the 1960s, has been over the extraordinary success of the United States in dominating the media around the world. Accusations have been made of U.S. cultural imperialism, a process whereby the political imperialism of the nineteenth and twentieth centuries has been superseded by the ideological capture of subordinate populations—this time through advertising and popular culture as much as guns and government, with the United States developing into a mass exporter of media products and a prominent owner of overseas media. And when the United States became a more and more indebted nation as a consequence of corporate welfare and military programs favored by successive federal governments, the mass media provided key sources of overseas revenue and capital to offset this crisis. The twentieth century saw the U.S. mass media multiply in their technological variety but grow ever more concentrated in their ownership and control. The twenty-first century promises more of the same, with an aggressively global strategy to boot.

"Popular press" redirects here; note that the University of Wisconsin Press publishes under the imprint "The Popular Press".

Mass media is a term used to denote a section of the media specifically envisioned and designed to reach a very large audience such as the population of a nation state. It was coined in the 1920s with the advent of nationwide radio networks, mass-circulation newspapers and magazines, although mass media was present centuries before the term became common. The term public media has a similar meaning: it is the sum of the public mass distributors of news and entertainment across mediums such as newspapers, television, radio, broadcasting, which require union membership in large markets such as Newspaper Guild and AFTRA, & text publishers. The concept of mass media is complicated in some internet media as now individuals have a means of potential exposure on a scale comparable to what was previously restricted to select group of mass media producers. These internet media can include personal web pages, podcasts and blogs. The communications audience has been viewed by some commentators as forming a mass society with special characteristics, notably atomization or lack of social connections, which render it especially susceptible to the influence of modern mass-media techniques such as advertising and propaganda. The term "MSM" or "mainstream media" has been widely used in the blogosphere in discussion of the mass media and media bias.

Types of drama in numerous cultures were probably the first mass-media, going back into the Ancient World. The first dated printed book known is the "Diamond Sutra", printed in China in 868 AD, although it is clear that books were printed earlier. Movable clay type was invented in 1041 in China.

However, due to the slow spread to the masses of literacy in China, and the relatively high cost of paper there, the earliest printed mass-medium was probably European popular prints from about 1400. Although these were produced in huge numbers, very few early examples survive, and even most known to be printed before about 1600 have not survived. Johannes Gutenberg printed the first book on a printing press with movable type in 1453. This invention transformed the way the world received printed materials, although books remained too expensive really to be called a mass-medium for at least a century after that. Newspapers developed around from 1605, with the first example in English in 1620 ; but they took until the nineteenth century to reach a mass-audience directly.

During the 20th century, the growth of mass media was driven by technology that allowed the massive duplication of material. Physical duplication technologies such as printing, record pressing and film duplication allowed the duplication of books, newspapers and movies at low prices to huge audiences. Radio and television allowed the electronic duplication of information for the first time. Mass media had the economics of linear replication: a single work could make money proportional to the number of copies sold, and as volumes went up, units costs went down, increasing profit margins further. Vast fortunes were to be made in mass media. In a democratic society, independent media serve to educate the public/electorate about issues regarding government and corporate entities. Some consider the concentration of media ownership to be a grave threat to democracy.

Purposes

Mass media can be used for various purposes:

- Advocacy, both for business and social concerns. This can include advertising, marketing, propaganda, public relations, and political communication.
- Enrichment and education.
- Entertainment, traditionally through performances of acting, music, and sports, along with light reading; since the late 20th century also through video and computer games.

- Journalism- news and blogging.
- Public service announcements.

Claimed Negative Characteristics of Mass Media

Another description of Mass Media is central media meaning they emanate from a central point, the same identical message to numerous recipients.

It is claimed this forces certain intrinsic constraints on the kind of messages and information that can be conveyed, such as:

- An inability to transmit tacit knowledge (or perhaps it can only transfer bad tacit knowledge as opposed to good),
- A focus on the unusual and sensational rather than a restatement of wisdom,
- The promotion of anxiety and fear to sell the newspaper / channel, etc.
- Simplification of complex issues so as to appeal to more sorts of people.
- It can be a conflict of interest when large corporations own large news outlets, and thusly, control what the people know, i.e. corporate propaganda.
- The manipulation of large groups of people through media outlets, for the benefit of a particular political party and/or group of people.

·One of the biggest critics in Media's history is Marshall McLuhan. He brought up the idea that "the medium is the message". This view of central media can be contrasted with lateral media, such as email networks, where messages are all slightly different and spread by a process of lateral diffusion.

JOURNALISM

Journalism is a discipline of collecting, analyzing, verifying, and presenting information regarding current events, trends, issues and people. Those who practice journalism are known as journalists. News-oriented journalism is sometimes described as the "first rough draft of history" (attributed to Phil Graham), because journalists often record important events, producing news articles on short deadlines.

While under pressure to be first with their stories, news media organizations usually edit and proofread their reports prior to publication, adhering to each organization's standards of accuracy, quality and style. Many news organizations claim proud traditions of holding government officials and institutions accountable to the public, while media critics have raised questions about holding the press itself accountable.

Public Relations

Public relations is the art and science of managing communication between an organization and its key publics to build, manage and sustain its positive image. Examples include:

- Corporations use marketing public relations (MPR) to convey information about the products they manufacture or services they provide to potential customers to support their direct sales efforts. Typically, they support sales in the short and long term, establishing and burnishing the corporation's branding for a strong, ongoing market.
- Corporations also use public-relations as a vehicle to reach legislators and other politicians, seeking favorable tax, regulatory, and other treatment, and they may use public relations to portray themselves as enlightened employers, in support of human-resources recruiting programs.
- Non-profit organizations, including schools and universities, hospitals, and human and social service agencies, use public relations in support of awareness programs, fund-raising programs, staff recruiting, and to increase patronage of their services.
- Politicians use public relations to attract votes and raise money, and, when successful at the ballot box, to promote and defend their service in office, with an eye to the next election or, at career's end, to their legacy.

Forms: Electronic media and print media include:

- Broadcasting, in the narrow sense, for radio and television.
- Various types of discs or tape. In the 20th century, these were mainly used for music. Video and computer uses followed.
- Film, most often used for entertainment, but also for documentaries.
- Internet, which has many uses and presents both opportunities and challenges. Blogs and podcasts, such as news, music, pre-recorded speech and video)
- Publishing, in the narrow sense, meaning on paper, mainly via books, magazines, and newspapers.
- Video games, which have developed into a mass form of media since devices such as the PlayStation 3 , Xbox 360, and the Wii broadened their use.

Audio recording and reproduction

Sound recording and reproduction is the electrical or mechanical re-creation and/or amplification of sound, often as music. This involves the use of audio equipment such as microphones, recording devices and loudspeakers. From early beginnings with the invention of the phonograph using purely mechanical techniques, the field has advanced with the invention of electrical recording, the mass production of the 78 record, the magnetic wire recorder followed by the tape recorder, the vinyl LP record.

The invention of the compact cassette in the 1960s, followed by Sony's Walkman, gave a major boost to the mass distribution of music recordings, and the invention of digital recording and the compact disc in 1983 brought massive improvements in ruggedness and quality. The most recent developments have been in digital audio players. An album is a collection of related audio tracks, released together to the public, usually commercially. The term record album originated from the fact that 78 RPM Phonograph disc records were kept together in a book resembling a photo album. The first collection of records to be called an "album" was Tchaikovsky's *Nutcracker Suite*, release in April 1909 as a four-disc set by Odeon records. It retailed for 16 shillings — about £15 in modern currency. A music video (also promo) is a short film or video that accompanies a complete piece of music, most commonly a song. Modern music videos were primarily made and used as a marketing device intended to promote the sale of music recordings. Although the origins of music videos go back much further, they came into their own in the 1980s, when Music Television's format was based around them. In the 1980s, the term "rock video" was often used to describe this form of entertainment, although the term has fallen into disuse.

Music videos can accommodate all styles of filmmaking, including animation, live action films, documentaries, and non-narrative, abstract film.

BROADCASTING

Broadcasting is the distribution of audio and/or video signals (programs) to a number of recipients ("listeners" or "viewers") that belong to a large group. This group may be the public in general, or a relatively large audience within the public. Thus, an Internet channel may distribute text or music world-wide, while a public address system in (for example) a workplace may broadcast very limited *ad hoc* soundbites to a small population within its range.

The sequencing of content in a broadcast is called a schedule. With all technological endeavours a number of technical terms and slang are developed please see the list of broadcasting terms for a glossary of terms used.

Television and radio programs are distributed through radio broadcasting or cable, often both simultaneously. By coding signals and having decoding equipment in homes, the latter also enables subscription-based channels and pay-per-view services. A broadcasting organisation may broadcast several programs at the same time, through several channels (frequencies), for example BBC One and Two. On the other hand, two or more organisations may share a channel and each use it during a fixed part of the day. Digital radio and digital television may also transmit multiplexed programming, with several channels compressed into one ensemble. When broadcasting is done via the Internet the term webcasting is often used. In 2004 a new phenomenon occurred when a number of technologies combined to produce podcasting. Podcasting is an asynchronous broadcast/narrowcast medium, with one of the main proponents being Adam Curry and his associates the Podshow. Broadcasting forms a very large segment of the mass media. Broadcasting to a very narrow range of audience is called narrowcasting. The term "broadcast" was coined by early radio engineers from the midwestern United States.

Film

Film is a term that encompasses motion pictures as individual projects, as well as the field in general. The origin of the name comes from the fact that photographic film (also called filmstock) has historically been the primary medium for recording and displaying motion pictures. Many other terms exist — *motion pictures* (or just *pictures* or "picture"), *the silver screen, photoplays, the cinema, picture shows, flicks* — and commonly *movies.*

Films are produced by recording people and objects with cameras, or by creating them using animation techniques and/or special effects. They comprise a series of individual frames, but when these images are shown rapidly in succession, the illusion of motion is given to the viewer. Flickering between frames is not seen due to an effect known as persistence of vision — whereby the eye retains a visual image for a fraction of a second after the source has been removed. Also of relevance is what causes the perception of motion; a psychological effect identified as beta movement. Film is considered by many to be an important art form; films entertain, educate, enlighten and inspire audiences. The visual elements of cinema need no translation, giving the motion picture a universal power of communication. Any film can become a worldwide attraction, especially with the addition of dubbing or subtitles that translate the dialogue. Films are also artifacts created by specific cultures, which reflect those cultures, and, in turn, affect them.

Internet

The Internet (also known simply as "the Net" or "the Web") can be briefly understood as "a network of networks". Specifically, it is the worldwide, publicly accessible network of interconnected computer networks that transmit data by packet switching using the standard Internet Protocol (IP). It consists of millions of smaller domestic, academic, business, and governmental networks, which together carry various information and services, such as electronic mail, online chat, file transfer, and the interlinked Web pages and other documents of the World Wide Web.

Contrary to some common usage, the Internet and the World Wide Web are not synonymous: the Internet is a collection of interconnected *computer networks*, linked by copper wires, fiber-optic cables, wireless connections etc.; the Web is a collection of interconnected *documents*, linked by hyperlinks and URLs. The World Wide Web is accessible via the Internet, along with many other services including e-mail, file sharing and others described below.

Toward the end of the 20th century, the advent of the World Wide Web marked the first era in which any individual could have a means of exposure on a scale comparable to that of mass media. For the first time, anyone with a web site can address a global audience, although serving to high levels of web traffic is still relatively expensive. It is possible that the rise of peer-to-peer technologies may have begun the process of making the cost of bandwidth manageable. Although a vast amount of information, imagery, and commentary (i.e. "content") has been made available, it is often difficult to determine the authenticity and reliability of information contained in web pages (in many cases, self-published). The invention of the Internet has also allowed breaking news stories to reach around the globe within minutes.

This rapid growth of instantaneous, decentralized communication is often deemed likely to change mass media and its relationship to society. "Cross-media" means the idea of distributing the same message through different media channels. A similar idea is expressed in the news industry as "convergence". Many authors understand cross-media publishing to be the ability to publish in both print and on the web without manual conversion effort. An increasing number of wireless devices with mutually incompatible data and screen formats make it even more difficult to achieve the objective "create once, publish many".The internet is quickly becoming the center of mass media. Everything is becoming accessible via the internet. Instead of picking up a newspaper, or watching the 10 o'clock news, people will log onto the internet to get the news they want, when they want it.

Many workers listen to the radio through the internet while sitting at their desk. Games are played through the internet. Blogging has become a huge form of media, popular through the internet. Even the education system relies on the internet . Teachers can contact the entire class by sending one e-mail. They have web pages where students can get another copy of the class outline or assignments. Some classes even have class blogs where students must post weekly, and are graded on their contributions. The internet thus far has become an extremely dominant form of media.

Publishing

Publishing is the industry concerned with the production of literature or information – the activity of making information available for public view. In some cases, authors may be their own publishers. Traditionally, the term refers to the distribution of printed works such as books and newspapers. With the advent of digital information systems and the Internet, the scope of publishing has expanded to include websites, blogs, and the like. As a business, publishing includes the development, marketing, production, and distribution of newspapers, magazines, books, literary works, musical works, software, other works dealing with information.

Publication is also important as a legal concept;

(1) as the process of giving formal notice to the world of a significant intention, for example, to marry or enter bankruptcy, and;

(2) as the essential precondition of being able to claim defamation; that is, the alleged libel must have been published.

A book is a collection of sheets of paper, parchment or other material with a piece of text written on them, bound together along one edge within covers. A book is also a literary work or a main division of such a work. A book produced in electronic format is known as an e-book. In library and information science, a book is called a monograph to distinguish it from serial publications such as magazines, journals or newspapers. Publishers may produce low-cost, pre-proof editions known as galleys or 'bound proofs' for promotional purposes, such as generating reviews in advance of publication. Galleys are usually made as cheaply as possible, since they are not intended for sale.

Magazine

A magazine is a periodical publication containing a variety of articles, generally financed by advertising and/or purchase by readers. Magazines are typically published weekly, biweekly, monthly, bimonthly or quarterly, with a date on the cover that is in advance of the date it is actually published. They are often printed in color on coated paper, and are bound with a soft cover. Magazines fall into two broad categories: consumer magazines and business magazines. In practice, magazines are a subset of periodicals, distinct from those periodicals produced by scientific, artistic, academic or special interest publishers which are subscription-only, more expensive, narrowly limited in circulation, and often have little or no advertising. Magazines can be classified as:

- General interest magazines (e.g. Frontline, India Today, The Week, etc)
- Special interest magazines (women's, sports, business, scuba diving, etc)

Newspaper

A newspaper is a publication containing news and information and advertising, usually printed on low-cost paper called newsprint. It may be general or special interest, most often published daily or weekly. The first printed newspaper was published in 1605, and the form has thrived even in the face of competition from technologies such as radio and television. Recent developments on the Internet are posing major threats to its business model, however. Paid circulation is declining in most countries, and advertising revenue, which makes up the bulk of a newspaper's income, is shifting from print to online; some commentators, nevertheless, point out that historically new media such as radio and television did not entirely supplant existing media.

Software Publishing

A software publisher is a publishing company in the software industry between the developer and the distributor. In some companies, two or all three of these roles may be combined (and indeed, may reside in a single person, especially in the case of shareware). Software publishers often license software from developers with specific limitations, such as a time limit or geographical region. The terms of licensing vary enormously, and are typically secret. Developers may use publishers to reach larger or foreign markets, or to avoid focussing on marketing. Or publishers may use developers to create software to meet a market need that the publisher has identified. Major reasons why media has an influence on our society is because the people who control it (the government and rich people) are the people who control what news is given to us, therefore the information we are could either be bias or "exaggerated". This is why many people do not trust the media, but sometimes they may have to because it is the only source of news bulletins available. Therefore we may be forced into believing something when it may not even be true. Sometimes newspapers try and compete with each other to sell their newspapers by giving dramatic headlines to entice the public.

Mass Wire Media

Mass wire media is a new frontier of news reporting in the high-tech age. A few decades ago news reporting was through newspapers and radio and television. The radio broadcasts that were made famous by Franklin D. Roosevelt during World War II changed the way radio was looked at. These fireside chats made the radio news and news radio. Things are different now as we are witnessing a revolution of people-oriented reporting in real time and other times. This element of intimate knowledge of the event or story being reported has dramatically changed the way we all view news stories.

This is called by some the Social Media Revolution. This revolution has intrinsically altered the way news is reported almost the way it happens. The trend of people-oriented reporting is only on the rise as reporting news becomes more personal and more accurate.

Video Games

A video game is a computer-controlled game where a video display such as a monitor or television is the primary feedback device. The term "computer game" also includes games which display only text (and which can therefore theoretically be played on a teletypewriter) or which use other methods, such as sound or vibration, as their primary feedback device, but there are very few new games in these categories. There always must also be some sort of input device, usually in the form of button/joystick combinations (on arcade games), a keyboard & mouse/trackball combination (computer games), or a controller (console games), or a combination of any of the above. Also, more esoteric devices have been used for input. Usually there are rules and goals, but in more open-ended games the player may be free to do whatever they like within the confines of the virtual universe. The phrase interactive entertainment is the formal reference to computer and video games. To avoid ambiguity, this game software is referred to as "*computer and video games*" throughout this article, which explores properties common to both types of game.

In common usage, a "computer game" or a "PC game" refers to a game that is played on a personal computer. "Console game" refers to one that is played on a device specifically designed for the use of such, while interfacing with a standard television set. "Video game" (or "videogame") has evolved into a catchall phrase that encompasses the aforementioned along with any game made for any other device, including, but not limited to, mobile phones, PDAs, advanced calculators, etc.

Contrast with Non-mass Media

Non-mass or "personal" media (point-to-point and person-to-person communication) include:

- Speech
- Gestures
- Telephony
- Postal mail
- Some uses of the Internet
- Some Interactive media

Arguably, blogs and other first-person, web-based communications are non-mass media.

Problems with the Term "Mass Media"

The term "mass communication" invokes ideas of whole societies consuming homogenous messages through singular forms. It often provokes criticisms such as "mass culture" and "mass society" and implies a negative impact on the creativity, independency and academia of modern social life. Within twenty-first century society such a term is no longer an accurate explanation of the contemporary media environment nor the products that operate within it.

This notion coincides with the arguments of media theorist John Thompson who suggests that if the term was ill-suited to traditional media forms, it is undoubtedly irrelevant to the digital media forms of today.

He proposes the abandoning of the assumption that audiences are passive recipients of media messages; 'Assumptions of this kind have little to do with the actual character of reception activities and with the complex way in which media products are taken up by individuals, interpreted by them and incorporated into their lives.'

This theme has also been proposed by media and cultural theorist Henry Jenkins, who places emphasis on media audiences rather than the media institution itself. He explains the contemporary media audience as 'active, critically aware and discriminating' and discusses the rise of niche markets and participatory culture. His text 'Interactive Audiences' opens with the statement 'You've got fifteen seconds. Impress me', encapsulating the recent re-positioning of relationship between media audiences and the "mass media".

In this environment, the emphasis is taken away from the industry and supplanted on the individual user, who is as Jenkins states; *'No longer a coach potato, he determines what, when and how he watches media. He is a media consumer, perhaps even a media fan, but he is also a media producer, distributor, publicist and critic'.*

In such demanding and competitive conditions major industries can no longer afford to produce standardized, homogenous programming that has single indicative meaning but rather are forced to involve, entertain and grasp viewers in ways which render different to variable forms of modified users rather than merely the "masses".

MULTIMEDIA LITERACY

Multimedia literacy is a new aspect of literacy that is being recognised as technology expands the way people communicate. The concept of Literacy emerged as a measure of the ability to read and write. In modern context, the word means reading and writing at a level adequate for written communication.

A more fundamental meaning is now needed to cope with the numerous media in use, perhaps meaning a level that enables one to successfully function at certain levels of a society. Multimedia is the use of several different forms of media to convey information. Several are already a part of the canon of global communication and publication: (text, audio, graphics, animation, video, and interactivity).

Others, such as virtual reality, computer programming and robotics are possible candidates for future inclusion. With widespread use of computers, the basic literacy of 'reading' and 'writing' are often done via a computer, providing a foundation stone for more advanced levels of multimedia literacy.

Definition Wars

Critics of the concept of multimedia literacy question whether the term literacy can be extended beyond its original definition. Others question whether the 'literacy' skills and concepts in multimedia literacy are new at all, being found in the theatre, film, radio etc. for many years. The expansion of basic literacy through history and across geography provides perspective on those seeking to draw hard lines about what literacy is and is not. Thousands of years ago, a few early cultures invented the skills and technologies of reading and writing. Many languages today still have no written form.

Of those with the invention of writing, only a small percentage of the citizens of these early cultures needed literacy. Each culture and time decides its needed technologies of thought and communication. Those who teach in a society respond to these needs. All societies have relatively recently (in the last 200 years) found that traditional literacy is essential. Not all have achieved it yet. Today there is a very rapid growth in forms of literacy, largely due to the arrival of the personal computer and the internet.

There was a tipping point in the demand for universal (reading and writing) literacy as an effect of the Industrial Revolution. Paper, writing instruments and printing also became much cheaper at about this time. Today there is a revolution in the development of new communication media. There is a demand for literate people to become skilled in the new literacies related to the use of a variety of online tools - blogs, social networking, video and audio sharing and so on.

The impact of these internet related media is different from that of the earlier multimedia revolution when film and radio became widespread. These media were powerful, but were largely in the hands of a small number of people with the mass of the population being a passive audience. The new media, particularly those described as Web 2.0 tools tend to actively involve the users in responding and creating material.

There is considerable debate in progress about the nature and significance of these new media. Traditionalist educators may argue that the long standing media form of text has and will continue to be the foundation of learning. Others will argue that the new forms are displacing the old forms of literacy and that schools must teach the full range of multimedia literacies.

Changing Digital Technology

As personal computers and their software become more powerful they have the capacity to not only record and edit text, sound, still images, motion pictures and manage interactivity individually, but synthesize all of them onto the same page, screen or viewing, creating new plateaus or forms of composition. Personal computer technology has placed multimedia creation in the hands of any computer user. As multimedia becomes a more prevalent form of communication it is argued that the literacy of 'reading' and 'writing' using multimedia be taught in schools and other education institutions.

The related study of mass media has long been part of the school program in many school systems either as a separate subject option in secondary schools or more often as a part of general literacy learning.

Film Study has also been a school subject in many schools for some time using relatively expensive and complicated equipment to make film or video. The rapid development of multimedia via personal computing means that it is becoming a routine form for a widening group of people not only for just "reading" but for creating the media. The line between mass media and personally authored media is becoming much more blurred if not obliterated. Non professional authors on the web already have audiences larger than major commercial publications such as major newspapers and TV stations, whether text based blogs or multimedia podcasts.

Bibliography

Briggs, Asa and Peter Burke: *A Social History of the Media from Gutenberg to the Internet*, Malden, Blackwell, 2001.

Cannadine, David: *History and the Media, New York*, Palgrave Macmillian, 2004.

Carey, James W.: *Public Opinion and the Communication of Consent*, New York: Guilford Publications, 1995.

Crowley, David. J. and Paul Heyer: *Communication in History*, Boston, Allyn and Bacon, 2003.

Earl, R.: *Writing for Mass Communication*, White Plains, NY: Longman, 1996.

Ehrlich, Matthew C. *Journalism in the Movies*. Urbana: University of Illinois Press, 2004.

Graber, Doris A.: *Processing the News*, N.Y., Longman, 1984.

Hudson, Robert V.: *Mass Media*, New York, Garland Publishing, 1987.

Hutchison, Earl R.: *Writing for Mass Communication*, White Plains, NY: Longman, 1996.

Langman, Larry: *The Media in the Movies*, Jefferson, NC: McFarland & Company, 1997.

Robert W. Snyder: *Defining Moments in Journalism*, New Brunswick, NJ: Transaction Publishers, 1998.

Sachsman, David B.: *The Civil War and the Press*, New Brunswick, NJ: Transaction Publishers, 2000.

Sloan, W. David: *Perspectives on Mass Communication History*, Hillsdale, NJ: Lawrence Erlbaum, 1991.

Suggs, Henry Lewis: *The Black Press in the Middle West*, 1865-1985, Westport, CT: Greenwood Press, 1996.

Index

□□□